PSI

PSI

Scientific Studies of the Psychic Realm

Charles T. Tart

E. P. DUTTON
New York

Library of Congress Cataloging in Publication Data

Tart, Charles T   1937–
    Psi: scientific studies of the psychic realm.

    Bibliography: p.
    Includes index.
    1. Psychical research.   I.   Title.
BF1031.T29 1977   133.8   77-5033

ISBN: 0-525-18575-5 (cloth)
          0-525-47472-2 (paper)

Published simultaneously in Canada by Clarke, Irwin & Company Limited, Toronto and Vancouver

10 9 8 7 6 5 4 3 2 1

First Edition

This book is dedicated to my wife, Judy, who has shared my interest in the psychic from the day we met, twenty years ago, in the Parapsychology Laboratory of Duke University, to the present.

Contents

Acknowledgments

Although this book focuses on my own understanding and investigations of the paranormal, it would not have been possible without the inspiration and foundation created by many others. To name just a few, there are the founders of modern parapsychology whose works and personal contact I have found invaluable, particularly Jule Eisenbud, Gardner Murphy, J. B. Rhine, and Gertrude Schmeidler. Arthur Hastings, Stanley Krippner, and Russell Targ have been sources of stimulation and critical feedback for more than a decade. In the last few years, John Palmer, my colleague at the University of California at Davis, Lila Gatlin, John Jungerman, Ed May, Hal Puthoff, and Elizabeth Rauscher have further enriched my understanding with their ideas and experimental work. The work of many other colleagues will be mentioned throughout the book, but even those citations do not list all those to whom I am indebted because this book is not a comprehensive survey of all parapsychological literature. Financial support for my research has been generously given by the Parapsychology Foundation and the est Foundation. Enormous amounts of practical assistance, inspiration, and moral support have come from my assistant, Irene Segrest, and my wife, Judy. Finally, my acknowledgments would not be complete without thanking my many students, who have acted as experimenters or percipients in my studies.

Preface

Like many scientists, I was raised with a strong religious background, which in my case was Lutheranism. In my early teens, as I began to think independently I encountered and adopted the scientific world view and became increasingly aware of the conflicts between what I had been taught in church and what science taught about the nature of the world. Most scientists I know who experienced a similar conflict went on to reject their religious upbringing totally or, at most, to abstract from it a vague system of ethics that would fit in with the prevailing intellectual climate. Although I am not sure why, I did not follow this route.

It would be romantic to say that I had some profound mystical experience that affected me to the core of my being and showed me the real values and truths in religion, but such was not the case. Looking back, I can see that although the science of the time clearly had much more precise and useful things to say about the nature of the physical world, religion, for all its shortcomings, was attempting to deal with some very important dimensions of human experience that science was totally neglecting. Conventional religion was obviously filled with superstition and irrationality, but some very crucial things seemed to be at the core of religious systems that science had not dealt with.

Because I was so impressed with the power and accomplishments of the scientific enterprise, I found it hard to believe that science could have *totally* ignored the spiritual dimensions of human existence. I began reading intensively in the fringe areas of science and discovered the greatly neglected field of psychical research (as it was then called). There, I found that others had wrestled with the question of the existence of truth in various spiritual views of the world and that others had applied scientific method to the study of what we might loosely call *miracles,* the sorts of happenings frequently cited as proof of religious beliefs. These miracles were apparently continuing to occur among ordinary people in our scientific age, even though they were supposed to be scientifically impossible. Records of large numbers of inexplicable happenings existed and had been analyzed for patterns. There were data, for example, about the British mother who dreamed that her son, in government service in faraway India, had been trampled to death by an elephant; later she received confirmation that he had indeed been trampled to death within a few minutes of the time that she had the dream. There were even stranger events. People had dreams that successfully predicted the future. People reported that their consciousness had left the body and functioned independently of it. Objects fell off shelves when no one was nearby to knock them over.

Psychical research had gone beyond the point of collecting these accounts and had begun to develop as an experimental science. Inexplicable events continued to happen even under highly controlled laboratory conditions. The year of my birth, 1937, was the first year of publication of the *Journal of Parapsychology,* which was founded by J. B. Rhine and others. By the time I began to read the books in this area, hundreds of experiments had already been carried out in the field of psychical research (currently known as parapsychology) establishing the reality of apparently inexplicable (in terms of *current* physics) phenomena by the strictest scientific standards.

I had happened upon a partial resolution of my personal (and my culture's) conflict between science and religion. Parapsychology validated the existence of basic phenomena that could partially account for, and fit in with, some of the spiritual views of the universe. Although it could not yet provide very specific answers about the meaning of these phenomena, it did demonstrate that scientific method could be used to explore these areas and move toward a more knowledgeable understanding and synthesis.

I read the old literature of psychical research and the literature of parapsychology voraciously during my late teens, but it was an isolated intellectual quest. No one I knew really shared my interest in the subject. When I entered the Massachusetts Institute of Technology to study electrical engineering in 1955, I found other students interested in this subject, and we formed a club to further our mutual study of it. During my sophomore year, I carried out my first serious study of psi: an attempt to produce out-of-the-body experiences by hypnosis.

Although my research interests have broadened considerably since that time, in the last twenty years (all my work is referenced in the Bibliography) I have been a part-time parapsychologist, investigating a wide variety of psi phenomena. This book is my attempt to share some of the adventure, the frustration, and the satisfaction of those twenty years. I now understand that the personal conflict I experienced between my religious upbringing and the scientific world view was and *is* shared by many of us.

Part I: Psi

Introduction

✿✿

Psi is a general term that includes a wide variety of human experiences having the common characteristic that, in terms of our contemporary understanding of the physical world, they cannot have happened. Psi includes the three well-studied forms of extrasensory perception (ESP) : telepathy, clairvoyance, and precognition. In our contemporary picture of the physical world, there can be no telepathy (mind-to-mind contact over a distance) because there is no known physical energy to carry the information. The idea of clairvoyance, which, for example, enables a person to identify cards in the middle of a pack of shuffled cards successfully without looking at them, makes no sense either because all the light energy that would provide information about the pattern on the card is screened from the person. Precognition—knowledge of the future before it happens (but not by using the mundane method of logically predicting from the known state of physical affairs) —similarly makes no sense in terms of widely accepted physics because the future does not yet exist.

Psi also includes psychokinesis, which is the ability to produce physical effects on objects by simply wishing for them to take on such and such a condition. A person tries to influence the fall of dice that are thrown by a machine or the internal electronic circuitry of a machine that he does not understand in the least, and sometimes he is successful. But contemporary physics provides no explanation of how the action is performed.

Psi may be the mechanism behind many other exotic phenomena, such as the experience of consciousness leaving the body, of healing when no healing can be expected, of a person possibly surviving physical death and communicating through mediums. Even more exotic reports of experiences, such as walking over burning coals without burns, floating through the air, magic, and perhaps even the spiritual beings religions talk about, may fall under the psi label. The category of uncanny, seemingly impossible things that could be termed psi phenomena is very large. However, in this book, I will confine myself largely to those I have personally investigated and of which we have some scientific knowledge, omitting the more exotic and possibly nonexistent ones.

This book is not intended to prove the existence of particular psi phenomena to anyone. When I was young and more naïve about this field, I believed that if people would only read the existing evidence or if we could collect even more evidence, people in general and scientists in particular would see the reality of these phenomena and begin studying them. As a psychologist, I have come to realize that people's beliefs are formed in much more complex ways than simply looking at the evidence about something and that we frequently have intense and largely implicit emotional commitments to our beliefs. So I have stopped attempting to prove the existence of psi phenomena. This has also been true for parapsychologists in general. Almost all the work in the field for a long time now has been attempts to find out the *nature* of these phenomena and how they work. For skeptics who want to read the background evidence first, I recommend some of the dozens of good books that are listed in the Bibliography and the more than 600 reports of successful experiments that are gathering dust on library shelves in back issues of the *Journal of Parapsychology,* the *Journal of the American Society for Psychical Research,* the *Journal of the Society for Psychical Research,* and the *Interna-*

tional Journal of Parapsychology. The *European Journal of Parapsychology,* which has just begun publication, will contain more research reports.

My personal and professional interests have broadened considerably beyond the nature of psi phenomena, and today I would describe myself as primarily a psychologist interested in the nature of human consciousness, particularly those radical reorganizations of the mind that we call *altered states of consciousness.* My investigations and understandings about states of consciousness can be found in my book *States of Consciousness* and elsewhere [149, 151, 153, 155, 159, 160, 164, 168, 172, 173, 175, 180, 181, 183, 184].* As a member of our Western culture, I am particularly interested in altered states of consciousness because of the mystical experiences and the changes in belief systems that people have experienced during them. Altered states are a tremendously important factor in determining where our society will go. We are desperately searching for a new value system, and the bright, shiny scientism I learned early in my life has not provided it. A fanatic religious revival is a possible future for us, coupled with a strong rejection of free scientific inquiry about human nature. I would rather see an expansion of scientific inquiry into the neglected aspects of the human mind and human spirituality so that we can develop an integration of the scientific and the spiritual.

This brings us to the point in which my interests in psi again become quite important. If a person has a mystical experience in an altered state of consciousness, the orthodox scientific view of it is that it is no more than an *illusory* experience, demonstrating only that the brain, the human biocomputer, can program itself in the oddest ways that have no relation to reality. Such emotional excesses should not be taken seriously because they demonstrate impaired contact with reality, and we need to be realistic about our world if we are going to solve its problems. This orthodox view completely ignores the point that many decades of investigation of psi have demonstrated, using the best scientific method: that there are vital *human* phe-

* These numbers refer to entries in the Bibliography section at the end of this book.

nomena which, precisely because they are inexplicable in terms of our current scientific world view, mean that we need to investigate and develop a much wider world view. It is quite stupid for us to dismiss the spiritual in the name of scientific realism. I have investigated many unusual phenomena in altered states of consciousness, and I believe that some of these are purely internal experiences, but my interest in psi keeps me open to the fact that there may be much more reality to some of them than just an internal trip. If this book and the findings of parapsychology in general help to sensitize other investigators to this psi dimension in studying human consciousness, it will have served its purpose.

Although I am trying to write without jargon and excessive detail, this is primarily a scientific book, reflecting my commitment to science as a way of refining our knowledge, an approach discussed at greater length in the text. Most of my friends and colleagues who accept the existence of psi do so, not because of scientific evidence, but because of vivid personal experience. Yet, with many of my friends and colleagues, I see these experiences being incorporated into belief systems whose validity is rather dubious. These systems may fulfill personal needs, but they do not give a more accurate picture of reality than either naïve religion or naïve scientism. Thus, in describing the studies I have carried out, I shall try to make it clear why particular methods were used, and what kind of alternative explanations they indicated or guarded against so that I can illustrate how scientific investigation works in practice and what it contributes. I have not gone into the meticulous detail that makes science so precise in describing my experiments lest I bore most readers, but the researcher interested in the fine details can consult the original journal publications of my studies. I am all for "feeling the vibes" and forming opinions on the basis of personal experience, but my experience has also taught me how important it is to apply the critical methodology of science. I hope these demonstrations of it will be valuable to others.

Many people are put off by the common stereotypes of science as a cold, hyperintellectual process and of scientists as glorified computers. The formal scientific reports in the journals certainly give that impression. But in reality, science is a human adventure, full of hopes and fears, successes and failures, personal maturation and neurotic game playing, and most interestingly, surprises. For a long time, it was—in fact, still is—conventional to gloss over the whole human dimension in science in order to demonstrate one's objectivity. I have tried to leave the human side of my studies in this book because I have learned that objectivity in science comes, not from falsely omitting the human element, but from submitting this human element to the discipline of scientific method.

I began this book by noting how important my personal experience of the conflict between science and religion had been in interesting me in parapsychology. I have been studying parapsychology for almost twenty-five years now and actively working in it for almost twenty years. The reader may rightly wonder whether my conflict has been resolved.

Yes and no. On the *yes* side, I am more certain than ever of the reality of psi events that point toward a much wider, more meaningful picture of the universe and our place in it than orthodox science has provided. I do not believe in the teachings of any particular spiritual tradition, but I am inclined to be open-minded about the ideas in them and respect the impulse behind spiritual seeking. On the *no* side, my work as a psychologist has made me frustratingly and disappointingly aware of the degree to which we fool ourselves to satisfy our often neurotic desires. It has also made me see that we all (including myself) live in a personally and socially shared illusion (see Chapter 19, "Ordinary Consciousness as a State of Illusion," in *States of Consciousness* [173] and another work [176] for a detailed exposition of this idea). Most movements and systems labeled *spiritual* or *religious* are full of nonsense covering small nuggets of truth, often so thoroughly that they are not worth digging for. Not that religious and spiritual systems have any monopoly on nonsense and illusion. It is found abundantly in all areas of human life (including universities and laboratories).

No, I would not say that the conflict has been resolved. Rather I would say that the stakes have gone up and that the realities of both sides of the conflict stand out more precisely and clearly than ever before. Perhaps a greater synthesis will come out of it, perhaps not. The jacket painting "Roads," by the noted psychic and artist Ingo Swann symbolizes my approach to psi. I am intensely interested in the starry, cosmic ideas and experiences that imply a much vaster conception of human potentials than orthodox science gives us. But, as a psychologist, I am all too aware of the airy illusions we can weave around the theme of human potential if we do not keep our feet solidly planted on the earth. Science is a hard road but a solid one. If we keep our eyes open to a wider vision *and* our feet firmly planted on that road, we can make some progress toward greater understanding.

I.

Science and Psi

✿✿✿

Although psi refers to real events, a great deal of superstition, misperception, distorted belief, and just plain nonsense is covered by that heading. Today those of us who have conducted scientific research in parapsychology are more often upset by some of the people who want to be our "friends," claiming that they are "scientific parapsychologists," than we are by our critics. Because I emphasize a scientific understanding of psi throughout this book, this chapter will be devoted to clarifying what scientific method is and to sketching the basic scientific procedures that have led to the proof of the existence of psi. My hope is that the reader will then be able to distinguish scientific parapsychology from its imitations.

Science is basically a technique or disciplined style of observing and thinking in order to refine knowledge. We start with the assumption that we know some things about those portions of the world we are interested in. However, some of this knowledge is too general to be useful in the study of specific questions, and some of it may be just plain wrong. What is knowledge? Our knowledge is a set of mental maps, concepts and theories about the nature of the reality (both outside of us and inside our heads), that direct our dealings with reality. To deal with it most effectively, we need extremely accurate maps of the territory we are going to function in. But our present maps are rough and contain many errors and blank spots. We need to refine them.

Traditional Ways of Knowing

For those who have wanted to know more, there have always been many ways of refining knowledge. We can roughly identify three major ways: the way of direct experience, the way of authority, and the way of reason. Each has its strong and its weak points. A brief examination of each will demonstrate how they are combined to create the scientific method.

The *way of direct experience* is embodied in such sayings as "seeing is believing" and "he who tastes, knows." If I want to know how people behave under stress, I can find a situation in which people are under stress, and I can watch them. If I want to know what the taste of a banana is, I can buy a banana and eat it. This may give me much better knowledge of behavior under stress or the taste of bananas than I could gain if I simply read about them or had someone else tell me about them. Unfortunately, as we have learned from psychology, our internal experiences may be rather poor representations or outright distortions of the reality that stimulates them. He who tastes does not necessarily know much at all about the taste because he may not have been paying very good attention at the time. Anyone who has attended a court trial in which five eyewitnesses, all of whom presumably looked at the same event from essentially the same vantage point, describe five different versions of what happened will understand that direct experience of something does not necessarily lead to knowledge, to a good conceptual map of the experience. The old saying ought to be rephrased: "He who tastes has an *opportunity* to know." Whether he makes very good use of that opportunity is not guaranteed.

The *way of authority* refers to getting knowledge from other people who are supposed to know. Someone may explain to us how something works, or we may read an explanation in a book by a recognized expert. There are obvious advantages to the way of authority: It immensely extends our own experience by making available to us the experiences and thoughts of others about situations that we might never have an opportunity to experience for ourselves. It can be a magnificent time-saver. I do not have to redevelop the entire arts of metallurgy and electricity in order to make and wire up a doorbell.

But it is painfully clear that apparent authorities are often stubbornly wrong. Many authorities once wrote that the earth was flat. Believing someone simply because that person is an authority may greatly mislead us. Therefore, although it is valuable to have the benefit of other people's experiences, we cannot rely too heavily on them.

The *way of reason* stems from a widespread and largely implicit belief that there is one valid logic, one absolutely correct way of thinking about things, and that if we just define the elements of a situation clearly and apply the rules of logic to them correctly, we are bound to come out with the correct understanding of the situation. We will be rational. Clearly, logic can be extremely helpful in allowing us to go beyond our immediate observations and experiences, to extrapolate into the unknown, to play ahead. But the other side of this coin is that philosophers and logicians are widely known to quarrel, often vehemently, with each other about what is true.

Quite aside from the rather important fact that what often passes as logic and rationality is actually *rationalization* (making up reasons for what we emotionally believe) this sort of contention over what is true by logic comes about because, as we now understand, there is no *one* absolutely true logic. There are *many* logics. We can have many grammatical logics; we can have various kinds of mathematical logics; we can have a muscular logic for riding a bicycle; etc. *Any* logic stems from making some *assumptions:* Two plus two equals four, not by some cosmic decree, but because in our mathematical system we *define* two plus two as equaling four. Parallel lines, if extended to infinity, remain the same distance apart according to conventional, Euclidian geometry. But if you change the assumptions, you come up with two other geometries: one in which parallel lines eventually come closer together and meet as you extend them to infinity and another in which parallel lines begin diverging and eventually are an infinite distance apart when extended to infinity. All three geometries have useful scientific applications.

Thus, we cannot rely on logic alone because it is an inherently self-contained map. Although it may be flawless in and of itself, it may not guide us through our territory very well.

Science

Science accepts the drawbacks of the three ways of achieving knowledge but combines them into a method that, if systematically and carefully applied over and over again, will lead to a progressive refinement of knowledge, an increasingly better match between our cognitive maps and the various territories they depict. The essence of science consists of a cyclical flow of information about some area of reality. This flow begins with an observational process, moves on to a theorizing process, and ends in a predictive process that comes back to observable reality, all constantly linked into a social framework by communication. Figure 1-1 represents this scheme as a mandala. The circles represent processes; the arrows indicate information flow. This simplified representation does not take into account a number of complexities introduced by our humanness. We will deal with these complexities later.

We begin with some segment of reality that we are interested in—biology, behavior under stress, psi phenomena, whatever. We observe what goes on, what the phenomena seem to be, what changes occur in them, their intensity, their possible causal sequences, and so forth. This constitutes a flow of information from the field of interest to our observational process and gives us our data.

In science we assume that we are probably poor observers, that we do not look at the correct time and so miss things, that sometimes things happen too fast for us to observe them adequately, or that our senses are simply not keen enough. So we commit ourselves to a constant refinement of the observational

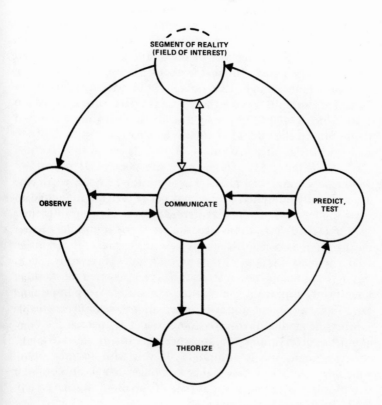

Figure 1-1. Essence of science.

process, looking for our flaws and ways of correcting them. We may invent instruments or techniques to accomplish this. If I am interested in the structure of leaves, I can see only so much with my naked eye, so I may invent a magnifying glass or a microscope to improve my observations. If I am interested in the behavior of people under stress, I may find that in various stressful situations, everybody runs around so frantically that I cannot begin to keep track of all that is happening. I may invent a technique of using multiple observers, each with a specialized task he can carry out adequately, or some other technique for making more intense observations of selected phenomena at selected times, rather than attempting to cover everything at once. These may improve the quality of my data. Thus, we collect better sets of observations or facts. (Official science makes a great hullabaloo about dealing with the *facts*.)

It turns out, though, that nobody is interested primarily in facts. For example, assume that there is a structure in a certain town which is 100.63 feet long, 214 feet high, with an S-shaped depression in the middle of what might correspond to the roof, and that inside this structure is a 1949 Nash, a 1974 Ford, 6 clerical assistants, 247 pounds of white paper, 304 pounds of yellow paper, and 4 monkeys. These are the facts. So what? We are not really interested in the facts per se. We are interested in what the facts *mean*. This is often expressed as being interested in "important" facts, those facts that verify or contradict certain meanings, certain cognitive maps we want to make. In a murder trial, the precise weight of the suspect's shoes is certainly a fact, but it is probably not relevant; whereas whether or not his fingerprints appear on the murder weapon is a very important fact. Thus, we do not stop with observations; we *interpret* them.

Scientific method involves a commitment to theorize logically about the observations you are working with. If you are going to use a logic, use it accurately. If you wish to prove that your new refining process makes a stronger metal, do not have two plus two equaling seven as part of the proof. Recheck your logic, run cross-checks, make sure you have obeyed its rules. Further, your theory must logically account for all the important facts you already know about the phenomena.

In many ways, science is a refined version of common sense. Unfortunately, common sense usually stops at this second step. Once we have figured out what the facts mean (theorized), we feel satisfied and forget about the situation. We have taken some experiences that initially did not make sense and finally matched them with or created a cognitive map that seems logical, and our curiosity or fear of the unknown is satisfied.

The capacity of the human mind to build a cognitive structure from any assorted set of facts is absolutely amazing. I sometimes demonstrate this to people by describing some very odd and senseless act that they could do and then asking them immediately to give me three reasons why it would be a good thing to do. Some people can turn out logical, plausible-sounding reasons almost as fast as they can talk. Scientific method recognizes that logic may have no relation to reality and therefore *insists* that investigation must not stop just because ideas seem logical and plausible. You have to go on to the next step of continuing to work out the logical consequences of a theory and make some *predictions* about aspects of reality that you have not yet observed but that are implied by the theory. Then you have to set up the conditions to test your predictions, go back to reality, and see whether they come out. If they do not, the theory must be either modified or thrown out entirely.

Suppose I observe some people under stress and see that they wave their arms frantically. I also take blood samples and observe that there is an abnormally high amount of adrenalin in their blood. I might then construct a theory that adrenalin is released in response to stress and that the presence of adrenalin in the bloodstream directly affects muscular coordination, with the result that people wave their arms wildly. It sounds plausible. But if the theory is true, where can it lead? I might then go on to reason that if this is true, in the absence of a stressful situation, the direct injection of adrenalin into the bloodstream should make people wave their arms wildly. I test this prediction and find that it is not true.

The process described so far constitutes a flow of information from some area of reality to observation and reasoning processes that result in predictions that lead back to the area of reality. All this can take place in one person's mind. We have combined the way of direct experience and the way of reasoning, and if we kept repeating this process, our knowledge should continue to improve. However, science is a social enterprise carried out by colleagues. This gives science far greater power than a single individual can have. This communications process is represented in the center of Figure 1-1. Information flows both to and from the processes of observation, theorizing, and predicting. The dotted arrows to and from reality symbolize the communication between scientific method and reality. That is how science deals with the drawbacks each of the three traditional ways of knowledge has when practiced in isolation.

A scientist must communicate his observations to his colleagues freely and fully. No secrets are allowed; he must communicate *all* the relevant data. His colleagues then attempt to duplicate similar observations under the conditions he described. If they cannot repeat his observations, or if they come up with different ones, then there was something wrong with the original scientist's report. Either his senses or observational powers were not in good order, or he did not describe all the conditions needed to make his observations.

To return to our earlier example, another colleague may subject a new group of subjects to stress and find that their adrenalin levels are elevated, but they do not wave their arms wildly. He communicates this to me. This makes me reexamine my original observations or conduct new experiments, and I might find, for example, that I used a group of subjects from a certain cultural background in which they were taught to express tension by physical agitation and that my colleague used subjects from a different background. Clearly, our observations become more precise through this communication with others.

Similarly, I must freely communicate the reasoning that goes into my theorizing and the predictions based on my theory. Colleagues will study these and may detect logical errors in my theorizing, suggest other logical consequences from my theorizing, see other testable predictions stemming from the theorizing. By this full communication, I gain the advantage of consensual validation from my peers; they give me feedback on whether I am using my abilities of observation and reasoning in ways that we agree are correct. That is, I, as an individual, may have certain flaws as an observer and a thinker. Although my colleagues also have flaws, it is unlikely that they have *exactly* the same flaws, so they may help me correct my flaws and I theirs.

This, then, is the scientific method, a constant flow of information from parts of reality through observation, theorizing, predicting, a flow shared and enriched by free communication among colleagues working in that area. The whole process is continually repeated. Each time, our observations become more precise and detailed, and the theories (our cognitive maps about the nature of reality) fit more precisely and have wider coverage. How can this method be used to establish the reality of psi phenomena?

Spontaneous Psi Experiences

Many people have had the experience of thinking about a friend, hearing the telephone ring, and finding that it is that friend calling. People who have such experiences have frequently gone on to theorize that this is a form of telepathy or some other mind-to-mind contact. Somehow they picked up the friend's intention to call before the friend actually began dialing, and so were thinking about the friend when the phone rang. This shows that there must be some form of communication that goes directly from one mind to another, even if science cannot explain it.

This kind of real-life happening underlies many people's belief in psi, but any good scientist would say that it is not sufficient evidence to postulate some unknown form of mind-to-mind communication. Alternative theories could be advanced to explain the observation. The story is anecdotal and might not really have happened that way. Perhaps the friend had called hundreds of times over a period of years, and once or twice, our reporter happened to be thinking of the friend just before the telephone rang. Or the person might think of that friend practically all the time, in which case there would naturally be many coincidences with phone calls. Or it might not have happened at all. The account could be imagination, rather than reporting. Because people forget or make up things that they honestly believe are memories, because people are often vague about the details of such events, you need not take them seriously. Then there is the matter of simple coincidence.

It would be appropriate at this point to dispel the widely accepted, orthodox myth that apparent spontaneous psi is a rare event that happens only to weird, unhappy, uneducated, or neurotic people and therefore is not of interest to the majority of us. I have always known that psi experiences are much more widespread than the orthodox intellectual culture allows. This has been based on my experience with the many people who have come up to me after lectures and told me about personal psi experiences that they have never mentioned to others. However, my personal knowing was a very selected form of knowledge. What was needed was a good general survey of the population. Until very recently, there had been very little sampling of this sort because parapsychologists have not had the resources and funds to conduct such surveys. Two years ago, however, Andrew Greeley [28], a sociologist at the National Opinion Research Center, reported an excellent survey of 1,460 Americans who had been carefully selected to be representative of the population in general. His findings indicate that although *apparent* psi and related phenomena may be rare as far as official culture is concerned, they are actually very widespread. Fully 58 percent of the sample felt that they had had some sort of telepathic experience (the feeling that they were in touch with someone far away) at least once. The figures showed that 32 percent of Americans believed that they have experienced telepathy several times or often, that 24 percent felt that they had experienced some sort of clairvoyance (seeing events that happened at a great distance as they were happening) at least once, and that 10 percent had experienced clairvoyance several times or often. The young, women, and blacks were more likely to have psychic experiences, although these differences were small. Perhaps even more surprising was Greeley's finding that 27 percent of the population (50 million people) felt they had had real contact with the dead and that 11 percent reported having such experiences several times or often.

Greeley's interviewers also asked about mystical experiences ("Have you ever felt as though you were very close to a powerful, spiritual force that seemed to lift you out of yourself?"), brief alterations of consciousness that generally are ineffable (cannot be really communicated with words), revelatory (provide certain knowledge about basic human concerns), transient, and passive (in the sense that they happen to, rather than being directly caused by, the person). Much to their amazement, they found that 36 percent had had such an experience at least once or twice. Extrapolating to the population at large, some 70 million Americans have had some sort of mystical experience, and about 10 million have these experiences frequently.

Furthermore, Greeley found no evidence to support the orthodox belief that frequent mystic experiences or psychic experiences stem from deprivation or psychopathology. His "mystics" were generally better educated, more successful economically, and less racist, and they were rated substantially happier on measures of psychological well-being than those who had not had such experiences. Greeley's survey indicates that it is normal to have apparently paranormal experiences. The paranormal is not the exclusive province of a few deranged people. Certainly, some such people have paranormal experiences, but I suspect that their proportion is probably not much higher than it is in most other areas of ordinary life.

If apparently paranormal experiences happen to the majority of us, does that mean that most of us are deluded? The fact that many people believe something does not make it true. But it is possible to go just so far in refuting alternative, normal explanations of apparent psi with spontaneous case collections. Of necessity, psychical research moved into an experimental stage so that *specific* alternative theories could be *specifically* ruled out.

A Basic ESP Experiment

Suppose that you put two people in a room in accordance with a written plan and designate one the sender and the other the receiver or *percipient*. In parapsychological literature, they are usually called *agent* and *subject*. The percipient and the sender sit back to back so that they cannot see each other. A third person, the experimenter, observes the procedure. The sender is asked to think of some simple thing, draw a sketch of it, and try to send the image mentally to the percipient. The percipient is asked to make a sketch of whatever impressions come to mind. When the percipient has sketched his impression as well as he can, you compare the two sketches.

Suppose they look like the sketches shown in Figure 1-2. The sender has drawn a crude sketch of a bird; the percipient, a picture of a balloon floating through a cloudy sky. Because both birds and balloons fly through cloudy skies, you may feel there is a great deal of similarity between the two drawings and conclude that there was indeed telepathic transmission, although it was not completely clear (the idea of flying in the sky came through, but not the particular representation of a bird). You have only the crudest kind of theory to interpret your observation at this point: that a mysterious something (telepathy) can transmit information directly from mind to mind. The predictions you could make from such an incompletely articulated theory are very rough. For example, you may predict that other people may sometimes demonstrate telepathy and that conventional theories about the nature of reality that restrict communication solely to known physical energies are incomplete.

This simple experiment strongly excludes our first alternative theory. We are not dealing with an anecdote. This situation involves controlled observations. We have written down a description of the experimental procedure, and the drawings can be put in front of us at any time, so there is no need to worry about a failure of memory.

However, although we may all accept the observation that drawings of a bird and a balloon do have similar associations of *flying* and *sky*, we may not want to accept the theory that telepathy was responsible for this similarity. At least seven other alternative theories can be proposed to make sense of the data. Some of these will have already occurred to you.

Alternative theory 2 is that because the sender and percipient were members of the same culture and people of one culture think about many things in common, the similarity between the two drawings is simply a matter of coincidence or chance.

Alternative theory 3 is that the resemblance between the drawings is a subjective judgment and that we only see them as similar because we want to. The apparent similarity is not an objective fact; a bird and a balloon do not look alike. Because

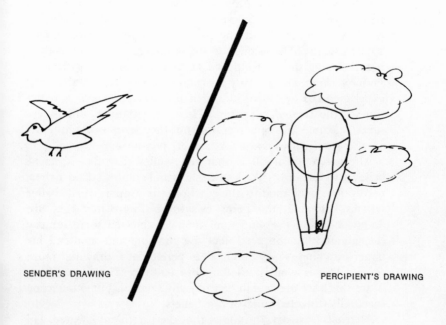

SENDER'S DRAWING   PERCIPIENT'S DRAWING

Figure 1-2. Drawings by sender and percipient in simple telepathy experiment.

science is (or should be) based on objective data, the results of this experiment are too subjective to take seriously.

Alternative theory 4 is that the similarity may have been suggested by some common external stimulus. For example, an airplane may have flown overhead a few minutes before the experiment began, and even though it was only semiconsciously perceived (and not remembered in reporting the experiment), the sound of this airplane may have triggered mental processes related to flying, suggesting a bird to the sender and a balloon to the percipient. Thus, the results show only that a common stimulus can result in similar chains of thought in different people.

Alternative theory 5 is that there was communication between the sender and percipient but that it was probably ordinary sensory communication. While sketching, the sender might have unconsciously whispered something about flying that the percipient overheard, or the percipient consciously or unconsciously might have listened to the sounds made by the sender's pencil during the drawing and figured out something from it. Perhaps there was a shiny surface in the room (such as the experimenter's eyeballs) in which the percipient saw a reflection of the sender's drawing. These are unusual and exceptionally acute kinds of perception, but they are possible in terms of what we already know about sensory perception.

Alternative theory 6 is that the sender may have been a believer in telepathy. We know that people tend to distort their perceptions and modify their actions to support their belief systems, often without being consciously aware that they are doing so. Thus, the sender might have detected some sensory cues about what the percipient was drawing and modified his target drawing to resemble the percipient's drawing more closely. This is what is called a *motivated recording error*. That is, we think we are making an objective record, but our record is actually distorted to favor our beliefs.

Alternative theory 7 proposes that the percipient cheated. He might have sneaked over behind the sender and looked over his shoulder or taken a mirror out of his pocket and looked over his shoulder with it when the experimenter was not looking.

Alternative theory 8 takes the cheating hypothesis one step farther and proposes that the experimenter tampered with the record and perhaps made up the whole experiment.

All these alternative theories predict that if you eliminate the particular ordinary method by which information can be transmitted, you will not get these kinds of results in future experiments. They further support the orthodox physical theories of human nature and the universe because they say that nothing inexplicable is happening.

This hypothetical experiment was similar to work done in the very early days of psychical research and still often done by amateurs today. As good scientists, however, we have to set up an experiment in such a way that if results are produced, various alternative theories will be ruled out. Specifically, we must continue to rule out alternative theory 1 (that it is all anecdotal) by recording precise observations at the time so that they can be inspected later. We must rule out alternative 2 (that it is all coincidence or chance) by being able to define precisely what coincidence would be in this case and demonstrate that our results are not due to it. We must rule out alternative 3 (that we are being subjective in our judgment of similarity) by making objective ratings of our results, ratings that any educated rater can agree with or that are at least immune to systematic bias. We must rule out alternative 4 (that a common stimulus triggered similar associations in sender and percipient) by selecting the target to be transmitted in a way that is independent of any possible common stimulus. We must rule out alternative 5 (that there was acute but ordinary sensory communication of the information) by making it impossible for such sensory communication to occur. Alternative 6 (motivated recording errors) must be ruled out by mechanizing the recording process so it cannot be unwittingly tampered with by the experimenter and/or by eliminating the experimenter's knowledge of the target so that he cannot systematically slant the record. That is, we can try to make sure that any recording errors are *random* so that they will cancel out, rather than *systematic* (in which case, they add up). Alternative 7 (cheating by the percipient) must be ruled out by making cheating impossible. Alternative 8 (that the experimenter cheats) can be made very unlikely but is impossible to rule out entirely if someone wants to believe this alternative badly enough.

Now let us jump ahead some fifty years from the beginnings of experimental psychical research to the 1930s and look at the kind of sophisticated parapsychological experiment that established the reality of psi phenomena by ruling out these various alternatives.

The Pearce-Pratt Experiment

In 1933, J. B. Rhine and J. Gaither Pratt [98] conducted a complex experiment with a promising percipient, Hubert

Pearce, a student at the Divinity School of Duke University. Pratt was the experimenter, and Rhine acted as data collector for all series and coexperimenter on the last. Procedurally, this was a clairvoyance experiment. The experimenter put cards in a designated spot at a designated time without turning them over and looking at them. Thus, there was no one trying to act as a sender. The targets were the well-known Zener cards, a deck of twenty-five cards, five each of five different symbols (a cross, a square, a circle, wavy lines, and a star).

Here is the basic procedure as the experimenters described it:

At the time agreed upon, Pearce visited Pratt in his research room on the top floor of what is now the Social Science Building on the main Duke campus. The two men synchronized their watches and set an exact time for starting the test, allowing enough time for Pearce to cross the quadrangle to the Duke Library where he occupied a cubicle in the stacks at the back of the building. From his window, Pratt could see Pearce enter the Library.

Pratt then selected a pack of ESP cards from several packs always available in the room. He gave this pack of cards a number of dovetail shuffles and a final cut, keeping them face-down throughout. He then placed the pack on the right-hand side of the table at which he was sitting. In the center of the table was a closed book on which it had been agreed with Pearce that the card for each trial would be placed. At the minute set for starting the test, Pratt lifted the top card from the inverted deck, placed it face-down on the book, and allowed it to remain there for approximately a full minute. At the beginning of the next minute, this card was picked up with the left hand and laid, still face-down, on the left-hand side of the table, while with the right hand Pratt picked up the next card and put it on the book. At the end of the second minute, this card was placed on top of the one on the left and the next one was put on the book. In this way, at the rate of one card per minute, the entire pack of twenty-five cards went through the process of being isolated, one card at a time, on the book in the center of the table, where it was the target or stimulus object for that ESP trial.

In his cubicle in the library, Pearce attempted to identify the target cards, minute by minute, and recorded his responses in pencil. At the end of the run, there was on most test days a rest period of five minutes before a second run followed in exactly the same way. Pearce made a duplicate of his call record, signed one copy, and sealed it in an envelope for Rhine. The two sealed records were delivered personally to Rhine, most of the time before Pratt and Pearce compared their records and scored the number of successes. On the few occasions when Pratt and Pearce met and compared their unsealed duplicates before both of them had delivered their sealed records to Rhine, the data could not have been changed without collusion, as Pratt kept the results from the unsealed records and any discrepancy between them and Rhine's results would have been noticed. In subseries D, Rhine was on hand to receive the duplicates as the two other men met immediately after each session for the checkup. [98]

Let us examine how this actual experiment successfully rules out the alternative theories proposed to explain the results of our earlier, primitive experiment.

First, we are clearly not dealing with anecdotal data. We have a contemporary account of the work; all targets and responses were written down. Indeed, they were written in duplicate and checked by Rhine, acting as an experimenter independent of Pratt, who was conducting the test procedure. Furthermore, when three independent psychologists later examined the photostats of the original records, they found only a single scoring error in the entire series, and that one was a matter of overlooking a hit [96]. We can say with great confidence that we know precisely what happened in this experiment and therefore must give this evidence serious consideration.

As for the second alternative, in the Pearce-Pratt experiment, we can objectively and precisely define what chance is and determine whether the results are significantly different from it. When you are guessing the identity of a deck of Zener cards (without looking at each card after guessing it), it is obvious (to scientifically accepted logic systems) that you have a 1-in-5 chance of simply guessing the correct identity of each card. In a run through a deck of 25, you should average 5 right guesses by chance alone. Sometimes you will get 4 or 3, sometimes 6 or 7, sometimes more extreme values. But by applying basic probability statistics, which are used in many major branches of science, you can make a rather precise estimate of how likely or unlikely a given observed result is if no psi is involved. The exact methods can be gleaned from any basic statistics book or from the extensive parapsychological literature. In this context it is sufficient to say that for a given experiment, you can objectively evaluate the probability of getting any particular result. The conventional scientific rule is that if the results observed would have happened 5 or less in 100 tries by chance (conventionally expressed as $P \leq 0.05$), something in addition to chance is probably involved. If the probability is 1 in 100 $(P = 0.01)$ or even less $(P < 0.01)$, something else is almost certainly taking place.

Table 1-1
Results of the Pearce-Pratt Distance Series

Subseries	Number of Runs	Hits Above Chance	Odds of Occurrence by Chance Alone
A	12	+59	$P < 10^{-14}$
B	44	+75	$P < 10^{-6}$
C	12	+28	$P < 10^{-4}$
D	6	+26	$P < 10^{-6}$
Combined	74	+188	$P < 10^{-22}$

Table 1-1 gives the results for the four subseries and the combined results of the Pearce-Pratt experiment. In all subseries, Pearce scored far more correct items than would occur by chance alone, and even in the least significant series, subseries C, such results would occur by chance less than 1 in 10,000 times (conventionally noted in the table and throughout this book as $P < 10^{-4}$).* In the most successful subseries, the odds

---

* A probability of 10^{-3} is 1 in 1,000;, 10^{-6} is 1 in 1 million, 10^{-9} is 1 in 1 billion; 10^{-12} is 1 in 1 trillion; and so forth.

against chance were enormous $(P < 10^{-14})$. The four series as a whole were exceptionally significant. Results such as these have a probability of 10^{-22}. Clearly, it is ridiculous to ascribe the results to coincidence. These results are far more significant than those regarded as successful in many other branches of science.

Alternative theory 3, that the similarity is a subjective judgment, is clearly ruled out by the procedure of guessing at the identity of cards. Everyone in our culture can agree that a square on the sender's record sheet for trial 4 and a square on the percipient's record sheet for trial 4 on a given run is exact similarity. Furthermore, the use of probability statistics to evaluate the significance of the series is also objective; anyone who knows how to do the mathematics would come up with the same figures.

Alternative 4 (that some common stimulus might have triggered similar associations in sender and percipient) is similarly ruled out by this experimental procedure. Pratt thoroughly shuffled the decks of target cards without looking at them. No matter what common stimuli he and Pearce had been subjected to, these could not affect the shuffling of the cards in any conventional way. Thus, the determination of the target (in this case, the sequence of cards) was completely independent of sender and percipient.

Alternative theory 5 (that there was some sort of sensory leakage to convey the information) is clearly ruled out here. The only sensorily perceivable information was the pattern of ink on the face of each card, a pattern that was exposed only to the tabletop and the book the card was placed on. Pratt did not know what each card was. There were no eyes or television cameras embedded in the tabletop to pick up this information, and Pearce was shielded from the cards by distance and building walls. The information was later transferred to Pratt's record sheet, but Pearce could not see that procedure by normal means.

Alternative theory 6 (that of motivated recording errors) clearly cannot apply here because Pratt did not know what Pearce's responses were at the time he copied down the order of the target deck. Pratt might have made errors in copying down this order, but they would be random errors with respect to Pearce's responses. As such, they would lower Pearce's scores as frequently as they would raise them and so would cancel out.

Alternative 7 (cheating by Pearce) seems effectively ruled out by the fact that Pearce sat in a separate building. Yet devoted critics such as Charles Hansel [31] try to explain away the results of the Pearce-Pratt study on this basis. Hansel believes a priori that psi is exceptionally unlikely or impossible (a common position, but not one in accordance with the open-mindedness and primacy of observation called for in science) and so argues that if there is *any* possibility of a normal explanation of results, such as cheating, *no matter how remote and regardless of whether there is any evidence to support it,* an experiment should be considered invalid. He proposed that Pearce might have snuck out of the library and entered a room across the hall from Pratt's room. There, he presumably stood on a chair and looked through a transom across the hall and into Pratt's room through that room's transom and was presumably able to see Pratt writing down the order of the target cards at the end of the experiment. His eyesight must have been exceptional indeed. According to this theory, he could quickly alter his own record sheets (on the run?) while sneaking back into the library so that Pratt could see him coming out of the library at the right time. Pearce would have to run rather fast to do this. Hansel supports his theory with a diagram of the room arrangements, based on his personal observations of the building some years later, showing that the two room doors were opposite one another

Aside from the strained complexity of this sequence of actions, Charles Honorton [34] noted that Hansel's diagram, which is the main support of his conjectures, is labeled "not to scale." If the drawing were to scale, it would be obvious that the two doors were actually too far apart for such a scenario to be possible. This certainly raises the question of whether the critics of parapsychology make motivated errors themselves.

If we take the position that psi is so improbable or impossible that *any* alternative explanation is preferable, then we can never rule out alternative theory 8. The possibility of fraud on the part of the experimenter was the line seriously taken by George Price [88] in one of the last major attacks on parapsychology to appear in a major scientific journal.* He reasoned that no intelligent person could read the evidence for ESP and still doubt that it existed, *but because ESP was a priori impossible,* we had to conclude that all the good evidence could be accounted for by errors and downright fraud on the part of parapsychologists and percipients.

There have, regrettably, been some cases of deliberate cheating by (former) parapsychologists. Judging by J. B. Rhine's review of this problem [99], there have been thirteen proven cases since 1930, including the well-publicized Levy case [100]. Most of these cases are quite old and occurred at a time when methodological standards were not so high as they are today. These cases were all exposed by other parapsychologists. I do not know whether the percentage of experimenters who cheat is higher or lower in parapsychology than in more orthodox sciences, but I suspect that it is much lower because parapsychologists are much more sensitive to this issue and so are on guard about it.

Ian St. James-Roberts [124] recently conducted a survey of cheating in ordinary science and published his findings in the *New Scientist.* Although he could not estimate the actual incidence of cheating, he did report one finding that I considered extremely discouraging: No punishment of any sort was given to 80 percent of those caught cheating. Indeed, some continued to be promoted. *All* thirteen investigators definitely caught cheating in parapsychology were cut out of the field, and *all* of their results have subsequently been considered quite dubious unless independently replicated by others.

The position taken by Price and some other critics is psychologically understandable. People go to very strange and irrational lengths to protect their systems of belief. However, although I can understand this position, I do not believe that it has a legitimate place in scientific inquiry.

* Price later retracted and apologized for these unfounded accusations of fraud [89].

When all these alternatives have been ruled out, the theory best able to explain the data of the Pearce-Pratt experiment is that some form of psi (clairvoyance) was operating. The implied prediction that other 'people will be able to perform similarly under similar conditions has been validated in hundreds of successful experiments documented in the parapsychological literature.

Thus we have a straightforward example of the application of scientific procedure of the sort originally used to prove the existence of psi phenomena. We went from a stage of anecdote and crude experimentation to sophisticated experimentation that gave us precise information in which we could put great confidence. Now let us look at some of the human complexities that frequently enter into the scientific process in general and into parapsychological research.

Science as Practiced by Human Beings

The diagram of scientific method presented in Figure 1-1 was quite simplified. Figure 1-3 offers a more realistic mandala of science because it puts the human realities back into the process. I have made three changes in the basic diagram to reflect these: the circles around the various processes as partially open rather than closed, a clockwise flow of information is indicated in addition to the formal counterclockwise flow (from Reality to Observation to Theorizing to Prediction to Reality) flow, and a ring labeled "Mind" is drawn outside of, but connected to, the formal process of scientific method.

The formal processes of Observation, Theorizing, Predicting, and Communicating have been opened to reflect the fact that scientists seldom give much explicit thought to what they are doing as they work. Their work habits are partly automatic and routinized and therefore are unknowingly influenced by many implicit assumptions and nonconscious processes. These are the sorts of things (later called creative) that allow a scientist to see important facts in a situation that has been investigated but not really observed. But they are also the sorts of things that make some scientists positively blind to things that happen

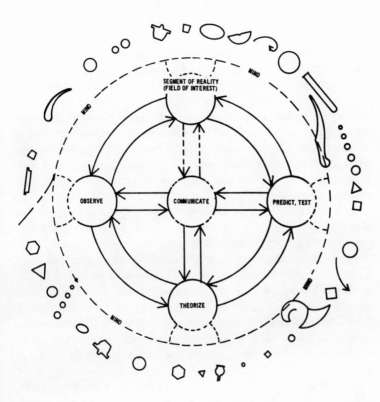

Figure 1-3. Mandala of science.

right in front of them. Human perceptual mental processes are far more complex than we realize, as I have detailed in *States of Consciousness* [173].

The counterclockwise flow of information reflects the fact that scientists do not start out as totally open, naïve observers who are stimulated by something and then go on to theorize, communicate, and test their theories. We all approach almost every situation from a committed, prejudiced point of view. We already have some explicit (conscious) and many implicit (unconscious) ideas about what is important, worth observing, or worth thinking about. A botanist looking about in the fields is full of ideas about which plants are useful and which are weeds.

At an extreme, we talk about scientists who are rigidly bound by their training and instruments: they will only look at things they already have the tools to study well. Some will only look at things for which they have ready-made theories to use as explanations. Some will only theorize about things that they already have the equipment and procedures to test. What we can test is partly or wholly determined by the particular segment of reality with which we are working. Some will not look at or think about things that would be difficult to communicate to their colleagues.

Parapsychologists have been forced to see many of these human "failings" in the practice of science because of the frequently biased way nonparapsychologist scientists have criticized and rejected their work. The history of parapsychology is full of examples of outside scientists who would not, for example, bother to look at the experimental data: since they already knew there could be nothing to it, they wouldn't waste their time. They were so committed to certain theories about reality that had no place for psi phenomena that they would not look at evidence which might contradict theses theories. Or they would selectively look at a fraction of the evidence, sternly criticizing a few experiments that even parapsychologists agreed were invalid, for example, and ignoring the hundreds of others which they could not criticize according to generally accepted scientific rules.

These sorts of human failings are, of course, not limited to scientists who do not accept parapsychological findings. They happen in all fields of science, including parapsychology itself. As Abraham Maslow pointed out in a too little-known but brilliant book, *The Psychology of Science* [50], any individual scientist can use science as an open-ended, personal growth system or as one of the best neurotic defense mechanisms known.

The third ring represents an area I call *Mind*. It is the totality of functioning of the human mind that goes beyond the relatively straightforward perceptual and reasoning processes involved in formal scientific method. This is where intuition, hunches, and gut feelings come in, where a mathematician has a mental image of a certain kind of space that determines the kind of formula that he writes on paper, or where a scientist gets a funny feeling in his gut as he argues for a particular theory that makes him suspect that no matter how logical it seems, something is wrong. We have learned about some of these processes through psychology, but we have only the barest sort of information about most of them, so the figure represents them only as (yet) undefined shapes.

Beyond the level of Mind is an outermost ring that is not even labeled. I have added this ring as a reminder that we are part of the universe, not isolated reasoners who have figured it all out.

Let me further illustrate these humanizing, complicating factors with examples from parapsychology.

Consider how this field of interest affects our ability to observe. Suppose I would like to have a percipient perform a continuous, highly successful telepathy receiving task while I vary the degree of electromagnetic shielding around him to see what effect it would have on the accuracy of telepathic transmission. The nature of psi prevents me from doing this, however. Even the best percipients are quite erratic in their performance, and there is no guarantee that telepathy will be working at the time I have my instruments set up. Further, the whole social context of psi phenomena, the rejection by the orthodox establishment, means that I won't be able to get research money to carry out that kind of expensive experiment anyway! So I am constrained in my observations.

Our theorizing constrains our observations. As a personal example, I have never conducted a study of precognition. Technically, it would be easier to do than many of the other studies I have done, but my conceptual system, my interlocking network of current theories about reality, simply cannot deal with the idea of knowing about an event before it occurs, before it has been caused. While I never say consciously to myself "I will not work with precognition because I don't understand it," somehow I just never get around to doing precognition studies. I don't want to collect data I don't feel able to think clearly about.*

Our ability to make predictions in order to test the consequences of our theorizing affects what sort of theories we develop. We do not have many good theories (even small-scale theories) in parapsychology. Aside from the fact that only a small number of scientists are working in the field, this seems to have come about partly because of a fixation on card-guessing tests as the main method of parapsychological research. For several decades, it dominated all parapsychological research. Percipients had occasionally reported that the quality of their mental imagery affected how well their psi was working (see Chapter 3). But mental imagery is not reflected in whether a percipient calls circle, wave, or star, so researchers did not think much about imagery or develop the tools for measuring it. If imagery cannot be measured very well, theories that must be tested by effects of imagery cannot be developed. Fortunately, psychologists and parapsychologists are again becoming interested in imagery, as will be illustrated later.

Finally, parapsychology may have a certain perverse quality to it that affects our ability to make predictions and test them. In studying manifestations of psi in psychoanalytic situations in which he had a good knowledge of his patients' dynamics, Jule Eisenbud [24] reports many instances in which psi phenomena would apparently interfere with expectations and predictions, as if there were some inherent capriciousness or perverseness in the phenomena themselves.

The communication process is also affected by all these other variables. Sometimes, there are things you have observed or ideas you have come up with that you just do not know how to communicate properly or that are communicated in a distorted form. Sometimes, this is caused by social inhibitions about frank discussion of things that are taboo; sometimes, it results from the fact that scientific communication is so overwhelmingly confined to words and that words are not adequate to

---

* Since writing this statement I have been *forced* to deal with precognition! See Chapter 7.

express certain things. Because we are human beings, with fears, compulsions, ambitions, and ego needs, our communications are sometimes distorted to impress our colleagues and win recognition, rather than to carry out the scientific process adequately. At the very least, we all tend to interpret complex data selectively in ways that promote our favorite theories. This is usually only a minor problem because there are always colleagues around who will argue with an interpretation! This illustrates how science as a social enterprise can compensate for individual biases.

In spite of all these human failings, scientific method works very well. We now have very precise knowledge in a wide variety of sciences that simply did not exist even a few generations ago. Parapsychology is a very small-scale science. Very few people (a couple of dozen full-time scientists at the most for most of its history) have been engaged in scientific parapsychological research. Its funds have been woefully inadequate to deal with the complexities and importance of psi. Nevertheless, our knowledge is much more precise than it was a few decades ago. I hope that more scientists, with better training and more equipment, will work in parapsychology, and as the field slowly gains acceptance, I believe this will eventually come about.

Resistance to Knowledge

For most of its history, and in many cases today, reactions to parapsychological data have illustrated another aspect of the humanness of the scientific process. Allison [1] carried out a sociological study of parapsychology and its relationship with the rest of science. As a result, he likened the last three decades of this relationship to the covert way racial prejudice is often manifested among educated persons. He notes that J. B. Rhine's pioneering work at Duke University in the 1930s generated considerable public and academic attention, and there were numerous attempts, mainly by psychologists, to explain his results in conventional ways. Attacks were based on the possibility of recording errors, sensory leakage, improper statistics, and so on, but rapid improvements in the Duke work quickly eliminated all these grounds for criticism. Since then, the response of orthodox science has been largely one of silent and covert resistance.

Except for an occasional bitter attack based on the charge that parapsychologists *must* have faked all their data, silent resistance has been the norm. Parapsychologists have been denied academic positions and ignored as much as possible in the hope that their presence and data will somehow fade away. Denial of academic positions is a tremendous obstacle to research because it makes it difficult for researchers to get funds, to get reports published in the journals that are widely read by other scientists, and to have access to graduate students who can be trained to become the next generation of researchers.

In some ways, the strong prejudice that orthodox scientists have shown toward parapsychology is not unique. Many new areas of science have had to fight against unreasonable prejudice and have eventually won. Indeed, Thomas Kuhn [47] has argued that some degree of closed-mindedness toward unusual ideas is useful in keeping ordinary science from being easily distracted from its work. What is unusual about parapsychology, compared with other new areas of science, is the very long time that this prejudiced rejection has lasted in spite of the exceptionally high quality of scientific research in the area. I suspect that it is because the implications of psi are so revolutionary. Nevertheless, as a social system, science has built-in safeguards against being blind about some particular area for too long. New scientists enter the field with different sets of implicit blindnesses, old scientists die, and developments in other areas alter our prejudices. I believe that parapsychology will enter the mainstream of science within a few generations, possibly within one.

2.

Getting the Message from There to Here: The Beginning of the Psi Process

✤✤

In looking at the nature of scientific inquiry in the previous chapter, we saw that scientists are always trying to make sense out of things, to devise theories and explanations for things they have observed that fit in with our general knowledge about these things and help us to predict similar things we have not yet observed.

The great difficulty with, and challenge of, psi phenomena is that in so many ways they do not make sense. Indeed, at this stage of our knowledge, they are *defined* as unexplainable in terms of our generally accepted physical world model. Information is received about a distant event, and desires affect a distant event with no plausible way for the information or energy to get from the event to the percipient or vice versa.

This is not to say that we know nothing about psi. As a *psychological* phenomenon, we know some things about it and are learning more. I believe that we are capable of much greater psychological understanding of how psi is related to mental events, but fitting it in with our current physical world view is exceptionally difficult and may be a problem for a long time.*

What follows in this chapter and chapters 3 and 4 is an overview of the processes involved in the four main psi phenomena: clairvoyance, telepathy, precognition, and psychokinesis. The overview will be a *model* of these processes, rather than a theory.

What is the difference between a model and a theory? We all want models and theories to explain things, but what exactly does the word *explain* mean in this context? We can distinguish two major uses of the word *explanation*.

The first use, *horizontal* explanation, is a matter of drawing comparisons with something familiar, of pointing out that what you are puzzled by is similar to something else with which you are already familiar and not puzzled about. For instance, you might ask someone for an explanation of the fact that when you carry your transistor radio behind a steel building, the station you are listening to fades out but that when you continue around the building or walk far behind it, the reception comes in again. Your friend might explain this by saying that it is like dropping a stone in a lake. The radio waves are like the ripples that spread out from the place where the stone is dropped, and the steel building is like a rock sticking up from the surface of the water. There will be a small area of calmness behind the rock because it interrupts the ripples, but a little farther in back of the rock, the ripples join again. It is the same for radio waves and the steel building; the radio waves cannot go through the steel just as the ripples cannot go through the stone, but they come together at the sides and behind it. This is an analogy to something familiar. It makes us feel more comfortable because we think that we understand the behavior of our radio.

The second kind of explanation, *vertical* explanation, deals with the unknown by talking about it on a level that is differ-

---

* I shall be delighted, however, if my physicist friends extend modern physics far enough to help explain psi and so disprove my prediction. I suspect, though, that it will not be a very straightforward kind of extension.

ent from the level of the things you want to explain. It is an abstract explanation. For example, a horizontal explanation of how electricity flows through wire might compare the electricity with water flowing through a pipe. The voltage would be like the pressure behind the water; the amperage would be like the quantity of water flowing through the pipe; the resistance would be like the effect of obstructions in the pipe or the friction of its walls. A vertical explanation of the flow of electricity in a wire would talk about electricity as a flow of electrons, about how electrons transfer from atom to atom, about electric force fields on the atomic level, about the number of electrons passing through a unit of volume in a unit of time as a measure of the flow of electric current, and so forth.

A model is generally a horizontal explanation, an analogy. In science, we use both types of explanations, but the vertical explanation is preferred and is what I described in Chapter 1 as theorizing. We already have the data in their obvious form. We do not want simply to feel more comfortable by seeing that they show patterns familiar to us. We want to know what lies behind the obvious. We want something that is more generalizable than the particular data you happen to have looked at; we want predictive power to lead us to new data.

Theories perform several functions in science. They help us to organize observations, which I like to call their *filing cabinet* or *mapping* function. Instead of memorizing thousands of separate observations, you memorize a theory from which you can predict these observations, which constitutes quite a saving of work. Theories also make predictions about where we should look for other data that may be of value to us. But they are never quite final. A theory is always subject to test as new predictions evolve from it. This applies even to so-called scientific laws. A *scientific law* is simply a theory that has worked so exceptionally well in untold thousands of trials that we have taken the human step of believing that it is a true statement about the ultimate nature of the universe, rather than a theory or concept that we have about it. The so-called law of gravity, for example, is a scientific theory about the effect of two masses upon each other in the absence of interfering forces. It has worked so well that we call it a law. But even this law is subject, in principle, to repeal or modification if evidence of conflicting instances should be discovered.

There is an important difference between a theory or vertical explanation and a model or horizontal explanation. A model can perform some of the same functions as a theory. That is, it can organize data and make some predictions about other, potentially useful observations we could make. But we do not expect a model always to be true; we know we are only using it for convenience. A theory, however, must *always* predict correctly (in principle); if it does not, it must be modified or scrapped. The analogy between electricity flowing in a wire and water flowing in a pipe is an excellent model for teaching many things about electricity, but some of the predictions you could draw from it are not correct. For example, if you greatly increase the flow of current through wire, the wire will get hot; whereas if you increase the flow of water in a pipe, the pipe obviously will not get hotter.

We simply do not have any really good theories or models of psi today in the sense of comprehensive or really detailed understandings of basic phenomena. What general theories we have so far in parapsychology tend to be *too* general, too cosmological in scope, and they are more philosophical positions than precise formulations that could lead to predictions whereby we could test their validity. We desperately need smaller-scale theories that are testable. We are starting to get them, but we do not have many yet.

What I shall present in this and the next two chapters are models for the basic psi processes, but I do want the reader to understand that they are primarily models, although they can function like theories in some instances. They look at the data about psi in terms of familiar things we know, about how information in general is handled and how some psychological processes work, and while they are good for giving an overview of psi phenomena and organizing our knowledge, they do not represent any ultimate understanding of how psi works.

Clairvoyance

Clairvoyance (from the French *clair* and *voyance,* clear seeing) is defined as the extrasensory perception of objects or events without the presence or knowledge of such objects or events in another person's mind as an intervening factor. Clairvoyance is a direct perception of external reality without any known physical energy or sensory receptor conveying the information.

The classical experimental design that established the reality of clairvoyance was the sort used in the Pearce-Pratt experiment described in Chapter 1. A deck of cards is thoroughly shuffled to randomize their order, and the percipient then guesses what this order is before anyone looks at the cards to learn their order.* Each card can be put, face down, in a special location while the percipient is trying to identify it, as in the Pearce-Pratt study (the *broken* technique), or the cards can be left in the deck and the order guessed without removing them one by one (the *down-through* technique). Scores significantly beyond chance expectation indicate the operation of clairvoyance. That is, in addition to guessing, the percipient in some way becomes aware of the identities of at least some of the cards. Readers interested in variations on this basic clairvoyance-testing design should see the discussions by Rao [96].

Figure 2-1 presents a model of the clairvoyance process. The rectangular blocks (also used in subsequent figures) indicate processes or mechanisms of some sort by which information is transformed or used. The arrows indicate the direction of information flow within the model. We will look at this first model in considerable detail because many points relevant to it will also apply to other models.

---

* This standard design does not eliminate an alternative theory of pre-cognitive telepathy. However, studies of pure clairvoyance have been successfully carried out in which a machine gives a *total* score for assessing significance but the target order is never known. The computer generates the targets, scores the responses against them, prints out the total number of hits, and then permanently erases the targets and responses from its memory.

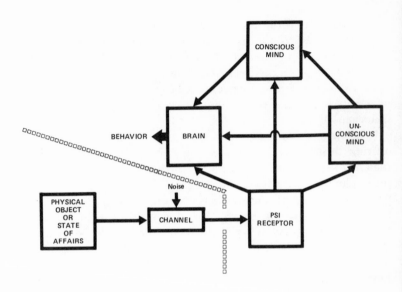

Figure 2-1. Model for clairvoyance.

We begin with the target, a physical event or state of affairs from which information flows through some channel of transmission and reaches the percipient. After reaching the percipient, the information is transformed into mental and/or neural impulses by some sort of receptor and eventually results in knowledge and/or observable behavior, from which we infer that information about the target event has reached the percipient.

Consider an ordinary example of this model. Someone asks you, "What is on your lap?" This book is the physical object on your lap. Light rays reflected from it flow through the channel of the space between you and the book, reaching a receptor mechanism, your eyes, that transforms those light rays into neural impulses by which the information can be transmitted to your brain. Your brain-mind considers the question and the incoming data and you say, "This is a book about psi."

When we apply this model to clairvoyance, we begin with some physical object or event, which is the target about which we wish to acquire information. Any object has a certain set of physical properties that define it and constitute its uniqueness. The book on your lap has a set of properties such as a certain mass, the ability to reflect certain wavelengths of light (its color), a certain surface texture, and a specific collection of printed words within it that make it not only a book but one specific book.

Parapsychological data also make it necessary for us to remain open to the idea that an object may have *psychical* properties that can be detected by psi even if they do not have any physically detectable correlates. For example, J. G Pratt reported a *focusing effect* on certain target cards in the research he and Milan Rýzl carried out with a very talented Czech percipient, Pavel Stepanek [109]. Physically, these target cards were virtually identical: pieces of cardboard that were green on one side and white on the other. Yet there was significantly higher ESP scoring on some of these target cards than on others. It would seem that some of the cards had psychical properties that made them more distinctive to the clairvoyant process than others. A large number of studies have been carried out on the physical and psychological nature of this focusing effect [43, 44, 81, 82, 83, 84, 86, 87].

We should also distinguish between active and passive properties. An *active* property emits or sends out some sort of information-carrying energy that is intrinsic to the object's nature. My desk lamp has an active property; it emits light waves. If an object has *passive* properties, it does not emit such energy. This book is passive. If no light impinges on it from the outside to be reflected back, you will not be able to see it.

Figure 2-2 presents the model of the clairvoyance process for active and passive objects. The object may have active physical or psychical properties that are detected simply because they are constantly being sent out through space by the object. In the case of psi, relevant physical examinations are screened out, by definition. We have no idea of what the nature of active psychic radiation from an object might be. On the other hand, the object may have only passive properties and so may be clairvoyantly detectable only when some sort of psychical activating energy impinges on it and is reflected by it. This reflected psi energy might result from a process within the percipient that is analogous to the way a radar set sends out a scanning beam of electromagnetic energy for targets to reflect back, or it might be some general background activating energy not specifically dependent on the human percipient for its origin, that is analogous to the way objects are visible during the day because of the background radiation of sunlight. Some researchers have proposed that extremely low frequency (ELF) electromagnetic waves, which are constantly traveling through the earth's atmosphere to varying degrees, might constitute such a background radiation and that target objects might reflect or modulate these in some fashion [79]. However, it is not clear how such a process could occur or how we could be sensitive to this modulated radiation from the *particular* target object we were trying for if it is in fact being reflected by all objects in the world.

We very much need some specific, testable theories to help us understand the clairvoyance process. We do not know what physical properties of an object or event are psychically detectable. Are all possible properties detectable, or only certain kinds of properties? Perhaps clairvoyance can detect an object's surface patterns without being able to tell us anything about its molecular structure? At the present time, we have no empirical evidence to support such limitations. Clairvoyance tests have succeeded with a very wide range of target objects, but we can hardly claim to have come anywhere near sampling the whole range of physical properties for clairvoyant detectability. The aspects of target objects that have been investigated to date, such as size, shape, color and form, do not seem to have any limiting properties [96]. The most we can say is that a wide variety of targets have been clairvoyantly detected, including various kinds of cards, musical selections played from a tape to which no one is listening [2], and the internal electronic state of electronic equipment of which the percipients had not the slightest understanding [113].

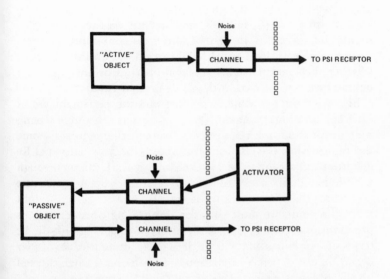

Figure 2-2. The target.

We also need to know what kinds of psychical properties there are; whether they interact with, or are related to, physical properties; whether there are deliberate ways of creating psychical properties, such as concentrating on an object in a specific way; and whether there are ways of eliminating such psychical properties so that an object might become clairvoyantly undetectable.

Here is an example of a small-scale, testable parapsychological theory concerning the nature of psychically detectable objects. It was formulated by William Roll of the Psychical Research Foundation [104]. The theory postulated that physical objects have some sort of psychical properties that are created by their individual associational histories. This leads to a testable prediction: If the associational history of an object is varied systematically, it should be possible to make that object more or less psychically detectable in proportion to the differences in its history. That is, if I have one object that has been carried for years in the pocket of a very colorful, adventurous person and a physically identical object that has simply remained in a drawer for the same length of time, a psychic should be successful in clairvoyantly discriminating between these two objects. Roll and I [106] carried out an initial test of whether such postulated psychical properties of an object can be clairvoyantly detected, with mildly positive results.

Because the target object or event and the percipient are at different locations, a model that makes sense in our ordinary state of consciousness requires some sort of channel over which the information travels from the object to the percipient. By definition, this cannot be any known physical channel. A psi experiment deliberately blocks all relevant physical channels over which the information could travel.

At this point, we must consider the baffling phenomenon of precognition—baffling, that is, in terms of understanding it; in terms of experimenting with it, it is quite straightforward. *Precognition* is the correct prediction of future events when there is no way of inferring what those events will be from knowledge of the present.* People have always had dreams that they believed predicted the future or consulted oracles who they thought could predict the future. The laboratory evidence for the existence of precognition is very straightforward. You perform the usual clairvoyance test with cards, but you ask the percipient to write down the order of the cards at some time before you actually randomize them. The nature of the randomizing process (thorough hand shuffling, usually followed by a number of cuts to be determined by extraneous factors such as the high temperature in Kansas City two days from now) means that there is no knowledge present at the time the percipient makes the calls. Significant results have been obtained in many such studies.

* The converse of precognition, *retrocognition* or *postcognition,* is also recognized as a concept. The mind somehow gets information directly from past events. There is obviously a methodological problem here. If you can verify the knowledge, then a record of it must exist. Practically no research has been done on retrocognition. The interested reader should consult E. Douglas Dean's review [20].

The model of the clairvoyance process can also serve as a model of the precognition (and retrocognition) process if we postulate some kind of channel over which information can flow backward (or forward) in time (i.e., if we assume that psi information about a future object or event can somehow flow to our present space and time location and be detectable). It is simple to say this is what happens in terms of the model we need, but the idea that only the present exists and that therefore the past is long gone and the future does not yet exist is deeply imbedded in the assumptive structive of our ordinary consciousness. It is difficult to be really open to the idea of information from the future reaching the present, much less to envision *how* this works.

Some physicists interested in parapsychological phenomena note that although the bulk of theories about time in physics are grounded in commonsense thinking, there are a number of important equations in physics that can be mathematically solved to give a solution of energy traveling either forward *or* backward in time. These time-backward solutions have been regarded as not being physically meaningful and ignored in accordance with our commonsense assumptions, but they may yet tell us something about the nature of time [91, 134].

Although I shall focus on this model as simply a model of present-time clairvoyance, it is also a model of precognitive clairvoyance. Similarly, the telepathy model, which will be discussed in Chapter 4, also becomes a model of precognitive telepathy if we postulate a channel to conduct information backward through time.

What then is the nature of the channel through which psi information flows? If I hear someone talking, it is obvious that the air carries the sound waves the speaker is producing; therefore, the air is the channel. If I see something, I know that the space between me and the thing seen carries the light energy; therefore, the space is the channel. But if I correctly guess the order of a deck of cards that I cannot see because it is in a distant room, what is it that carries the information to me?

One way of dealing with this question is to recognize the

possibility that although both space and time are *concepts* that we use in dealing with experience, they may have no absolute reality. This goes against our commonsense assumptions, but it is a useful position. (It is also a matter of direct experience in some altered states of consciousness.) If space and time do not actually exist in some ultimate form out there, then it becomes possible to bypass the whole idea that the clairvoyantly or precognitively perceived object is separated from you and so has to be reached. There is no spatial-temporal distance between you and the target; therefore, there is no problem concerning how the information travels.

This sort of thinking seems to be a good description of the psychological experiences and concepts of many psychics and mystics [49], as well as stemming from experiences in altered states of consciousness, but until someone tells us how to translate this idea into testable predictions that would be different from those generated from the idea of some kind of channel extending through space or time, we cannot consider it a scientific theory. So, in our model we shall stick with the idea of a channel.

All channels have two important properties: noise and loss. Information conveyed over most channels is subject to various degrees of distortion as a result of mixing with information other than the signal (*noise*) and to a falling off of intensity of the information-carrying energy with distance (*loss*). If the intensity of the energy conveying the information falls too far below the intensity of the energy of the noise, we may not be able to detect it. I can stand on the other side of a room and whisper, and you can hear me clearly if the room is quiet (i.e., if the channel, the air between us, is not filled with noise). But if a dozen people, all conversing loudly, are in the room, the channel between us will be filled with so much noise that you will not be able to understand me. Even though some of the energy of the sound of my whispering is still reaching you, it is undetectable because of the noise created by the other people talking. In the first case, we had a channel with a good signal-to-noise ratio; and in the second case, the channel had such a poor signal-to-noise ratio that the signal could not be heard.

What is the nature of the channel? For example, does it depend simply on space (and time) existing between target and percipient, so that there is always a channel between a percipient and *any* event in the universe? Or must there be a more tangible physical medium, such as air, between the target and the subject? All terrestrial parapsychological experiments allow for an air channel between the percipient and target. However, a telepathy* experiment conducted (without asking NASA for permission!) by astronaut Edgar Mitchell [54] while he was orbiting the earth outside the earth's atmosphere seemed to show some transfer of psi information, so perhaps physical matter between target and percipient is not necessary.

Ordinary physical channels can be shielded and blocked to varying degrees. But can the psychical channel be shielded? Both Russian [197] and American [90] studies (telepathy has been the main form of psi tested) suggest that electromagnetic shielding does not block psi. Indeed, electromagnetic shielding might even enhance ESP in gifted subjects. E. Douglas Dean [19] conducted a telepathy study in which the percipient was in Zurich, Switzerland, and the sender was skin diving off Florida (and therefore under water), yet neither this great distance nor the shielding effect of the water, which would seriously attenuate most known physical energies, kept the experiment from succeeding.

Most forms of physical energy decrease in intensity with distance, usually in proportion to the square of the distance, as the energy spreads out over a widening area. The heat from a

* I use examples from procedurally telepathic studies even though we are discussing clairvoyance because almost all such studies use physical targets, which means that there is a possibility that clairvoyance is the mechanism. Technically, we speak of GESP studies (general ESP studies) because although we have a sender trying to send, we have no way of telling whether the percipient gets the information from the sender's mind or directly from the target material. Whenever I use the word *telepathy* in this book, I am referring to the fact that someone was *trying* to send a message, without worrying about whether the percipient used telepathy or clairvoyance unless it is particularly important to make this distinction.

bright light bulb may be unpleasant and burn you if your hand is only half an inch from it. But if you move your hand a few feet away, the heat energy is now spread over such an area that its intensity is well below the harmful level. Some preliminary work by Karlis Osis and his colleagues with a GESP experiment [65, 68, 69, 105, 106] suggested that distance might produce a slight amount of attenuation (on the order of 0.7 to 1.7 units of information per thousand miles), but there are so many well-documented spontaneous instances of apparent telepathy or clairvoyance halfway around the earth in which immense amounts of information have been transmitted that the most conservative statement about distance and ESP that we could make today would be that distance has no obvious effect on clairvoyance or telepathy within terrestrial limits.

There is one exception to this general rapid falloff of the intensity of physical energy with distance: the tightly focused beam. A laser beam, for example, can remain a tight spot of intense energy over distances of many miles. Could the lack of obvious falloff of psi energy with distance indicate that the information travels in some kind of tight beam? Perhaps. But this introduces as great a problem as the lack of effect of distance. How do you aim a tight beam, say, only 1 foot wide, at someone 100 miles away when you have only the vaguest idea of the direction, as has been the case in many psi experiments? The probability of aiming the beam correctly by chance is infinitesimal.

Another possible implication of the lack of apparent falloff of psi with distance is that the energy conveying the information is so intense that even though it falls off rapidly with distance, it is still high enough above the noise level at the percipient's end to provide a clear message. A radio transmitter, by analogy, may put out 100 kilowatts of power right at the transmitting antenna; and although the power at a location 100 miles away is negligible compared with the original power, it is still enough above the natural level of electromagnetic noise to allow static-free radio reception. This is an interesting line of speculation, but it is hard to imagine how a small piece of cardboard with an inked pattern on it (a target card in an ESP experiment) can somehow generate such an enormous amount of power of an unknown nature or that the mind could aim and send out an enormous pulse of this power to be reflected back like a radar beam.

Can we increase or decrease the noise in the channel? Apparently, we can, although it is not clear whether we are affecting the channel directly or the percipient. (We shall look at this possibility in discussing the channel for a telepathy model in Chapter 4.)

There is some evidence to suggest a loss or lessening of information with distance in the psi channel with respect to precognition when the distance is temporal* rather than spatial. Jeremy Orme [63] has compared the relative frequency of spontaneous precognitive events with the temporal distance of the event predicted and found an overall falloff; that is, he found more precognitions of events just before the events than long before them. Russell Targ [134] has theorized that any event propagates energy both forward (ordinary causality) and backward through time, but with a definite falloff in intensity as temporal distance increases, so that short-term precognition would generally be more successful (produce a stronger signal to work with) than long-term precognition. Targ also postulates that some events ("significant" ones) create stronger signals than others and that therefore a highly meaningful event could be precognized earlier than a minor one. The possibilities for experimental work in this area are interesting, but unfortunately, very little research has been done on precognition over various temporal intervals, and the little that has been done has not always shown that increasing temporal distance makes precognition more difficult [96].

Note that there is a confusing factor here: What a person

---

* Although there has been little thought given to it yet, there is no such thing as exclusively temporal distance between two events. Because the earth is moving, there is always a spatial as well as a temporal distance. Furthermore, not only is the earth moving around the sun but the entire solar system is also moving in space. Therefore, the spatial distance does not always increase linearly with the temporal distance; it increases in a more complex, although still describable way. Future theorists can have fun working out this relationship.

believes about the nature of the psi channel may very well affect his performance in such a way that it will support belief. If a person believes that his psi performance will fall off with distance, it may do so; if he believes it may increase with distance, it may do so. From what we now understand in general psychological terms about the importance of people's belief systems, a general experimental rule should be to assume that what the percipient believes, including his implicit and unconscious beliefs, will have an important effect on experimental results unless specifically proved otherwise.

So far, our model includes information originating at a target object or event and flowing through a channel to reach the percipient. For known sensory processes, the information is not in a form that is directly perceivable to us. Light, sound, touch, and the chemical information that we call taste and smell do not directly affect our brains. Rather, they go through a converting or transforming mechanism, a *receptor,* that receives the physical energy carrying the desired information and transforms it into neural impulses that can be further processed within the nervous system and brain. For the ordinary senses, we know in considerable detail what the receptor organs are (eyes, ears, and so forth), how they work, and the routes over which the neural impulses travel from them to the brain for further information processing. But for psi information in general and clairvoyant information in particular, we do not have the slightest idea what the receptor may be.

There are metaphysical statements about the nature of the psi receptor. In some traditions, psi supposedly works through the third eye (pineal body); in others, through the heart *chakra.* But these statements are not scientifically useful because they do not provide sufficient detail that can be tested and thus verified or disproved. At present, we have no idea what the organ for psi reception might be, or indeed whether it is one general-purpose receptor or a variety of them.

We need a receptor in our model because our model incorporates the commonly accepted assumption that consciousness is somehow generated or produced by the action of the brain and nervous system. Thus, we start with a target consisting of a physical object with properties that could not *directly* stimulate the brain and nervous system unless a specific receptor organ exists. For psi, we then have a problem in understanding how targets can affect consciousness via our brains and nervous systems. This problem can be solved if an organ that acts as a receptor can be found. Such reasoning follows from the ortho- dox view of consciousness that I have discussed in *States of Consciousness* [173].

There are a number of other views about consciousness or awareness that I shall treat as radical views. These views con- sider basic awareness to be something other than brain or nervous system functioning, even though it is clearly associated with and affected by brain functioning. The radical views are generally associated with the spiritual psychologies (which I discuss at length in *Transpersonal Psychologies* [172]) or with people's experiences in altered states of consciousness. An in- teresting consequence of these views is that if awareness per se differs from brain functioning, then the nature of basic aware- ness might be the same as the nature of psychical properties of objects that are functioning as targets, in which case we may not need a special psi receptor after all.

This would be easiest to imagine for telepathy because we could say that thought travels through a channel and directly affects thought, rather than undergoing some unknown conver- sion process in between. At present, however, we cannot express this position precisely enough to turn it into a testable scientific theory. In our model, therefore, we shall stay with a receptor that turns whatever form of energy in which psi information travels into neural impulses.

Any receptor not only transforms information from a nonuse- ful to a useful form but also has a limited capacity for pro- cessing information. Your eyes can see the light reflected from this page, but they cannot see infrared light or ultraviolet light, even though these kinds of light are all around us. Most re- ceptors limit the kind of information we can respond to and may add their own characteristics to the information, whether or not those characteristics are appropriate. If someone presses hard on your eyes you will see patterned flashes of light, called *mechanical phosphenes,* that color the mechanical pressure information with the quality of that particular receptor (patterned visual sensations). Although we do not know if the psi receptor (s) has limitations and coloring characteristics of this sort, our model suggests that they may have. In other words, psi seems to represent an expansion of the information-gathering capacity available through our physical senses, but it may not be an unlimited expansion. There may be certain things we cannot become aware of psychically, even if they are somehow emitting some sort of psychic energy or information.

Receptor processes must also be selective. You can usually carry on a conversation with one person at a party if the overall noise is not too loud because you can select his or her speech sounds over the many speech sounds available in the room and focus on some to get the desired information. The reception process and the selection process in the ear do not involve the same mechanical and neural parts, but for the sake of simplicity, we will talk of reception processes as including the selectivity factor and the conversion factor.

Psi can obviously be incredibly selective. The percipient can show success in clairvoyantly guessing the order of a deck of cards sitting face down on the experimenter's desk. To do this, he must focus sequentially on each card in the deck to the exclusion of all the other cards. There may be a dozen decks of cards in the experimenter's desk drawer, but the percipient does not respond to them. In telepathy experiments, the percipient tries to pick up one person's thoughts, yet there are billions of people on this earth who may be sending out thoughts at that moment. But just as we have no idea how psi information is converted into neural impulses or mental events, we have no idea how this incredible selectivity is achieved.

3.

Inside the Percipient:
The Psychology of Psi

✿✿✿

At this point, in our modeling we have gotten target information from a distant space or time location to the inside of the percipient. This is what is clearly *para* in parapsychological processes; it is the thing that is totally inexplicable in terms of our current physical understanding of the world. Once the information is inside the percipient's body, what happens to it is very important, but this may not be *para*psychological. Although we are far from a comprehensive understanding of the route that information takes from the psi receptor to its manifestation in consciousness or behavior, we do know something about various parts of the process, and we know that these are similar to other kinds of psychological processes of which we do have some understanding. I suspect that this is where we can make the greatest progress in studying psi phenomena in the immediate future. I advise students who want to know how best to prepare for parapsychological research to get a Ph.D. in psychology.* We know that psychological factors such as mood or belief affect the psi process, but we are not at all sure that

* Students interested in a possible career in parapsychology *must* read the recent *Education in Parapsychology* [121], which can be purchased from the Parapsychology Foundation, 29 West 57th Street, New York, N.Y. 10019.

physical factors do. Although I hope that some brilliant physicists prove me wrong, I would bet on a much faster understanding of the psychology of psi than of its nature with respect to the physical universe.

Using our model of clairvoyance and precognition, let us now consider four major possible routes of information flow from the psi receptor to its eventual manifestation in the percipient's behavior: receptor to brain, receptor to conscious mind, receptor to unconscious mind, and receptor to unconscious mind to conscious mind.

Psi Receptor to Brain

It is possible that psi information flows directly from the psi receptor to the brain and then results in overt behavior. An everyday example of this would be your reaction if someone sneaks up behind you and makes a loud noise. You jump! We would then talk about the reception and conversion of the sound waves into a barrage of neural impulses from the ear and their direct effect on various startle reflex mechanisms within the nervous system and brain, resulting in your behavior—jumping. The whole thing happens before consciousness has time to get involved.

This is a purely behavioristic approach to psi that might be appealing to those who find such an approach useful. More important, however, we need to consider this route of information flow because we have experimental data indicating that psi can have a direct effect on the nervous system without consciousness being involved. One example of such evidence comes from a study I carried out some years ago [137] in which percipients showed a physiological reaction to the psi event of a shock apparatus being operated in a remote room. John Beloff [5] has recently reviewed a number of studies showing that physiological responses can function as indicators of psi.

A friend told me of an apparent psi experience that illustrates this receptor-to-nervous-system-to-behavior route in a life situation. The event occurred during World War II. One evening, she went to bed quite exhausted after weeks of strenuous work. She suddenly woke from deep sleep and leaped out of bed, overwhelmed with a feeling of utter horror and the conviction that she had to do *something* to stop some awful thing that was happening. But she had not the slightest idea of what this awful thing was and did not remember any sort of dream or mental activity before her sudden awakening. A few minutes later (she recalls that it was not more than two or three, probably less), a loud explosion shook her house, rattling the windows with tremendous force. She later learned that an ammunition ship being loaded at Port Chicago, about sixteen miles from where she lived in Berkeley, California, had exploded, practically leveling Port Chicago and killing many people. Because it would have taken the sound waves of the explosion sixty to seventy seconds to travel sixteen miles, it appears that she awakened with the feeling of horror at about the time that the explosion actually killed people, and heard the explosion a minute or so later. Her consciousness was only secondarily involved in this receptor-to-brain-to-behavior manifestation of psi.

What are the nervous system connections from the psi receptor to the eventual behavior? This is a very general question for psychophysiology, but we can make it more specific by asking whether it is the same sort of neural pathway that is used for nonparanormal reactions. What sorts of general brain and nervous system conditions affect this receptor-to-behavior pathway? Might a high level of arousal be favorable to information flow along this route, or a state of relaxation? Many parapsychological studies have found relaxation to be generally favorable to psi, although they have not looked specifically at purely behavioral responses. A number of studies reviewed by Honorton, Davidson, and Bindler [36] suggest that brain wave states characterized by an abundance of alpha rhythms, which indicate relaxed alertness, might be favorable to the operation of psi, although there are exceptions to this finding [58].

A purely behavioristic approach to the psi process model was undertaken independently by Christopher Scott [120] in England, and Remi Cadoret [11] in Canada. Each postulated four ways in which ESP could occur. The first was continuous transmission of ESP information to a behavioral output that consisted of all relevant facts about the target material. The second was also a continuous transmission, but the information itself was not comprehensive (i.e., not all the information was getting through). The third was a discontinuous transmission of information in which all relevant aspects of the target were present when transmission occurred. The fourth was a discontinuous and incomplete information flow. Both investigators proposed statistical techniques for deciding which model was correct. Although these models have not yet been tested, they illustrate a purely behavioral approach to explaining psi that could lead to fruitful research.

Psi Receptor to Conscious Mind

Psi information may flow from receptor to conscious mind to brain to behavior. This possibility gives importance to the mental processes of the percipient, even though they eventually affect the brain processes and overt behavior and so have the same final manifestations found in the behavioristic approach; but in this case, the percipient is at least partially conscious of what is going on.

The question of how consciousness affects the brain and the subsequent behavior is a general psychological question that will not be solved until the mind-body problem is solved. Nevertheless, we can explore questions about the receptor-to-consciousness link. For example, what sorts of conscious mental attitudes and characteristics affect the flow of psi information? We can investigate the percipient's beliefs, attitudes, emotional states, and so on. Gertrude Schmeidler and others [112] have repeatedly shown one of the most striking effects: that percipients who believe in ESP tend to score above the level of chance in card-guessing tests, thus confirming their beliefs, but that percipients who do not believe in ESP tend to score below chance expectation, thus thinking they are confirming their negative beliefs. Others (see [70, 71] for an excellent review) have found similar results. Schmeidler called the believers *sheep* because they went along with the request to show psi and the disbelievers *goats* because they resisted and went in the opposite direction. The sheep-goat effect clearly reveals that personality factors can affect psi operation because a percipient cannot score significantly below chance expectation unless he is using psi on an unconscious level to identify some targets *correctly* and then altering the information on this unconscious level to guide consciousness to deliberately wrong guesses. Here, a conscious attitude activates an unconscious process. Unconscious processes may distort psi operation in numerous ways. (We shall examine this further in the section "Psi Receptor to Unconscious Mind.") Their manifestations are very complex, and the interested reader should see Jule Eisenbud's excellent study [24].

The kinds of relatively conscious characteristics that have been studied include mood, values, introversion and extroversion, neuroticism, intelligence, self-confidence, ego-involvement, social adjustment, and aggressiveness. Although such characteristics have been shown to affect psi operation in various studies (see [96, 112] for reviews of the literature), all the correlations are of very low magnitude. That is, although they are *statistically* significant and thus reflect real processes, the size of the effects is quite low. Although they can be confirmed in *groups* of people, they do not allow the researcher to predict the performance of any given individual very accurately.

The conscious mind is not a simple, steady thing; it is an extremely complex structure. Although it holds to a certain kind of pattern we call our *ordinary state of consciousness,* it nevertheless shows important and rapid variations within that pattern. Changing attitudes and the workings of various mental functions within the ordinary state of consciousness can affect the way in which psi operates. This can sometimes be seen in simple ways: by encouraging a percipient who is starting to score poorly or offering incentives for better performance. Even more interestingly, *altered state of consciousness,* which are radically different ways of organizing consciousness, can sometimes dramatically facilitate psi operation. Hypnotic states have sometimes facilitated psi [37, 108, 196]; so have states induced by meditation [67] and effects produced by the psychedelic drugs [155, 180]. (We shall look at this aspect in detail in Chapter 5.)

In any psi test, we are asking the percipient to make a conscious attempt to use psi; therefore, one would think that the nature of the associated conscious mental processes would have been studied very thoroughly. Unfortunately, this is not the case. The historical reason seems to be that in the 1930s, when J. B. Rhine's highly successful experiments [97] were receiving wide attention and provoking a great deal of critical attack, the major efforts in parapsychology became focused almost exclusively on making experimental conditions absolutely airtight so that no alternatives to the psi hypothesis could be reasonably argued. A shift to working with groups of percipients, rather than individuals, occurred at about the same time and resulted in a great neglect of the mental processes of individual percipients. Indeed, there was often a feeling that if the percipient was made too introspective and self-conscious about what he was doing, it would interfere with the process. This is beginning to change, particularly with the increased interest in altered states of consciousness and psi, but we are still very ignorant about what sort of conscious strategies are most likely to activate the psi receptor and bring psi information into conscious awareness.

The best analysis we have so far of the conscious mental processes of outstanding subjects was provided by Rhea White [202], who analyzed descriptions of percipients' mental processes that were obtained in the early days of psychical research. These percipients usually worked under far from ideal conditions, in terms of getting proof that psi was responsible for their successes, but White rightly felt that because we now had good evidence of the existence of psi from very well controlled studies, the older material could be examined for clues about the process. She found a very high degree of unanimity in the way these outstanding percipients had described their mental processes, and she worked out a description of a four-stage process that they used. Although important individual differences may be hidden in this general process, it is well worth reviewing here for the hints it gives us about successful psi operation. White's four steps were called relaxation; engaging the conscious mind; the waiting, the tension, and the release; and the entry of the response into consciousness. For two outstanding percipients, a substep called the demand followed the second step (engaging the conscious mind) .

The first step, relaxation, involved achieving not only deep physical relaxation but also deep mental relaxation. The induction of such a relaxed state often required a considerable length of time, especially in the beginning; it was not unusual for percipients to spend five to ten minutes on this step alone, even after they had learned it well. Modern systematic techniques for relaxing the body, such as Jacobson's progressive relaxation [38], autogenic training [119], or biofeedback procedures would probably work well. Comfortable meditative postures would probably also be effective.

Deeply relaxing the physical body became an integral part of relaxing the mind. In our ordinary state of consciousness our minds tend to flit about from thought to thought, so these outstanding percipients devised various ways to engage their conscious minds in order to relax into a relatively blank state. Some tried to achieve a blank state relatively directly, attempting to suppress their thought processes and just passively contemplate a blank field. Others would use a concentrative technique first, trying to take some single mental image, such as a yellow rose, and picture it vividly and steadily before their mind's eye for a long period of time. Then they could suddenly let go of this mental image and experience a relatively blank state as a consequence. The concentration was never directed to an object in the external environment, nor to the psi target itself, but to some mental image kept in the center of attention in order to still the restlessness of the mind.

The substep, demand, taken by a couple of outstanding percipients was deliberately to demand the psi response from some unknown part of their minds after reaching a relatively blank state. Although other percipients did not make a conscious demand, the very fact that they went through these often elaborate and quite precise and ritualistic relaxation procedures in order to come up with a psi response constituted an implicit demand to a nonconscious part of their minds to give a psi answer. Step 2, the deliberate blanking of the conscious mind, creates a state of inner tension, particularly because the percipient cannot try *actively* to quiet his mind in the characteristic style he is accustomed to using in his ordinary state of consciousness.

This tension leads to the third step, the stage of waiting, tension, and release. Our ordinary conscious attitude is *instantly* to demand what we want, but here the percipient must be prepared to wait, possibly a long time, perhaps hours, for some sort of phenomena containing the psi information to happen. The impulse to just guess or otherwise do *something* to get through this step is very strong. There must be a kind of passive waiting here that, in some sense, is still filled with tension. That mental tension or desire may very well be the activating factor that makes the psi receptor work to pick up the psi message and deliver it to consciousness.

The final step, some experiential event that constitutes the response to the target, conveys the psi information. Here, there was a great deal of variation among percipients. Sometimes, a sharp image or vision would occur, along with a feeling of *knowing* that this was the correct response; but quite often, various things would happen in the relatively blank space of the preceding stage, and the percipient would have to learn, through experience, which events constituted an actual flow of information from the psi receptor and which were unrelated. This final process of learning to discriminate between a useful psi image and random noise helped to inspire me to apply learning theory to the psi process and to propose that immediate feedback to the percipient about results would be extremely helpful here. The highly successful results of my studies of feedback training are described in *Learning to Use Extrasensory Perception* [178].

Almost no work has been done to test White's concepts. One exception is a study by John Beloff and Ian Mandleberg [8] of some college students; however, it produced no evidence for psi. Because Beloff's Edinburgh laboratory has a long-standing reputation for never getting psi results in spite of Beloff's personal charm and in spite of whatever techniques are used, I suspect that this result does not cast doubt on White's conceptualizations but merely reflects some psychological or parapsychological factors about the Edinburgh laboratory. I believe that White's conceptualizations provide very useful keys to learning how to activate the psi process consciously, and I refer the interested reader to her original article [202] for many details that I cannot go into here.

It is well to note that White's fourth step implies that there will be some sort of quality or qualities associated with a genuine information flow from the psi receptor that will not be associated with just guessing; thus, there will be some sort of operating signal or quality of the imagery or whatever form the perceptions take that will eventually enable percipients to discriminate experiences that contain psi information from experiences that do not. Some formal research has been devoted to the question of whether percipients can have some idea of when they are using psi. In psi studies on apparent telepathy (GESP), clairvoyance, and precognition, percipients have been asked to indicate when they have particular confidence in a call. Several studies have found that the proposition of correct psi responses on these designated confidence calls is significantly higher than on calls for which the percipients did not indicate confidence. These studies have recently been reviewed in a paper by H. Kanthamani and Edward Kelly [40] that also reports what was probably the most outstanding success in this confidence-call procedure. Using an exceptionally talented percipient, BD, who had shown a variety of psi manifestations in other studies, they reported on three series of tests. Two were tests of clairvoyance using the psychic-shuffle technique, in which the percipient repeatedly shuffles cards that are out of sight in a closed box until he feels that they match some predetermined target order. In each series, BD, who was using ordinary playing cards, made twenty-five confidence calls, and he was completely correct on every one of these (i.e., he identified both the suit and the number of each card). In a third clairvoyance series, in which each card was presented, one at a time, inside a blank, opaque envelope, he made twenty confidence calls, four-

teen of which were completely correct and six of which were
partially correct. These results with BD are exceptionally significant and indicate that a gifted percipient can have a high
awareness of when he is receiving psi information. For ordinary
percipients, however, the effect is much smaller.

Many specific questions about conscious attitudes and psi
remain. What sorts of conscious acts can aid the information
flow from the psi receptor to consciousness? Mental relaxation?
An attitude of expectancy? Free play of imagery? Occult ex-
ercises? Will the kinds of procedures outlined by White work
for everyone? If there is some kind of activating mechanism
within the percipient that sends out some kind of psi energy
the reflections of which constitute the clairvoyant information
from target objects? The same sort of questions can be asked
about what conscious acts make this mechanism function.

Psi Receptor to Unconscious Mind

The third possible information route is from psi receptor to
unconscious mind to brain to behavior. The unconscious mind
is an important and dynamic area of the mind that significantly
influences our behavior and feelings but that is ordinarily inaccessible to direct awareness.* I will use the concept of the
unconscious mind both in this general sense and in the specific
Freudian and Jungian senses.

In our ordinary state of consciousness, we infer the existence
of the unconscious mind because people behave in ways that do
not make sense in terms of what they can describe about their
conscious processes but that do fit a theory that they are being
influenced by certain kinds of mental processes going on outside
their awareness. For example, a psychoanalytic patient might be
talking about how much he loves his brother, but the analyst
notices that the patient's hands make strangling movements,

---

* The degree of inaccessability of such processes varies. For example, we
could distinguish preconscious processes (which can become accessible with
effort) from totally unconscious processes (which must remain forever
inferential) . This sort of elaboration of our model will be left for a future
study.

and so he infers that on an unconscious level the patient feels a lot of unresolved hostility toward his brother.

In the case of psi, we must postulate this information flow route because a percipient's behavior sometimes suggests that he is operating on the basis of psi information although he is unaware of it. Rex Stanford [125] has stated this quite precisely in his concept of the *psi-mediated instrumental response* (*PMIR*). *Instrumental response* is a psychological term meaning some kind of behavior or response to a situation that is instrumental in satisfying needs. Eating when you are hungry is an instrumental response that satisfies the need for nourishment. Thus, a PMIR is something you do that is useful in fulfilling your needs, but the fact that you do it or the way that you do it is unknowingly influenced by psi-acquired information. Basically, Stanford proposes that sometimes we unknowingly and without conscious intention use psi to some degree to scan our environment for need-relevant objects or events or for information crucially related to such events and that when such information is obtained, we unknowingly act in ways that are instrumental in satisfying our needs in relation to the particular objects or events in question. The PMIR can occur without any conscious effort to use psi, without conscious effort to fill the needs that are served by a particular PMIR, without prior sensory knowledge of the need-relevant circumstances, without conscious awareness of the need-relevant circumstances, and even without any realization that anything extraordinary is happening.

What Stanford is proposing, then, is that we use psi far more often than we think and that most of the time the outcome is not such that we would think something unusual has happened and thus check to see if it is psi. There are many ordinary life experiences that can be understood as PMIRs. You might, as Stanford reports in one case, make an apparent mistake while riding the subway, get off at the wrong station, and there meet the friend you were on your way to visit. You would probably just consider such an event luck.

The PMIR hypothesis is a broad theory, and although it may make many ordinary events more understandable, its very generality makes it difficult to prove or disprove with regard to ordinary events. However, good laboratory evidence in support of the PMIR hypothesis exists.

The first kind of experimental evidence, from which Stanford evolved his hypothesis, comes from results of psi experiments in which, in addition to the overt psi task that the percipients were doing, there was another aspect of the experiment, known only to the experimenter, that called for other psi effects.

For example, James Carpenter [12] conducted two studies in which percipients matched a deck of standard ESP cards against concealed target cards. However, the percipients did not know that half of the concealed cards had photographs showing human sexual intercourse enclosed with them and that the other cards had only blank cards, of the same size as the erotic photographs, enclosed with them. In the first study, involving sixteen college men, the percipients were significantly more accurate on the erotically associated targets than they were on the neutral cards. Assuming that most male college students have strong sexual needs (which does not seem to be a very improbable assumption), it seems they used significantly more psi on target material relevant to their needs.

In the second study, Carpenter tested male and female junior high school students using the same sort of procedure. He found an interaction between whether cards were associated with erotic material and the anxiety of the percipients (as measured by a psychological test). That interaction consisted largely of the more anxious percipients consistently missing the erotically associated targets and correctly guessing the neutral targets. Anxious percipients would have difficulty handling sexually arousing material and therefore would use a PMIR to avoid it. Other studies of this nature, reviewed by Stanford, indicate that percipients can react to hidden aspects of an experiment by psi and that this interaction is affected by their needs.

Stanford went on to more directly demonstrate the PMIR under laboratory conditions. Two of his recent studies illustrate this. Because each was complex, I shall report only the immediately relevant aspects here. In one study [128], forty college-age men were individually tested by a female experimenter. No mention of the PMIR hypothesis was made. Each percipient took a short word-association test; the experimenter recorded the time it took the percipient to make each response. None of the percipients knew that there was a sealed decision sheet (a different one for each of them) on which one of the words of the association list had been selected as a target. For half of the men, if their fastest (or tied for fastest) response was the target word, they would go on to participate in a much more interesting ESP experiment. The other half of the group had to give their slowest (or tied for slowest) response for the key word. Stanford believed that this would not work as well because it would be easier for psi to speed a response on such a test than to inhibit one. The experimenter giving the association test did not know what the key word was until the test was completed, so she could not make biased scoring errors. The percipients had no idea (by ordinary means) that their responses in the first part of the experiment would affect what happened in the second part, or even that there *was* a second part.

Requiring half the men to give their fastest response to the target word to achieve the desirable condition and the other half to give their slowest response is a standard experimental procedure called *counterbalancing*. It is used to eliminate possible confounding of results because of steady trends in irrelevant aspects of data, such as a tendency of percipients to respond more quickly as a word-association test moves along.

The favorable experiment consisted of participating in a picture-perception ESP task under pleasant, relaxed conditions and with positive suggestions. The female experimenter conducted this task, which would presumably be quite pleasant to the male percipients. The less interesting experiment consisted of sitting alone in a straight-backed chair in the experimental room doing card-guessing tests for twenty-five minutes.

The results supported the PMIR hypothesis. In the fast group, the correct associations occurred significantly faster than they would by chance. The speed increase in the fast-response condition was larger than the speed decrease in the slow-response condition.

In the favorable experiment of a similar complex study [129] college-age men participated in a picture-rating task showing college-age women in varying degrees of undress. In the unfavorable condition, they participated in a vigilance task that consisted of holding a stylus over a small patch of light on a pursuit rotor (a rotating disk) set to rotate at such a slow speed that the task was very easy, very boring, and physically tiring; The percipient had to keep this up for twenty-five minutes. Again, word association times were significantly changed.

I have long suspected that psi is used far more frequently in life, without awareness, than we generally believe, and Stanford's formalization of this idea into the PMIR hypothesis makes useful testing possible. Sometimes, we are lucky for a good reason; we have unknowingly used psi. Sometimes, we are unlucky for a good reason; because we often have conflicting motives, some of which are only partially conscious and which may be self-destructive or self-punishing, we unknowingly use PMIRs to walk into misfortune. If we think that PMIRs are relatively rare, that once in a great while our lives are influenced by nonconscious psi processes, the implications do not seem too important. However, I believe that if we drop that assumption (for which we have no good evidence), the implications are actually staggering. Although it is still too general to classify as a scientific (testable) hypothesis, I have always been very impressed by Maurice Nicoll's statement [61] that the universe is very responsive to prayer (i.e., any strong and relatively long-lasting desire). But as Nicoll, an expositor of the psychological system taught by Gurdjieff, indicates, we suffer from the illusion that we have a single unchanging "I"; whereas in reality, we have many selves that change rapidly. This means that we have a large number of important desires, each held by various subselves, many of which are contradictory. The statement that the universe is very responsive to prayer can be translated into the statement that PMIRs are actually very frequent. In other words, our unconscious psi relationship with the universe is very effective, and we tend to get what we want. It is too bad that the psychopathology of ordinary life often makes what we want quite unpleasant. I have observed some friends who have a type of personality that seem to thrive on stress and personal tragedy, even though they would consciously deny it. I am frequently amazed at how often the universe seems to cooperate in arranging life circumstances that generate tragedy for these people. For people who do not thrive on tragedy, life comes up with tragedies less frequently.

The basic model that we have been using for clairvoyance (Figure 2-1) can be used for the PMIR if one change is made. The clairvoyance model assumed that our conscious minds activate psi by desiring or otherwise informing unconscious processes or the psi receptor processes to search for and retrieve the desired psi information. In the PMIR model, we must assume that the psi receptor and the unconscious mind are active (at least sometimes, perhaps all the time) whether or not the conscious mind desires this. The scanning of the environment by psi activates unconscious mental processes, which may, in turn, call for more psi, and so on. Finally, this affects conscious mental processes or directly affects behavior and results in need-satisfying action.

In altered states of consciousness, a person sometimes becomes directly conscious of aspects of his mind that are normally unconscious. Thus, what is conscious in hypnosis or drug-induced states might be quite different from ordinary consciousness. The person may or may not recall these changed mental processes again in his ordinary state. Because some of the most talented psychics regularly go into an altered state of consciousness in order to activate their psi, an understanding of altered states would tell us a great deal about this normally unconscious information-flow route. Unfortunately, earlier investigators of trance mediums and psychics who worked in altered states were so concerned with whether there were indications of psi in the material or whether the alleged spirit communicators were genuine that they paid very little attention to the nature of the altered state.

Another reason our understanding of this particular psi information route is poor is that we know so little about the unconscious mind in general. If, as many parapsychologists suspect, this unconscious flow route is more favorable to psi operation than routes in our ordinary state of consciousness, it is very important for us to understand this route. At the moment there seems to be great variability in this route, difficult-to-decode symbolism and noise processes involved, but if there were a regular way that psi expressed itself on an unconscious level, even if it were different from the style of expression of our ordinary conscious minds, we could presumably learn to translate the unconscious processes into a meaningful code and get at our psi information that way.

Psi Receptor to Unconscious Mind to Conscious Mind

In this possible route, the information goes from the psi receptor to the unconscious mind to the conscious mind to the brain and then to behavior. Unlike the route discussed in the preceding section, this route does not deal directly with the unconscious manifestations; instead, it deals with changes in the content of consciousness which suggest that the unconscious has been processing and altering the psi information before it reaches consciousness. The case of psi-missing (scoring significantly below the level of chance), as in Schmeidler's sheep-goat effect, is an excellent example of this. The psi information is correctly picked up by the psi receptor and faithfully transmitted to the unconscious mind, which then deliberately influences the conscious mind to guess a wrong target.

These unconscious-mind effects can be more selective (thus calling for more psi ability) than the simple identification or incorrect identification of a target by psi. They can express conscious and unconscious personality characteristics (as noted in connection with the PMIR). For example, Martin Johnson and Bertil Nordbeck [39] studied a talented percipient in a matching study in which some of the targets (which were sealed in envelopes) were words relating to unpleasant experiences in the percipient's life and others were words relating to pleasant experiences. The percipient had no sensory knowledge that this mixture existed, but she showed hitting (above-chance scoring) on the pleasant-association targets and missing on the unpleasant-association targets.

Psi manifestations in nocturnal dreams are also an excellent example of this receptor-to-unconscious-to-conscious route, although the situation is a little more complex because the consciousness we are dealing with is the altered state of dreaming consciousness. A good illustration of this sort of processing comes from one of the early studies of telepathically influenced dreams [194] conducted at the Maimonides Medical Center. The target that a sender was attempting to transmit telepathically to a sleeping percipient was a reproduction of Salvador Dali's strange and beautiful painting *The Sacrament of the Last Supper,* which portrays Christ seated at the center of a table, surrounded by his twelve disciples. A glass of wine and a broken loaf of bread are on the table, and a large body of water and three fishing boats can be seen far in the background. The following are relevant excerpts from the percipient's dreams as recounted to an experimenter who awakened the percipient after each period of stage 1-rapid eye movement sleep (dreaming sleep) throughout the night:

S's first dream: "There was one scene of an ocean . . . It had a strange beauty about it and a strange formation."

S's second dream: "I haven't any reason to say this, but somehow boats come to mind. Fishing boats. Small-size fishing boats . . . There was a picture in the Sea Fare Restaurant that came to mind as I was describing it. It's a very large painting. Enormous. It shows, oh, I'd say about a dozen or so men pulling a fishing boat ashore right after having returned from a catch."

S's third dream: "I was looking at a catalog . . . a Christmas catalog. Christmas season."

S's fourth dream: "I had some sort of a brief dream about an M.D. . . . I was talking to someone and . . . the discussion had to do with why . . . a doctor becomes a doctor because he's supposed to be an M.D., or something of that nature."

S's fifth dream: "It had to do with doctors again . . . The picture . . . that I'm thinking of now is the doctor sitting beside a child that is ill . . . It's one of those classical ones . . . It's called 'The Physician.' "

S's sixth dream: "I was in this office—a doctor's office again . . . We were talking about Preston . . . He's a psychiatrist. A supervisor I had. Before he became a psychiatrist he was a pathologist."

S's seventh dream: "The only part that comes to mind is the part where I'm in a kitchen, and there is a restaurant that I was planning to go to."

S's eighth dream: "I was sampling these different articles that looked like spices. Herbs. Grocery store. Place to eat. Food of different types."

From S's associations: "The fisherman dream makes me think of the Mediterranean area, perhaps even some sort of Biblical time. Right now my associations are of the fish and the loaf, or even the feeding of the multitudes . . . Once again I think of Christmas . . . Having to do with the ocean—water, fishermen, something in this area." [194, p. 592]

Ordinarily, it would be very difficult to come to an unbiased decisions about whether these dreams really represent psi transmission of information about the target picture. However, these dreams occurred on one night in a series of nights in the experiment, and the overall results of the series were judged to be statistically significant by having outside judges blindly match dream narratives against target pictures. Because we know objectively that psi was present in the experiment, it is legitimate to make a finer interpretation of these dreams. For example, we can see that although no particular dream portrays all the information in the target picture, each dream conveys one or more elements of it. In dreams, target elements are often put in different contexts, resulting in partial transmission of information and a scrambling of the overall pattern. Another relevant fact is that what comes through is often material that elicits an *association* to the target element rather than the target element itself. In this case, we have dreams about doctors, healers, all common associations to Christ as the Physician or the Healer; there were also comments about a Christmas catalog (rather than about Christ).*

* The extensive work on dream telepathy by the Maimonides group has recently been summarized in a technical monograph [193] and in two books, *Dream Telepathy* [195] and in Stanley Krippner's fascinating *Song of the Siren* [46].

We can ask numerous questions that we don't have answers to yet about this information flow, not only general psychological ones as to how information passes from the unconscious mind to the conscious mind and what sort of transformations our unconscious processes work on information, but even more specific ones about whether psi information is processed in the same or a different way as sensory and memory information is in the unconscious mind. In the telepathic dream reported in Chapter 6, for example, there was a different feeling quality associated with this dream than with ordinary dreams. We also need to know what sort of conditions in the conscious mind can facilitate the flow of information from the unconscious, i.e., how do we draw out information from this normally inaccessible part of the mind? What sorts of conscious conditions or actions minimize the distortion that seems to occur in the process? Given that our *direct,* conscious use of psi is so poor, these are very important questions.

4·

Getting the Message from Here to There: Modeling Psychokinesis and Telepathy

✿✿

The model of psychokinesis (PK) is in many ways a reverse of the clairvoyance model. PK occurs when people (we shall call them agents) affect the outcome of physical events by simply wishing for that outcome and when there is no known physical explanation for that outcome. The classic PK experiment involved throwing dice, usually by shaking them in a cup or having a machine shake and throw them. The agent, who could not touch the dice or use other normal means to affect them would, on some occasions, wish for a designated target face to come up and, on other occasions, wish for another target face, according to a prearranged schedule. By chance, we would expect the desired target face to come up 1 in 6 times; but in many PK experiments, it came up slightly more than that. This was, over a long period, statistically significant. The evidence for PK is not quite so overwhelming as that for telepathy and clairvoyance, but it is certainly sufficient to establish the existence of the phenomenon. Modern PK studies have involved a wide range of targets, as we shall see later in this chapter.

Figure 4-1 is a model of PK. We start with an external stimulus, typically the experimenter's request to an agent to try to carry out the PK task, (e.g., trying to make a particular die

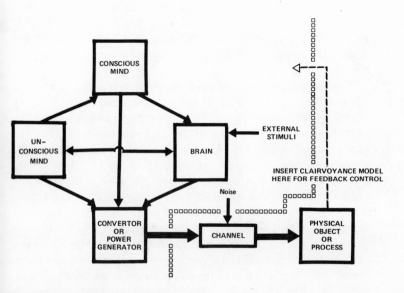

Figure 4-1. Model for PK.

face come up. This information is processed by conventional receptors (usually the eyes and ears) and passes into the brain, where it may then go to the conscious and/or the unconscious mind, ending up in a process I shall call the *PK converter,* or *power generator.* The heavy arrows indicate that from this point on, some sort of energy or power flows over a channel and finally affects the target object or process.

Information-Flow Routes

There are four possible routes of PK information flow within the agent, and there is also the possibility of simultaneous operation and interaction among the routes. Starting with the initiating request, the first route we can model is directly from brain to power generator, which represents a behavioristic or physiological approach. This route may be more than just a theoretical possibility because preliminary studies (reviewed in 59, 95*] suggest that lower animals such as lizards, cockroaches, and cats—all simple organisms to which we would not ordinarily attribute much consciousness—might exercise PK effects.

The second possible route is from brain to conscious mind to PK power generator. This is the commonsense route that we would ordinarily think of in a PK experiment. That is, the agent is consciously aware that the experimenter has requested that he exercise PK, and he consciously tries to operate the PK power generator (whatever it is) so that he can do the job. However, agents so seldom get direct PK effects (most of the time, the power generator does not operate) that our conscious minds clearly do not quite know what to do. The agent must simply hope that some sort of unknown process will intervene to activate the PK power generator and produce the PK effect.

The third route takes this mysterious something that intervenes into account; the route seems to be from brain to conscious mind to unconscious mind to power generator. There is very little that we can say about this route in terms of present knowledge. It simply reflects the fact that occasionally our conscious wishes do activate some unconscious part(s) of our minds and PK occurs. We would expect to see the same sort of personality flavoring as when ESP passes through the unconscious mind.

The fourth possible route is from brain to unconscious mind to power generator with no direct conscious involvement. Such a route seems to have been operating in a study by Helmut Schmidt and Lee Pantas [118]. They tested students with a four-choice, electronic random number generator. The ostensible task always appeared to be precognition: pressing one of the four buttons that corresponded to the lamp, which would light a moment later. This was precognition rather than clairvoyance because the machine continuously changed targets (many thousands of times per second) and did not make a final selec-

* John Randall's review was written before Walter Levy's fraudulent doctoring of data in animal psi studies [100] was discovered, so the reader is cautioned to read his review selectively.

tion until the instant one of the response buttons was pressed, an action occurring after a percipient's decision had been made. However, the task actually was precognition for only half the students working at it. For the other half, Schmidt pressed a concealed switch on the machine that changed its internal circuitry so that a hit occurred only if the machine was psychokinetically forced to generate a particular target. This change in the machine's operation could not be detected externally, and the students were not informed of the change. Schmidt wanted to test scoring rates on precognition and PK without the differences being attributable to differing conscious attitudes the students might have had about their precognitive and PK abilities.

Schmidt and Pantas found statistically significant hitting for both conditions: 29.8 percent for precognition and 31.4 percent for PK, instead of the 25 percent expected by chance, both likely to occur by chance alone less than 1 in 100 times. This clearly indicates an unconscious triggering of the PK power generator, bypassing any involvement of the conscious mind. What consciousness is doing is irrelevant; the unconscious must figure out (perhaps from the feedback in the task or by reading the experimenter's mind) that PK is what is required. All the questions raised in Chapter 3 about processes in the brain, the conscious mind, and the unconscious mind and their possible interactions within the clairvoyance and precognition model also apply here.

I have made this model a little more complicated than the model in Chapter 2 by adding an arrow labeled *Internal Stimuli* within each possible information process to reflect the fact that more events are occurring in the agent's mind and nervous system than the experimenter's request to influence the target. This is also true for our clairvoyance and precognition model. For example, there may be spontaneous neural discharges or noises within your brain that interfere with the flow of information between the various processes. Or you may consciously dislike the experimenter, so that when he tells you to make the dice come up fours, you say (mentally), "Nuts to you," and consciously try for a different target face. Or you may be cooperative consciously, but on an unconscious level, the experimenter reminds you of someone you dislike, so your unconscious mind tries to produce PK results that will be contrary to what the experimenter wants. You can imagine the complexity of a situation in which all these factors are at work. You might start scoring significantly on affecting dice, but then the machine that throws the dice unexpectedly breaks down. Thus, you consciously complied with the experimenter's request to exercise PK, but simultaneously (and perhaps with little conscious knowledge), you satisfactorily expressed your hostility toward the experimenter.* And, of course, there are always many other things on an agent's mind in addition to the experiment ("What shall I buy for dinner tonight?") that send his or her psychological energies elsewhere. We shall deal with the social aspects of the experimental situation at greater length in subsequent chapters.

All four possible information-flow routes have been modeled for a relatively simple situation in which there are straightforward instructions to the conscious mind of the person trying to use PK. But if we look at the Schmidt-Pantas experiment more deeply, we can see that a fifth possible information-flow route may be needed.

In that study, the students trying to score high† had to use PK unknowingly rather than precognition because their conscious understanding of the experimental instructions was of no use to them, yet they scored above chance. This could have happened via the proposed route from brain to unconscious to PK power generator; that is, they could have taken note of sensory cues in the situation that might have been unknowingly provided by Schmidt (he was physically present and knew he

---

* Note added in press: Irwin Silverman has just published an excellent survey of the research on resistance, effects of deception, etc., *The Human Subject in the Psychological Laboratory* (Pergamon Press, 1977) which should be read by everyone doing psychological and parapsychological research.

† The student subjects were actually trying to score *low*, but Schmidt and Pantas had deliberately set up the testing situation to encourage psi-missing. Therefore, the experimenters predicted high scoring for the students trying for low scores.

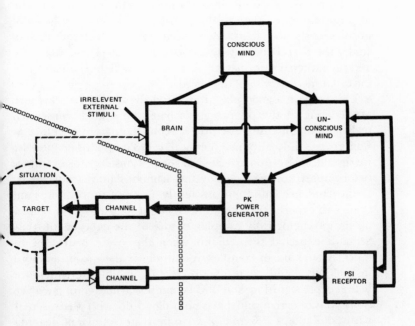

Figure 4-2. A model for psi-mediated instrumental response (PMIR), involving conscious use of PK as a result of information acquired by unconscious use of ESP.

had changed the machine's circuit, even if he did not say anything about it), and then their unconscious minds figured out that PK was required. However, Figure 4-2 models a possible fifth information-flow route, in which the relevant information flow involves unconscious use of psi (telepathy or clairvoyance). Using this route, the agent's mind uses telepathy to pick up Schmidt's knowledge of the experimental change and/or uses clairvoyance to pick up the change in the machine. Thus, this route is from target and/or situation to psi channel to psi receptor to unconscious mind to PK power generator to the PK channel to the target.

Thus, Figure 4-2 is a model of Stanford's PMIR theory [125, 126], which was discussed in Chapter 3. In this process, a part of the unconscious mind initiates psi to scan the environment for information relevant to the person's needs and then uses PK unconsciously to satisfy these needs. In the Schmidt-Pantas study, the overall need is to succeed at the experimental task, and psi-gathered information about the change in the nature of the task is necessary to fill this need.

This is again a good place to remind the reader that this sort of modeling of the psi process is based on shared, consensus-reality, commonsense assumptions about the nature of information processes. Reality may be more complex than our models; we should not get too attached to them! Consider, for example, two complexities suggested by the Schmidt-Pantas study. First, if the students could unconsciously use psi to pick up the change in experimental conditions, might they also have picked up the psychologically complex nature of the experiment, that Schmidt expected them to hit when they were instructed to miss? What kind of complex resolution of these contradictory instructions could come about? Second, might the difference between precognition and PK be simply a matter of how we *conceptualize* them and have nothing to do with their actual natures? Perhaps PK and precognition are simply misleading labels that we cling to in our ordinary state of consciousness, and perhaps the change in experimental conditions, which seems so basic to us, is really of no importance to whatever psi is.

Power Generator

To model the mysterious PK power generator, we need to hypothesize a totally novel process or mechanism. The known electromagnetic or chemical energies of the brain cannot influence external events of any magnitude except through muscular intervention. The electric and magnetic fields of your brain are the only things that really penetrate your skull, but they are far too weak to influence the course of dice falling a foot away, much less farther away, even if they could somehow be focused on it. Thus, we need a power generator, a process capable of taking the informational *desire* to influence the dice and generating some sort of psi *power* that would actually influence it.

For example, I am using power generators called *muscles* to enable me to write this book. The outputs of these power generators (mechanical pressures) go through channels (my skin) to the typewriter keys, printing ink on the paper. If you think about it, this normal process is actually very complex and not understood in many of its most important aspects, but because it is so familiar, we never think of it as a mystery. The PK power generator is just as mysterious, if not more so. Is there some special brain center for it? Is it some form of mental energy (whatever mental energy is in the first place)? It must be a nonphysical sort of energy in order to cross the physical space to the target without a known physical carrier. But how does this mental energy affect a physical object once it reaches it? What is the nature of the PK energy? Is there a way of converting physical energy to PK energy, or vice versa? For example, there are many mentions in the old psychical research literature that a room would seem to get cold when a spiritualist medium was apparently producing very strong PK effects. Does this imply that PK forces can somehow take heat energy out of the air and use it to produce physical movement?

As long as we conceptualize objects in purely physical terms (I do not know another way to conceptualize them), we must have a positive answer to the question of whether PK energy can be converted to physical energy. But since we are totally ignorant of the natures of the PK force and the power generator and of the way in which the PK force converts to a physical force, we are far from any precise theories.

However, there are ways in which we might develop good theories. Some years ago, I had a discussion with W. Edward Cox of the Parapsychology Laboratory at Duke University about some new machines that he had invented to test PK [13]; he had been getting statistically significant PK results with the devices. These machines involved an agent's attempting to influence a very large number of moving particles, such as drops of falling water or ions moving through a solution between two electrodes. It struck me that Cox's devices offered a chance to test two alternative propositions about the nature of the PK force: that PK is like a spatially discrete push or a jab and that PK is uniformly spread out over a fairly wide volume of space. If the first view were correct, we would expect maximum success in PK tests involving single objects. If the second were correct, many objects in this wider field would allow the PK force to be used more effectively and thus would give greater success.

We are, you will remember, discussing *models* of the psi process. The theory offered in the preceding paragraph is implicitly conditioned by our ordinary experience in manipulating objects. Because of this familiarity, it has a certain kind of sense to it. But that does not make it a more abstract theory nor guarantee that it is at all true. Given the existence of psi forces, the entire space-time framework of our ordinary existence is probably no more than a useful concept; therefore, modeling psi in that framework may be useful in some ways but misleading in others.

PK Channel

What is the nature of the channel, the medium through which the power transmitted from the PK power generator reaches the target? When I push down a key on my typewriter, the molecules of my skin serve as a channel for transmitting mechanical pressure from the muscles to the typewriter key. Some known physical energies, such as radio or light waves, require only space as a channel. Others require a physical medium; for example, sound waves require air, water, or solids to travel.

In the clairvoyance model (Chapter 2), I indicated that there could be noise on the channel; the same may be true with the PK model. In the case of PK, we can think of this noise as loss of power, slippage of aim, or the like. For example, when an arrow is shot at a target, any wind blowing across the range constitutes noise because it deflects the power in the arrow from being applied at the point you intend. At present, there are no experimental studies of noise in the PK channel.

We know essentially nothing about the nature of the channel in PK. Is it just space? Or must there be a physical medium between the subject and the PK target? There are some indications that a target surrounded by a vacuum, such as a beam of particles moving in an evacuated tube, can be affected by PK, so perhaps the channel is just space. Can PK be shielded so that you cannot affect something? We don't know. Is there any loss of PK force with distance? We know that *psychological* distance [96] affects performance; that is, if you *believe* distance hinders you, it proably will. But as yet, we have no systematic understanding of the effect of distance on PK.

Retrocognitive PK

Achieving an understanding of the PK channel will probably involve a major revision of our understanding of space and time. For example, I shall describe Helmut Schmidt's recent experiment on time-displaced PK, which I find especially disturbing to my concept of time. Schmidt [116, 117] would have a volunteer agent sit in front of a PK-test machine. The machine electronically generated either pair of a binary target, which we might call lefts and rights, at a rate of ten per second. The ratio of recent lefts and rights was displayed by both a meter needle and as a sound that the agent could hear with a pair of headphones. Whenever the needle deflected to the desired side and the sound pitch changed in the desired direction, the agent was hitting; that is, he was moving the ratio of lefts to rights in the direction specified as correct for that set of trials.

For part of this experiment, the targets were generated as the agents were trying to influence them (ordinary-time PK). The agents showed an average hit rate of 50.8 percent, instead of the chance-expected 50 percent, which would have occurred less than 1 in 100 times by chance alone. Clearly, PK was operating.

In the other part of the experiment, in which the agents still thought they were to use ordinary PK, all the targets had actually been generated and scored *before* they began any PK effort, while they had been talking with Schmidt and getting preliminary instructions. The display they saw as they later tried to use PK was actually only a playback of a recording of the targets generated and scored earlier. Indeed, these prescored targets were played back four times and interspersed with currently generated targets for the other part of the experiment because Schmidt hypothesized, on the basis of other work, that repeated interaction with the played-back targets would improve results. Indeed, the average scoring rate on these prerecorded targets was 52.95 percent, which was not only quite significant in itself but also significantly better than the score on the currently generated targets.

The effect seems to be the result of PK power flowing backward through time to influence the prerecorded targets at the time that they were generated. As information stored in the machine's memory, these targets were not changed by the PK; a printout of these targets made after the targets were generated but before the agents were asked to use PK (i.e., when the targets were prerecorded), matched a later printout.

Do you find this result difficult to comprehend? Well, so do I. I am tempted to imagine a very complex web of experimenter effects in order to explain it away as ordinary PK, but the answer may not be that easy.

We need the assistance of physicists (and paraphysicists) to answer the questions raised by the results. However, we cannot begin to work on these questions until we understand the psychology of the PK process well enough to make sure that the power generator is putting out *something* a good proportion of the time.

PK Target

Finally, we arrive at the physical target to be affected by PK, the point at which the nonphysical (by current standards) PK force must interact with matter to produce a physical effect. Are there any limitations on what the target can be?

The small amount of research done on PK cannot claim to have investigated a large number of specific targets, but the range on targets on which successful PK effects have occurred is so wide that it would be difficult to predict any limits on targets

Table 4-1
Targets Affected by Psychokinesis

Nonliving Targets

Subatomic Particles: radioactive decay rate; electronic random number generators.

Electromagnetic Waves: decay rate of oscillating magnetic field in magnetometer; generating magnetic field in magnetometer.

Molecular Action: changing temperature of thermistors; creating images on photographic film.

Static Objects: deflecting compass needles; bending metal keys; making stopped watches run.

Moving Physical Objects: which faces of dice fall up; which side of board dice fall on; which side rolling steel balls fall on; which face spinning silver coin falls to; psychic shuffle with cards.

Living Targets

Basic Biological Processes: rate of recovery of mice from anesthesia; electrical resistance of plants; rate of fungus growth; rate of enzyme activity; movement of protozoans; healing rates of injured mice; growth of plants.

Brain Function or Mental Processes: Is telepathy a matter of psychokinetic effects on the brain or mind?

at this time. Table 4-1 illustrates this range, although it does not attempt to include every type of target actually tested so far.

Most targets in PK experiments have been nonliving objects (the first category shown in Table 4-1). The classical targets for PK experiments were ordinary dice. The dice were usually shaken by a mechanical shaker to eliminate any skill effects that might possibly be exercised by the agent, and the order of target faces was systematically rotated to compensate for any mechanical imperfections in the dice. In the first experiments, agents attempted to influence which side of the dice fell face up (i.e., which number came up), and many experiments gave positive results. Other dice experiments asked agents to try to influence whether the dice would fall on the left or the right side of the table when the mechanical arrangement of shaker and table was such that we would expect a fifty-fifty distribution. These experiments also yielded positive results. Classical PK dice studies have been well reviewed in K. Ramakrishna Rao's *Experimental Parapsychology* [96].

We have reports of many variations in the ability to affect moving objects in the same size range as dice. Cox, for example, developed several machines that would roll steel ball bearings down chutes with barriers placed to cause random distributions, but agents were able to affect distributions systematically [14]. My students and I [165] built an apparatus that would spin a silver dollar on edge on a smooth, rotating table. The coin would spin for about twenty seconds before it slowed down enough to fall; during this time, an agent would attempt to make it fall head side or tail side up. In some short experiments, we observed significant results similar to those of many earlier PK studies of dice. That is, although the *total* number of hits did not differ significantly from the level of chance, the *pattern* of hits within the experiment showed a significant decline from beginning to end. Chance does not get tired or bored, but people do; such a falling off in performance with time is a common finding in all sorts of human-performance situations [80].

The *psychic shuffle* is an especially interesting type of PK effect. It was first observed in J. B. Rhine's laboratory in the 1930s [101]. The basic procedure involves an experimenter thoroughly shuffling a deck of cards that is designated as the target deck. The percipient-agent then shuffles a second deck of cards repeatedly without looking at them, until he believes the card order in his call deck matches the order in the target deck. The orders of the cards are then compared, and hits are scored. Because the order of the target deck is not known to anyone at the time that the percipient-agent's shuffling is going on, clairvoyance (or perhaps precognition) is required at an unconscious level on the percipient-agent's part, and PK may be required to affect the shuffle of the call deck. That is, with clairvoyant knowledge of the target deck, there are three possible ways to succeed in the psychic-shuffle method. The first involves only clairvoyance; the percipient keeps shuffling while maintaining clairvoyant contact with both the target and the call decks and stops shuffling when he clairvoyantly perceives that a good match with the target deck has been achieved simply through the chance mechanics of shuffling. The second also calls for unconscious clairvoyant contact with the cards in both decks; but the percipient-agent may sometimes use PK to affect the shuffling action to push matching cards into the right positions. The third way involves a combination of both methods, using PK to affect the initial shuffling of both the target deck and the call deck.

The most recent and probably the most successful results with the psychic shuffle method were reported in a study by H. Kanthamani and Edward Kelly [41] working with a specially talented subject, BD, whose performance on confidence calling was described in Chapter 3. They used ordinary playing cards. The target deck, randomly selected from a large pool of such decks, was randomly shuffled three times by Kanthamani before BD entered the room and then shuffled again ten times, out of BD's sight, after he entered the room. BD then shuffled his call deck until he thought there was a good match, and hits were scored by comparing the orders of the two decks. Six separate, preplanned series were carried out; and in all cases, the results were exceptionally significant. Looking simply at exact hits (both suit and number matching), in the best series, there were five runs, and we would expect five exact hits by chance alone. Instead, there were forty-three hits. The odds against this occurring by chance are fantastic—more than 10^{-26} by my calculations.

Kanthamani and Kelly were convinced that the results in this series had to involve a great deal of PK, rather than just clairvoyant perception and shuffling until the decks happened to match, because they statistically calculated the number of shuffles needed by chance alone to make various numbers of matches between the decks. For example, to score 5 exact hits by chance, one would have to shuffle the call deck an average of 325 times. Yet, BD usually shuffled 3 to 6 times and sometimes only one or two times, so he must have been using PK very strongly to get these results. The implications of the psychic shuffle for professional gamblers are most intriguing.

I have discussed the psychic-shuffle effect at length in order to indicate that we have to have clairvoyance operating simultaneously with PK in many PK experiments in order to be able to model PK. It would do no good at all to use PK randomly to push cards a little to one side or another while shuffling. To get results, *precise* control is needed, and that control depends on information about the order of cards in the call deck. We will see the necessity for this kind of clairvoyant feedback in many other manifestations of PK.

There is some feeling among parapsychologists that PK tends to be more successful in affecting moving objects than static objects, but there have occasionally been convincing demonstrations of PK affecting a static object, usually with outstanding psychics. J. Gaither Pratt and Herbert Keil [85], for instance, report having seen compass needle deflections caused by a Russian psychic, Nina Kulagina. Uri Geller's well-known and controversial feats often involve apparently affecting static objects, such as bending a spoon or key or starting a stopped watch. Geller's work onstage is simply not considered evidential by parapsychologists because he, rather than an experimenter, controls conditions there. But Geller has also done some PK feats under tightly controlled conditions [76, 186]. Cox [15], a professional magician and parapsychologist, observed Geller bend a steel key that never left Cox's hand and was far too stiff to be bent without tools; he has also observed Geller start a watch that Cox had stopped by jamming sticky foil into the works (unknown to Geller). By and large, however, parapsychologists have not had much luck in asking agents to affect static objects. There may be a psychological factor here. It seems easier to influence something that is already moving in some way.

PK has been demonstrated on microscopic objects. Temperature is an effect of molecular movement in solids. Gertrude Schmeidler [111] reported a successful experiment in which the well-known psychic Ingo Swann concentrated on thermistors (electronic devices for sensing temperature). They were sealed in thermos bottles to insulate them, but Swann successfully changed their temperature. The effect known as *psychic photography,* best studied in recent years in Jule Eisenbud's investigations [23, 25] of Ted Serios, seems to represent another form of PK on molecules because an image of some sort appears on photographic film, either in the absence of any light at all to affect the photographic film or in the absence of the proper kind of light patterns. In the latter case, the camera is pointed at a known scene, but an entirely different kind of image appears on the film.*

With the increasing availability of modern instrumentation for measuring small-scale physical effects, apparent PK effects on electromagnetic waves have also been observed. The Stanford Research Institute investigators Hal Puthoff and Russell Targ [91, 93] have reported PK effects on the rate at which an oscillating magnetic field in a highly sensitive, shielded magnetometer slowed down when Swann tried to influence it, and they have also reported momentary magnetic fields being generated inside a magnetometer where no magnetic field existed previously. Several investigators [6, 62, 199] have reported studies suggesting that the rate of emission of particles from the decay of radioactive elements can be influenced by PK, and we now have nineteen excellent experimental demonstrations (out of a total of twenty-four published experiments) showing that the outputs of electronic random number generators can be affected so that more of certain outputs occur than would be expected by chance [3, 9, 35, 51, 53, 114–118, 127, 130].

These kinds of effects are particularly interesting because in most cases the agents are sitting in front of a machine whose internal operations are a mystery to them. The agents usually see some kind of indicator (which of several lights comes on or whether a needle deflects to the left or the right of center), but the internal operation of the machine is controlled by complex electronic circuits that they know nothing about. Nevertheless, they succeed in exerting small PK effects. In order to model this in conventional terms, we must assume not only that the agent functions as a psi percipient on a nonconscious level clair-

* Much so-called psychic photography has been fraudulent, but Eisenbud's work is exceptionally well done and has survived considerable controversy in the parapsychological literature.

voyantly to keep track of the current state of the apparatus but that he also clairvoyantly figures out at least something about the general workings of the apparatus in order to know how to affect it. This often implies quite phenomenal nonconscious powers of understanding, which may be the case, or it may again be that our conventional modeling is limited.

Various kinds of living targets have been affected by PK, including basic biological processes such as the rate of recovery of mice from anesthesia. Successful results were obtained when agents tried to make some mice recover more rapidly from anesthesia [200, 201] (a kind of psychic healing). The electrical resistance of plants has been affected by PK [10]; so has the rate of fungus growth [4], the movement of protozoans on a slide [94], and the activity level of enzymes [122].

This gets us into the area in which some sort of PK may be used for healing. Bernard Grad [26, 27], of McGill University in Canada, has carried out a number of studies showing that psychic healing (by means of laying on of hands or by taking a certain mental attitude) has definite biological effects. These cannot be accounted for by the slight rise in the temperature of an object that has been held between the hands. The basic experimental procedure, used successfully by Grad in several experiments, was to wound barley seeds slightly by keeping them in a hot oven for a while. The seeds were then planted in various pots and the seedlings' sizes measured at fixed intervals, with the final measure in the experiment being the weight of the plants. A psychic healer, Colonel Estabani, gave a healing treatment, using some kind of PK, to sealed bottles of sterile saline solution. This treatment consisted of holding the bottles between his hands while he went through certain mental operations. A control set of bottles of sealed saline solution had nothing done to them. Every bottle had a code number. The treated bottles were allowed to sit along with the untreated bottles until their temperatures again were equal. An assistant, who did not know which saline bottles had received the healing treatment and which had not, then watered various seed pots with the saline solutions. After decoding the results, Grad consistently found that more seeds sprouted and that plants grew faster and weighed more at the end when watered with the saline solution that had received the PK healing treatment. He also found some evidence to suggest that depressed people can affect the saline solution in a way that *inhibits* plant growth. The implications for medicine are enormous.

The final possible PK target listed in Table 4-1 is brain functioning. Although we may not want to equate consciousness with brain functioning, brain and nervous system functioning are certainly intimately involved in consciousness, and it might be that the mechanism of at least some kinds of telepathy is a direct PK action by an agent on selected neurons in the percipient's brain. That is, the message is telepathically transmitted by using PK to inhibit the firing of some neurons and enhance the firing of others. We have no way of testing this explanation of telepathy as yet, but it is worth considering.

I have not attempted to ferret out information on every PK target that has ever been successfully affected, but I believe that the examples I have cited here illustrate the very wide range of targets. I also believe that these examples illustrate why we cannot very well make predictions of the order of "Such and such *cannot* be affected by PK."

Feedback in the PK Model

The final complication in the PK model (Figure 4-1) is the dotted line from the target back to the agent. Common sense tells you that you cannot influence a falling, tumbling, spinning die to land with a given face up just by exerting a momentary or continuous push on it. To affect the die, you have to know *exactly* where it is and all the components of its forward and rotational velocities in all three dimensions at the *precise* moment you are ready to push psychokinetically so that you can push with just the right amount of force at just the right spot on the die in just the right direction. Thus, for the falling die, the psychic shuffle, and similar situations, we have to insert the complete clairvoyance model to provide feedback between target and agent in order to make it a workable system. Obviously, this multiplies the possible interactions in our whole model. It is no wonder that the results of PK tests are generally less significant than the results of clairvoyance test.

I must qualify this, though, by reiterating that this model is based on our ordinary ways of thinking and that it may not adequately represent the reality of a situation. Consider again Schmidt's experiments on influencing electronic devices. These are essentially recycling electronic counters operated by noise sources. Agents are basically instructed to make a given number come up more or less frequently. If it is a binary random number generator, for example, rapidly generating the numbers zero or one, the agent might be able to make, say, 49 percent zeros and 51 percent ones when trying to increase the number of ones, which could be statistically quite significant if continued for a long series. Yet, the vast majority of agents in Schmidt's experiments have no real knowledge of electronics; they do not know what is behind the panels of the machines they are trying to influence. Our model for understanding the behavior of the target and knowing just when to push on it is not adequate, but it is the best we have at this time.

Telepathy Model

The basic laboratory experiment used to establish the reality of telepathy is similar to the clairvoyance card-guessing experiment except that another human being, the agent or sender, looks at each card in a deck at designated intervals and attempts to send it. Thus, at the time the percipient guesses at a card, that information exists in the agent's mind. Telepathy and clairvoyance experiments have been about equally successful, and many such experiments are described in the literature (see [96] for summaries) .

This experimental design (having an agent look at each card) is actually referred to as a GESP design because there is nothing to prevent the percipient from using clairvoyance to identify cards, even though we designate it as a telepathy experiment. For this reason, I will usually refer to the sender as the *agent,* the person actively involved in trying to send the target material, although we do not know whether the apparent sender actually sends anything at a particular time or whether the percipient is using clairvoyance. The designation *agent* simply implies that a participant is active, without committing us to a precise definition of that action.

There is a major experimental-design problem in trying to separate telepathy from clairvoyance. In order to avoid the possibility of errors in scoring responses, we *must* have an objective record of what the targets were; but as soon as we create this objective record, we raise the possibility of current-time clairvoyance or precognitive clairvoyance. If we do not know what limits (if any) exist for clairvoyance, how can we devise a pure telepathy experiment? A few such experiments have been done [52, 123] involving quite elaborate mental codes for translating a written target sequence into a different set of symbols for the telepathy experiment so that the telepathic targets are not obviously readable from the written record. Although they suggest that there is such a thing as pure telepathy (disregarding clairvoyance of the brain for the moment), these experiments are quite cumbersome to carry out.

An overall model for telepathy is presented in Figure 4-3. It combines the clairvoyance and PK models. For that reason, all the questions concerning reception raised about clairvoyance apply here. The general questions raised about activating the PK power generator also apply. More specifically, the problem is to discover how the information is translated into the telepathy-transmission mechanism that actually sends out whatever unknown form of energy is responsible for the telepathic transmission. Although the diagram of the model looks like a simple combination of the PK and the clairvoyance-precognition models, that does not necessarily mean that the mechanisms are the same.

We need to bring an important new consideration into the telepathy model with respect to the problem of noise in the channel. Earlier, we discussed unsystematic, random kinds of noise (i.e., noise involving no intentional or systematic distortion of the information) that might affect the clairvoyance channel. For telepathy, however, we have definite experimental

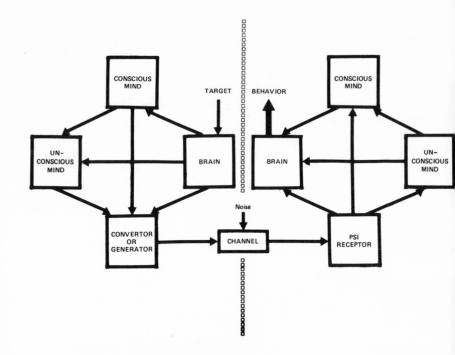

Figure 4-3. Model for telepathy.

evidence that systematic noise can be introduced into the channel to affect telepathic behavior. This can mean that the experimenter becomes an unrecognized part of the experiment.

The Experimenter Is Part of the Experiment

Practically all psychological and parapsychological experiments have been and are carried out under a rather outmoded model taken from classical physics that assumes that the observer or experimenter is somehow detached from what he observes, that he is not affecting it. This is a good approximation in physics on a macroscopic level. If a physicist is measuring the acceleration of freely falling bodies in a gravitational field, it probably does not matter, in terms of the accuracy of his reading of instruments, what he had for breakfast this morning or whether or not he had a quarrel with his wife. The light he uses to observe does not have any significant effect on the falling bodies themselves. There are some obvious situations in psychology where the presence of an observer taking notes might make people self-conscious and inhibited, but it has been assumed that by and large the psychological experimenter can set up an experiment and then be practically independent of it. Although most psychologists are not ready to accept it, it is now clear that this position is generally false. The experimenter *is* a part of the experiment.

Hidden experimenter effects have been discussed by Robert Rosenthal [107] as *experimenter bias* and by Martin Orne [64] as *demand characteristics* in psychology.* These effects are the implicit demands that an experimenter (usually unknowingly) makes on subjects to behave in a way that will make the experiment come out in accordance with the experimenter's expectations. When the experiment does come out as expected, the experimenter takes it as a tribute to his insight and intelligence and feels that he has learned something about the outside world, rather than realizing that it may have been largely a matter of his being able to influence other people.

For example, when I was a postgraduate fellow at Ernest Hilgard's Hypnosis Research Laboratory at Stanford University, we were carrying out an experiment to measure how much suggestibility would increase as a result of inducing hypnosis in student subjects. There had been some controversy in the research literature over whether people were simply suggestible to varying degrees, with hypnosis not really making much difference, or whether hypnotizing someone greatly increased his suggestibility. Almost all of us were of the latter opinion and were doing the experiment primarily to measure

* Note again the important new Silverman book, *The Human Subject in the Psychological Laboratory*. New York: Pergamon, 1977.

precisely how much suggestibility was increased, using some well-developed tests that were available. Each laboratory staff member ran many subjects in this experiment. For the hypnotized group, we would go through a standardized hypnotic-induction procedure and then administer a standardized suggestibility test. For the control (nonhypnotized) group, we chatted pleasantly with the subjects for the same length of time required to induce hypnosis and then proceeded directly to the suggestibility test. The implicit assumption was that the suggestibility-testing procedures were read to both groups of subjects in the precisely same way and therefore that any differences found between the groups would reflect the effect of hypnosis.

Early in the experiment, I found that if I had gone through the procedure of hypnotizing a subject, I did not give the suggestibility test in quite the same manner as if I had not, no matter how much I tried to standardize it. My voice would somehow be warmer, more intimate, and carried more conviction. I brought this up at staff meeting, and the rest of the staff were convinced that although I might have this problem, they were all reading the instructions in a perfectly standardized manner. With the full knowledge of the staff, Suzanne Troffer and I then set up an experiment to test this. We put a microphone in each lab room and made tape recordings of the suggestibility-test procedure for a number of subjects. After we had collected a large number of tapes, we got several staff members to act as judges and sat them down to listen to pairs of recordings. One of the pair was the suggestibility test following hypnosis; the other, carried out on an unhypnotized subject. The judges had to guess which condition was which.

The judges expected to find no differences, but when we analyzed their results, we found that they had been quite good at distinguishing the hypnotic and nonhypnotic conditions on the basis of the suggestibility-test procedure alone, thus indicating that the experimenters were indeed behaving differently in accordance with their bias that hypnosis would increase suggestibility. Interestingly, we found a certain amount of bias within bias. One judge, who was adamantly opposed to the idea that any differences would be detected, failed to detect significant differences, even though the other judges' results were individually significant. Details can be found in the original report [192].

To solve the problem of bias, we considered the study results with respect to hypnosis only tentative and redid the entire thing using a standardized tape recording of the suggestibility-test instructions for all subjects. In this way, we ruled out bias through auditory communication by controlling the communication between experimenter and subject. Because we had eliminated the clear source of bias, we had much more confidence in our results [144], which supported the idea that hypnosis increased suggestibility significantly.

Suppose that covert communications can reach a subject via telepathy and bias him in this way. If they could *not* we could generally control or at least standardize such kind of bias by standardizing all conditions as much as possible and eliminating any nonstandardized communication between experimenter and subjects, as in the hypnosis study. But if covert, nonconscious telepathy can bias subjects, the problem becomes much more difficult.

Consider the ordinary psychological experiment: the experimenter almost always has a very definite expectation of how the experiment should come out and may be quite emotionally involved in obtaining that outcome. The outcome may mean a lot to him theoretically: it may mean the difference as to whether he can publish a report about the experiment or not, and the number and success of reports he publishes is closely related to his promotion in the academic world. Emotional motivation usually favors the occurrence of psi. Although I fear that this idea will probably be emotionally rejected by most psychologists, I believe that almost all psychological experiments need to be reexamined to see to what extent they are accurate accounts of what actually goes on with people and to what extent they might be products of experimenter bias.

Thus, in looking at telepathy, we encounter the problem of systematic noise, as well as random noise, on the channel. Although it is most obvious in telepathy experiments, in which the percipient at least knows the agent is trying to send something, this kind of systematic noise may very well occur in other experiments. The percipient may believe that he is doing a clairvoyance or a PK or precognition experiment, but he may also be biased by telepathic demands from the experimenter.* How he responds to such telepathic demands will be affected by many things, such as his feelings about the experimenter and the experiment. It is a complicated picture indeed, but we cannot pretend that it is not there.

In Chapters 1 and 2 we discussed the scientific method, and I indicated that there are complexities entering into it because it is used by human beings, not by cold, unemotional, totally rational computers. This problem of experimenter bias is one of those complexities. We shall not go further into it here, but I leave you with the disturbing thought that if we can unknowingly telepathically bias a human subject to perform in such and such a manner in a psychological experiment, what happens if we bring in unconsciously used psychokinesis? If, as has been done, a physicist examines hundreds of thousands of photographs and, because one or two of them have a funny little patch on them, he declares he has discovered a new subatomic particle, has he really "discovered" a new particle, or has a small PK effect done something to the film? How far can such nonconscious psychokinetic shaping of the "outside" world, that we like to think of as totally independent of us, go?

Like our other models of psi processes, the model of telepathy has been chosen to fit in with commonsense assumptions about the nature of the universe, particularly about the identity of brain and nervous system functions and mental processes. And like the other models, this may not reflect reality so much as it reflects our attachment to our conceptions. Thus, the information-flow route that seems most likely (from external target stimulus via the sense organs to the brain to the transmitting process to the percipient, possibly with representation in the conscious or unconscious mind) may not be the case. The information-flow

---

* While this book was in press, this possibility and other aspects of experimenter influence via psi have been documented in three excellent review articles [45, 203, 204].

route after the sender knows what the stimulus is through brain processes may be directly from his conscious or unconscious mind to the conscious or unconscious mind of the percipient, without corresponding brain processes (except insofar as the percipient must use brain processes to control his muscles to express the received information). Although we still need to postulate some kind of channel (unless we want to think of space and time as not necessarily real), the transmission and reception may not be separate processes. It may be that the nature of thought itself is such that it is transmitted directly (over some channel) without requiring a special transmitting mechanism. We simply do not know enough to theorize more specifically about this, much less test it, but it is useful to think about.

5.

Altered States of Consciousness and Psi

✿✿

In all our attempts at modeling and understanding psi processes, we have largely taken for granted the stages of the process labeled *conscious mind* and *unconscious mind*. It is time we looked inside those labeled boxes, even though our current psychological understanding of consciousness is sketchy. We shall look at both the nature of psychological functions that affect the operation of psi in our ordinary state of consciousness and those radical changes in the way consciousness functions that I call *discrete altered states of consciousness* (d-ASCs), which includes such things as hypnosis, drug intoxication, dreaming, and meditative states.

I have spent most of my professional career investigating our ordinary state of consciousness and d-ASCs, and I can only touch on the ideas I have developed in these connections here. Although this chapter can be read by itself, the discussions will have greater meaning if the reader will refer to my recent *States of Consciousness* [173].

One way of looking at how consciousness functions and how psi may manifest through it is to observe the functioning of our own minds and listen to the reports others give us of the way in

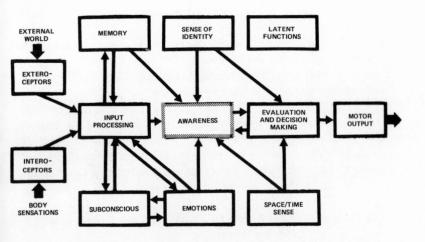

Figure 5-1. Major subsystems of consciousness.

which their minds function and try to decide what major categories of mental processes we need to be able to describe and explain mental functioning. In doing this several years ago, with particular concern for those mental functions that show quite large and radical changes in d-ASCs, I came up with ten major processes or *subsystems* that affect basic awareness and a rough idea of their main interactions with one another. There is nothing ultimate about these subsystems; they are simply convenient concepts for organizing what we presently know. Figure 5-1 is a simplified diagram of these subsystems and their main interactions.

We deal with two major classes of information in perceiving and reacting to the world: information about the environment or external world and information about what is going on in our own bodies. Information about the external world is taken in through the subsystem labeled Exteroceptors, the receptors for external stimulation. These include the eyes, ears, nose, and the other familiar sense organs. The network of receptors and nerve endings throughout our bodies that tell us what is going on internally are our Interoceptors, the receptors for internal processes.

We very seldom have direct contact with sensations from the external or internal world; usually, they pass through a very important subsystem called Input Processing. This subsystem is a set of automatic and largely unconscious learned processes which almost instantly scans the pattern of incoming sensations, identifies those that we have been taught to believe are important, and passes these on to awareness, discarding all the rest. It is analogous to the hierarchical management network in any large corporation, which passes on and condenses reports about reports until the president of the company gets a one-page memo telling him all that is important for him to know about his company without bothering him with the thousands of details that led up to that report.

Input Processing draws heavily on some kind of memory. That is, you need stored criteria of what is important in order for Input Processing to do its work. Much of this is implicit.

Awareness is the ghost in the machine, the part of us that is not an obvious, persistent structure; instead, it takes in information from all these other subsystems. It is a quality that inherently defies clear verbal definition because a verbal definition calls for the use of learned language structures, and awareness is more basic than any such structure. We seldom experience pure awareness; rather, we experience awareness as it is focused on and mixed with various activities of structures, the learned categories of recognizing and thinking. Thus, in Figure 5-1 awareness is shown as a dotted box to indicate that its quality is quite different from the more concrete structures that correspond to other psychological functions.

Ordinarily, we think that after we are faced with a situation and become aware of it, we may remember some relevant information, evaluate the nature of the situation and make a decision about it, and then act in some fashion, initiating Motor Output through our muscles to affect the external world or our own bodies. Sometimes, we consciously experience those special kinds of feelings from the Emotion subsystem along with our other psychological processes; for example, we may feel angry or elated about the situation. But there are three other not-so-obvious subsystems that have an important effect on all that we experience and do. One of these is our Sense of Identity, which is made up of those values we have about what kind of a person we are, what we stand for, how we like to present ourselves to others, and so on. Thus, we react to a situation not simply in terms of what is the best way to accomplish a certain end but also in terms of how can *I* accomplish that end and at the same time make other people think that *I* am brave or helpful or competent or whatever I like to present myself to others as. The Space/Time Sense subsystem is also a very implicit kind of psychological functioning, a kind of constant mental map we all carry that says, "Now I am at such and such a location on this planet and things are occurring in the present, which has a certain specific designation, such as 4:00 P.M. on a certain afternoon. Even our more abstract thinking about events usually puts them implicitly in a certain location at a certain time.

The Unconscious* subsystem is the catchall category for those psychological processes we do not experience directly but whose importance and existence we infer from the quirks in our actions, such as the slips of the tongue that psychoanalysts often refer to. Unconscious processes are often strongly emotionally tinged, such as by the drives of sex and aggression, and need to be kept in check for social reasons. The Unconscious system may get information directly from Input Processing before it even enters awareness and, in turn, affect Input Processing to control what we actually become aware of. The Unconscious may trigger particular emotions that may then further trigger particular parts of the Subconscious. Emotions also affect Input Processing (e.g., you can see examples of social injustice much more

---

* I have used the more general label "subconscious" rather than "unconscious" in Figures 5-1 and 5-2 to be consistent with similar drawings in my *States of Consciousness* [173], but I shall continue to use "unconscious" in the text.

readily if you are walking down the street angry than if you are elated), and information from Input Processing can sometimes directly trigger an emotion, even if that information does not get to awareness directly.

In the upper right-hand corner of Figure 5-1, there is another subsystem (or subsystems) labeled Latent Functions. These are psychological potentials that we did not develop in the course of growing up in our culture, that may indeed have been strongly inhibited by the culture, but that are potentially available. These include the psi potentials.

Psychological Functioning in Ordinary Consciousness

I have gotten fairly abstract in order to present an overview of our ordinary state of consciousness. Now, it will be helpful to illustrate how the total system of consciousness shown in Figure 5-1 ordinarily works for ordinary sensory perception. Suppose that while you are working on something a friend walks in, holds up a copy of a popular novel, and says, "What do you think of this book?" In a very general sense, we can see the whole system functioning by following the flow of information through it. The information conveyed by your friend's gestures and words are received by particular Exteroceptors, your eyes and ears, which turn them into patterns of neural impulses suitable for transmission within your nervous system. These immediately go to Input Processing, where the important meaning is abstracted from the large input of information. Most of the information coming to you from your friend is thrown away. You do not consciously notice the color of his shoes, the precise rate at which he moves across the floor, his posture, and so on. Rather, you immediately respond to the apparently important aspects of the situation—the sight of the book, the title and author's name printed on it, and the meaning of his words—so that you know he is asking you a question about your opinion of this particular book. This information is what is passed on to awareness. It is important because of your whole personal history of being brought up in a culture that has taught you that it is much more important to listen to the *words* of people than to focus on the rate at which they move across the floor and so forth. This Input Processing takes place quite automatically and almost instantly in terms of psychological time, so that you do not know you are throwing away most of the information and responding to only a small, semiarbitrarily selected part of it.

Input Processing automatically draws on stored information (Memory) in order to understand what was said. You will consciously draw on Memory to recall whether you have read the book and what opinions you formed about it at the time. With that question, your recall of the book, and your reactions to it in your awareness, you then decide what to say (Evaluation and Decision Making). Once you have made this decision, you use your Motor Output subsystem to say, perhaps, "It's entertaining enough, but there wasn't any real meat in it." The Space/Time Sense subsystem, usually operating implicitly and outside the focus of your awareness, causes you to say these words in a loud-enough voice for your friend to hear and to look toward him as you speak, rather than whispering while staring at the ceiling.

That is a simplified example of what can go on, although it is probably all that we would ordinarily be aware of. Yet, I deliberately chose the answer "It's entertaining enough, but there wasn't any real meat in it" to show how the other subsystems can affect your awareness and your final answer, even though you may not be immediately aware of them. Assume in this case that the book was rather racy and at the time you read it you had some intense and enjoyable sexual fantasies, tinged with some guilt. The friend who is asking you about the book is somewhat up-tight about sexual enjoyment, but you value his friendship, and so it is important to you that he have a good opinion of you. Therefore, although you are consciously trying to remember the book and formulate an opinion of it, some memory of how much it excited you is activated and this feeling of excitement in the Emotions subsystem also activates your Unconscious mind to generate some feelings of guilt about your earlier fantasy, an enjoyment that, if expressed, would bother your friend.

Rather than experience the guilt consciously, your Unconscious may literally affect Input Processing and Memory retrieval, coloring your perception of your friend's interruption. You may think that he walked in rather abruptly and is talking rather loudly, which makes you feel annoyed. Our evaluation processes are constantly affected by Unconscious processes and Emotions. By further identifying yourself as an active person who was working on something important, you decide that your friend's interruption *is* annoying, and although you suppress the expression of annoyance because of your friendship, you feel that you are a righteous, productive person who has been unjustly interrupted. Your answer, "It was entertaining enough, but there wasn't any real meat in it," is simultaneously a semiconscious opinion about the book and a symbolic expression of your annoyance at being interrupted. All this, of course, happens extremely rapidly and involves little or no awareness, but the net result has been that instead of feeling awkward at having had feelings that your friend would disapprove of and that you were a little guilty about yourself, you have inflated your own ego by feeling busy and important and given yourself credit for being a good friend by not expressing your annoyance at the interruption.

This is, of course, only a hypothetical example to illustrate the complexities of ordinary mental functioning, but it is not farfetched. Immense amounts of psychological data show that our minds frequently work in this way. Indeed, the (partially conscious) feelings generated may influence Input Processing so that even the perception of the book is affected. Perhaps the jacket design now looks rather garish to you; whereas when you originally read the book, you found it quite appealing.

This is an illustration of a particular situation and reaction being processed through the system within our ordinary state of consciousness, but it does not illustrate the overall nature of that ordinary state or show the limits of the variability of functioning within particular subsystems that the pattern of our ordinary state imposes.

Psi Functioning in Ordinary Consciousness

Now we are ready to return to our model of psi reception and stop taking the block labels *conscious mind* and *unconscious mind* for granted. Now we can look at some of the complexities that can occur and some of the possibilities produced by work with d-ASCs. We will consider only the case of clairvoyance, but the extension to other kinds of psi phenomena will be obvious because this section elaborates on our discussions in Chapters 3 and 4.

Figure 5-2 modifies Figure 5-1 to show four possible routes of information flow for psi information that correspond to known effects. The input from the external world to the Exteroceptors is blocked to remind us that for psi functioning, we deliberately

Figure 5-2. Four possible information-flow routes for psi.

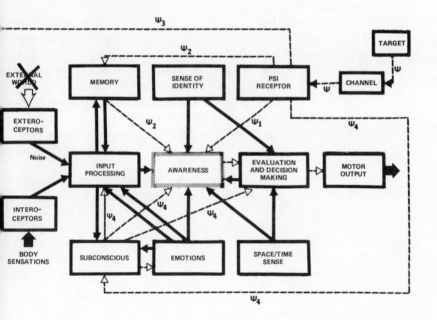

eliminate information flow relevant to the target from the outside world. Unless the percipient is in a sensory-isolation situation, there is still information about the immediate environment coming in, but because this information is irrelevant to the target, it constitutes only noise. To whatever extent you pay attention to this sensory input, you are distracting yourself from possible sources of information that contain the psi message. Some parapsychologists have recognized this input from the external world as a source of noise and employed sensory-isolation techniques, with some success, in an effort to reduce the interference [191].

The psi target and the psi channel (in the upper right-hand corner of Figure 5-2) feed into a function that is primarily latent in ordinary consciousness, the Psi Receptor, which is whatever process or processes that transform the psi information coming over the channel into a form useful for processing in the mind or the brain. Once this latent psi function is activated, four routes of information flow are are possible.*

The first, marked ψ_1, is shown by an arrow directly from the Psi Receptor to awareness. This represents occasional types of psi experiences in which a percipient finds that he is suddenly given an apparently perfect representation of the target. There is essentially no distortion; it is as if you had a complete and accurate look at the target for a short time. The information has a quality of intruding and temporarily displacing other ongoing mental processes that makes it seem relatively or completely independent of the structure of your state of consciousness.

Such experiences are relatively rare compared with more indirect psi experiences, but they are nevertheless quite striking when they do occur. I had one such experience myself in the summer of 1957 when I was working as a laboratory assistant at the Round Table Foundation, a parapsychological research organization that Andrija Puharich had set up in Maine. The well-known Dutch psychic Peter Hurkos was in residence at that

* For simplicity, I shall still leave out a Psi-specific Information Processing system between the Psi Receptor and the remainder of the information-flow routes.

time, and we were trying to find someone who could work as part of a good telepathic team with him. I already had tried several runs with Hurkos as both sender and percipient without making any really significant scores. The test, designed by Puharich and called the Matching Abacus Test [90], consisted of arranging transparent plastic boxes on two adjacent rows. Ten different target pictures could be seen through the boxes in one row; a matching set of pictures could be seen in the plastic boxes of the other row. The boxes were in random order within each row, and a shield covered the whole apparatus so that the sender could see the boxes but the percipient could not. As percipient, I would pick up a box and hold it so that Hurkos, as sender, could see it; then I would move it along the target row, waiting for a telepathic impression to tell me when to put it down across from its match.

During one of these tests, I was sitting there, immersed in my own familiar mental processes and guessing, when suddenly a vividly colored image of one of the target pictures, a sailboat, sprang full-blown into my mind and stayed there for a couple of seconds before fading. I was quite surprised because my immediate feeling was that this was obviously not *my* mental process. It felt alien. I asked Hurkos if the box I had in my hand at that moment was the one containing the sailboat. It was. It was as if, for an instant, the psi process (Hurkos's attempts to send the picture of that sailboat into my mind or my searching) had flowed directly into my awareness, bypassing all my usual mental processes.*

A second possible route for psi information is shown by the arrows labeled ψ_2. This route is from the Psi Receptor into Memory, where a memory image corresponding (to various degrees) to the target is triggered. The memory image, rather than the actual psi information, flows into awareness. William Roll [105] has proposed this as being an information route for psi, and this theory is able to account for some of the distortions

* Because this was an informal procedure it did not adequately control for possible sensory cueing from Hurkos, although I personally believe it was genuinely telepathic. I cite it here to illustrate personally the quality of the ψ_1 route, not to prove it.

and transformations frequently seen in the psi process. In this route, we never have a *direct* perception of the target, only an indirect impression via a memory image *associated* with the target. This would imply that if the psi target is something we have never experienced, we might not be able to get it or, at best, would be able to get only a composite image, made up of separate memory images.

Thus, the latent psi function is accessible only through the intermediary of Memory. The precise nature of the Memory mechanisms involved is still unknown. It is an interesting theory and seems to fit some experimental data [42].

The third information-flow route, ψ_3, is from the Psi Receptor to some body part or parts and thence to the Interoceptors. That is, the psi information is expressed as various kinds of bodily sensations that are being picked up by our Interoceptors, being subjected to various degress of Input Processing, going on to awareness, and then also having to be evaluated before the percipient can make a response to say something about what he thinks the target is. The bodily sensations may or may not be accompanied by Emotions. It is a route that we know very little about but that I think is quite important. It has received very little study, even though psychics in the past have sometimes described psi impressions as coming to them in terms of certain kinds of bodily feelings.

Both in operation and in terms of study, this route is complicated by our predominant cultural bias of not really paying much attention to our bodies. Our bodies are too seldom thought of as sources of information. Researchers in humanistic and transpersonal psychology are just beginning to find out that the body has a wisdom of its own—a brain of its own, as it were—that can provide us with information about ourselves and external reality and process that information. Carlos Castaneda, for example, has told me that in Don Juan's system, a sorcerer considers his body a major source of information about the world around him; the sensations in his body will tell him a great deal about events that otherwise would not be perceived through ordinary sensory channels.

The complication is that there is little use in having psi

(and other kinds of information) represented as sensations in your body if you do not pay attention to them. These sensations are automatically picked up by the Interoceptors, but then they go through Input Processing. In Westernized, overintellectualized people, the Input-Processing subsystem automatically throws away practically all body information, making this a relatively useless source of information for most of us.

This was vividly illustrated to me in the course of some personal growth work a few years ago. All my adult life I have found that I occasionally tend to become anxious and upset at social gatherings. Being psychologically minded, and knowing that my body is controlled by my mind, my reaction was always to try to figure out what was wrong with *me*, what psychological processes of mine were making me upset. Frequently, I could find no satisfactory answer.

As I began to practice a less attached attitude of trying simply to pay attention to and accept things without getting caught up in either my reactions to or my analyses of them, I paid more attention to these up-tight feelings when they occurred at social gatherings and also more attention to the other people in the room, sometimes asking them how *they* felt. I found, to my surprise, that my own bodily feelings, which made no sense to me, were quite frequently reflecting the fact that someone else in the room was feeling anxious.

Now I am not presenting this phenomenon as a case of psi; there were always innumerable sensory cues. The point is that my consciousness was not picking these up but my body was. By prematurely conceptualizing my own body feelings as being caused by my own psychological processes, I was throwing away a valuable source of information about the external reality around me. I suspect that this is a rather widespread phenomenon and that as people learn to become more sensitive to their own bodily feelings, they will not only get more sensory information about the environment around them but probably will also be able to pick up psi information that is being expressed by this route.

The fourth possible psi route, ψ_4, comes from the Psi Receptor to our Unconscious and thence has a variety of indirect effects on us. The psi information would be transformed more or less in accordance with the dynamics of each individual's Unconscious. As one possibility, the transformed information might then manifest by affecting the processing of other information in Input Processing, thus expressing the psi information. An excellent example of this would be in the use of external props, such as tarot cards or a person's palms, for a psychic reading. Sensory information of little or no relevance is modified by Input Processing so that certain aspects of it stand out more, and this might convey the psi information. As a second possibility, the Unconscious might send some mental contents directly into awareness as in a dream or a vision such as the earlier Christmas catalog dream, and so express the psi information this way. Or it might subtly affect our Evaluation and Decision-Making processes to distort them so that the decision made expresses the psi. E. Douglas Dean's and John Mihalaskys' work [21], showing that more successful executives have more precognitive abilities, could be interpreted in this fashion. These executives, believing they are making only rational decisions in their businesses, based on facts, have their evaluation processes subtly altered to incorporate the information they unconsciously pick up by precognition, thus arriving at a better decision. This is also the model for Stanford's PMIR, which has an adaptive effect on thinking or behavior, even though a person does not know he is using psi. Finally, the Unconscious could alter or generate various emotions that, in turn, selectively affect the way we saw things.

The operation of all these possible psi routes is very much affected by our *state* of consciousness. In our ordinary state, for example, our orientation is to deal with the important things in the world about us, which means that our available attention and energy are concentrated on information coming from the Exteroceptors and generally ignore Interoceptor information. This immediately takes away energy from subsystems that might convey psi information and possibly from the latent psi functions themselves. Furthermore, it loads our consciousness with information concerning the external world, so that even if psi information comes in by one of the suggested routes, it is unlikely to be noticed among the preponderant activity connected with dealing with the external world and our reactions to it.

In our ordinary state, Memory is put to use primarily in dealing with the external world and assisting the Evaluation and Decision-Making processes. This may prevent it from connecting with the Psi Receptor to allow information to get through by that route. Similarly, route ψ_1, is pretty well cut off because awareness is totally wrapped up in the ongoing processes of dealing with and reacting to the world. This also blocks route ψ_4, at least to our direct knowledge, and the more subtle distortions of conscious processes that are caused by the Unconscious in order to express psi may be either unnoticed in the press of ordinary activity or actively corrected for. For example, you notice that your thinking about what to do about a situation is going in a strange direction, a direction that is not so logical, and you deliberately force yourself away from that and come back to realistic thinking.

Furthermore, the Space/Time subsystem is active as an implicit background to all your thoughts, telling you that you are here in this place at this particular time and thus automatically implying that what is not in this particular place at this particular time cannot be reaching you. Your Sense of Identity subsystem makes you feel that you are an active, practical person and thus further discourages you from attending to illogical ideas and sensations. Thus, in our ordinary state of consciousness, there is both removal of attention energy from the psi processes and an active inhibition of mental processes that might be conducive to psi.

Nature of Altered States

To consider the possible effects of altered states of consciousness on psi functioning, it would be best to start with a thorough understanding of altered states. Unfortunately, scientific understanding of these states is in its infancy. Consequently, we are in the position of having to relate one poorly understood area to another poorly understood one. Nevertheless, I shall do what I can by briefly describing what I mean by a d-ASC in terms of my systems approach, which is presented fully in *States of Consciousness* [173].

The ten subsystems described in this chapter work together in our ordinary state (or any altered state) to form a *system,* so there is not only a specific range of functioning in each subsystem but also an overall, discrete *pattern* of functioning in the integrated system. It is the feel or quality of this pattern, as well as the specific functioning of the subsystems, that identifies and characterizes a *state* of consciousness. For instance, if you have to prove to yourself that you are awake, you can do it by scanning your experiential field and noting that some sorts of specific things are happening that do not happen in your dreams but do happen in wakefulness, or you could just judge the overall feel of your consciousness. The differences between the patterns of waking and dreaming or of waking and other altered states, such as meditative states, are *discretely* different. Hence, the adjective *discrete* (d) is affixed to the abbreviation ASC to emphasize these qualitative pattern differences.

The various subsystems that make up our ordinary state interact with each other to stabilize their overall pattern of functioning so that our state is stable. We do not, for example, have a mystical experience if there is a sudden, loud noise. But various induction techniques may break down the stability of our ordinary state and lead us into various d-ASCs in which there may be changes in the style and level of functioning of particular subsystems and in the overall pattern of functioning. These changes, which usually seem radical to the person experiencing them, offer interesting possibilities for affecting manifestations of psi.

Effects of Altered States on Psi Potentials

In d-ASCs, there are many possibilities of changing system functioning that might be favorable to psi. These could include the Psi Receptor somehow becoming activated, having more energy, and thus producing a stronger signal to begin with; other subsystems, whose normal operations inhibited psi, perhaps being inhibited themselves and so allowing readier access to psi information; and an overall change in the pattern of consciousness that might also allow readier expression of psi. What are some of the ways that subsystem change over the known range of d-ASCs might be favorable to psi?

Consider, first, route ψ_1, in which the psi information somehow comes directly into awareness. An experience many people report in various d-ASCs is that awareness is somehow freer, can focus on things it does not ordinarily focus on, or is somehow less tied down to the ordinary structure of the mind. This can be interpreted in two ways. In the conservative view of the mind, which considers awareness nothing but a byproduct of brain functioning, route ψ_1, means that brain functioning itself is somehow loosened up or at least moved into nonhabitual patterns, as if neural circuits that are ordinarily isolated from one another somehow leak into one another or temporarily form new connections. In the radical view of the mind, which sees basic awareness as qualitatively different in nature from brain and nervous system functioning, route ψ_1 could be interpreted as awareness literally being less involved in the structure of the brain, less intimately married to it, manifesting more in its own right. In either case, it gives the percipient the freedom or the ability to focus on the unusual, which could very well increase attentiveness to the psi message, regardless of the channel over which it comes

For the specific information-flow route ψ_1, if awareness per se is intrinsically different from brain functioning and more intimately related to psi information, this freeing of awareness from such intimate connection with brain structure would automatically make it more sensitive to psi impulses. Thus, d-ASCs in which people feel their awareness is less habituated, less bound to structure, such as hypnosis or some meditative states, might be particularly valuable for enhancing psi functioning. (Whether this would be *useful* psi functioning is another question because you not only have to free up awareness from habitual but irrelevant places, but also still have to be able to direct it to the relevant information.)

Consider route ψ_2, from Memory into awareness. Memory

functioning can show vast changes in various d-ASCs; it may work more efficiently or less so, or it may change in style. Your most recent memories may come up rather than the one you are searching for; or you may experience the phenomenon of *state-specific memory,* in which something learned in a particular d-ASC can be recalled fully in that d-ASC but only partially or not at all in some other state of consciousness, such as your ordinary state. If psi links with awareness through a kind of state-specific memory, it means that if we are in the appropriate d-ASC when this happens, we can remember psi information coming to us more effectively than in a state in which the retrieval mechanisms for this information do not work properly (such as our ordinary state). Or perhaps being in d-ASCs in which people feel that their memory is much more vivid might mean that psi information would come through more vividly.

Route ψ_3, in which psi is expressed as body sensations, is particularly interesting because in many d-ASCs people report a greatly enhanced contact with their bodies, experiencing some ordinary sensations much more vividly and often experiencing entirely new bodily sensations. Although they would probably still have to learn how to interpret what these various kinds of new bodily sensations mean in terms of the target, the possibilities here are intriguing. However, I suspect this will end up being a bigger research project than anyone realizes because with this society's neurotic attitude toward the body, we have a lot of remedial work to do before we can develop substantial body intelligence.

Route ψ_4, to the Unconscious mind and then to direct effects on the rest of consciousness, can also be greatly affected by d-ASCs. One way of describing some of the phenomena of d-ASCs is to say that what was *un*conscious in an ordinary state may become conscious in the d-ASC. That is, people may directly experience certain aspects of their minds and personalities that they or others could only *infer* in their ordinary state. This could mean that some of the psi information that reaches the Unconscious might be directly *experienceable,* possibly in a less distorted form, because although some of the distortion may take place in the Unconscious itself, other aspects of it may occur as a result of indirect interaction that influences ongoing conscious processes.

An important related problem is the degree to which a given percipient is at home in his own mind. If his Unconscious processes mainly represent repressed and unaccepted emotions as in ordinary kinds of psychopathology, the direct contact with those possible in some d-ASCs may not aid psi but instead be catastrophic. We should not expect to get more psi simply by putting people more directly in touch with their Unconscious minds. We also need to do some psychotherapy or growth work.

Remember that *any* state of consciousness is a system; the parts interact with each other to form a particular pattern. Thus, changes in other subsystems that might not be directly involved in one of the four psi transmission routes we have examined may still have important effects on psi functions. Consider, for instance, the functioning of our Sense of Identity subsystem. We all possess a variety of identities that change rapidly with various situations and emotions, but when a particular identity is functioning, it tends to organize the rest of our mental functioning into a consistent pattern.

It is hard to realize just how strong these various roles or identities can be because we so often identify totally with them. Suppose, in any discrete state, my Sense of Identity is that I am a rational, hardheaded person who is very practical and accepts no nonsense. If a psi impression comes in through any of the various routes, it will be at variance with my identity; and perhaps consciously, but more likely automatically and unconsciously, I will shift my attention away from that information or actively suppress it and get on with my realistic role.

On the other hand, consider the case of many psychics, who do have a socially acceptable (within a subculture) role of being "psychic." Regardless of whether or not they deliberately enter a d-ASC, under the appropriate circumstances, they take on the role of psychic, and the Sense of Identity subsystem tends to maximize those functions of consciousness that fit into the role of psychic and enhance psi functioning. We can, in a certain sense, be possessed by an identity that may help or hinder psi functioning.

Going into some d-ASCs may make it easier for us to accept the role of being persons with psychic abilities because we are so obviously not our ordinary selves. Some people who ordinarily think psi is nonsense will go to a party, get stoned on marijuana, and gladly read someone's palms, sometimes apparently showing psi in the process, because they feel so different in that d-ASC that they do not experience this psychic role as being in serious conflict with their ordinary roles.

Consider also the effects of the Emotions subsystem. Many outstanding spontaneous cases of psi and some laboratory experiments have suggested that when very strong Emotions are aroused, they can act as facilitators of psi. In some d-ASCs, it is much easier to arouse strong emotions than it is in our ordinary state, so such d-ASCs may facilitate psi. Because strong emotions themselves probably also induce d-ASCs, inducing a strong emotion in an ordinary state may produce a d-ASC that is favorable to psi. Inducing a strong emotion in a person who is already in a d-ASC may cause a transition to another d-ASC dominated by the emotion, and that may be favorable to psi. These ideas are elaborated for sexual arousal and marijuana intoxication elsewhere [183].

Finally, consider the Space/Time subsystem. It usually operates implicitly, and it always sets our experiences in a particular location at a particular time. This subsystem defines the psi targets as being somewhere else and thus hard to reach. In many d-ASCs, the Space/Time sense is drastically changed. Both may be experienced as nothing but conceptual categories, rather than as things that are inherently real. With such a change, all sorts of inhibitions against using psi may disappear. In your ordinary state of consciousness, using psi would mean doing something miraculous, somehow violating the barriers of real space and real time. But if you are in a d-ASC in which they are not real, then the target is not separated from you in any way that matters, and it is no extraordinary feat to pick up information about it.

Research Results on Psi and Altered States

I have tried to give an overview of the ways in which changes in d-ASCs may be favorable to the operation of psi. I would like to go on to give many specific illustrations of applications of these sorts of ideas that have increased psi functioning. Alas, I cannot. Of the hundreds of experimental studies of psi, only a tiny fraction deal with the effects of altered states such as hypnosis, meditation, or psychedelic drugs on psi functioning; and most of this handful of studies have methodological short-comings that make their results very tentative. They tend to be methodologically sophisticated in terms of ruling out alternatives to psi as explanations for their results, but they are rather poor in the handling of the d-ASC aspect of the experiment.

I shall give an example of one of the better studies here, more to whet the reader's appetite than to make any final pronouncements. In 1962, Milan Rýzl published a paper [108] describing his attempts to increase psi functioning in the hypnotic state. This is probably the most sophisticated research that has been done to date on hypnosis and psi. A common fallacy of many other studies was assuming that because a person was in a hypnotic d-ASC and was told he had psi faculties, he automatically had them. Rýzl assumed, more realistically, that although the hypnotic state might be favorable to manifesting psi, it was still necessary to *develop* that potential within the hypnotic state. He effectively used three specific properties of the hypnotic state and implicitly applied basic learning theory in the way I have described in *Learning to Use Extrasensory Perception* [178], and got very significant results.

Rýzl utilized the fact that hypnosis generally produces a very quiet state of mind. Typically, when a deeply hypnotized person is asked what he is thinking about, he will answer, "Nothing." By producing a quiet state through hypnosis, Rýzl eliminated most of the ordinary distractions to which the percipient would be exposed. He further utilized the fact that you can easily set up a high degree of motivation in the hypnotic state. He was able to motivate his percipients to want to develop psi and to keep this motivation high. Third, he utilized the fact that hypnotized people can usually visualize quite intensely. He trained the percipients by placing a tray in front of them while their eyes were closed and asking them to try to visualize the objects on the tray.* Once a percipient achieved and described a vivid visual image of the objects that he thought were before him, he could open his eyes and immediately compare his visual image with what was actually on the tray.

I believe that this immediate feedback contributed importantly to the results Rýzl got, although he himself emphasized the hypnotic state. Because the training went on over a long period, his percipients would have an opportunity to learn to discriminate which qualities of imagery went with successful use of psi and which did not.

Rýzl claims to have used this kind of training to develop strong psi abilities in a number of people. One such percipient, Pavel Stepanek, was able to demonstrate significant psi abilities to other investigators for many years. Rýzl's studies are a good example of relatively sophisticated use of a d-ASC because he used the specific properties of the hypnotic d-ASC in a way that might help psi and recognized that psi potential must be learned in the d-ASC, rather than simply expected to manifest. Unfortunately, there has never been any adequate attempt at replication of Rýzl's results; the few published attempts [7, 30] did not duplicate his main conditions.

I end this survey of psi and altered states of consciousness, then, in a most unsatisfactory way, leaving the reader's appetite whetted with what I believe are very real and important possibilities, but without being able to supply more concrete results. Again, my *States of Consciousness* [173] will greatly expand the view of altered states presented here, and I have given specific research ideas for the parapsychological investigator in two other papers [168, 180].

---

* Simply having a percipient sit with closed eyes in front of a target is an unacceptable condition in any attempt to *demonstrate* psi. But Rýzl used this for training, not for demonstration.

Part II: Studies

Introduction

✿✿

The task of science can be viewed as a kind of map making. We live and operate in a territory, a world, and we decide where we will go and what we will do on the basis of our internal and external maps of that territory. The conceptual map you consult when faced with a given situation may enable you literally to move yourself to another physical location that you value more, or it may tell you how to understand the situation you are in and how to act on it and modify it in ways that will be to your benefit. Clearly, we need to have good maps. If a car is racing toward us as we walk across an intersection, a mental map for dealing with this situation should adequately reflect its danger and indicate that we ought to move. A mental map that indicated we should cast our eyes skyward and think about the meaning of existence right then would not be a good map for survival. Scientific method is a set of procedures for continually upgrading the quality of our maps, for testing our concepts about the territory against our experiences in it (data) .

In Part I of this book, I attempted to make some global maps of the paranormal, to sketch in the shape of the continents and mark the major cities. We need these kinds of maps to get a general orientation to the territory. Unfortunately, the present state of our knowledge of psi allows us only the most general kind of maps. There are many blank spaces on them, and there are many places about which we can say only that some travelers report a city here but it may be over there or perhaps just be a mirage. Time, experience, and research will be the tools for making the maps more precise.

Alfred Korzybski, the founder of semantics, exhorted us to remember that the map is not the territory. Any map is only an abstraction *about* the territory. No matter how many places on your maps are marked "productive agricultural area," you won't get much nourishment from eating the paper on which those words are printed. We must remember then that scientific data, observation, and experience are *primary* and that the theories (the maps) are secondary. If the maps do not agree with the territory, we must redraw them.

As a psychologist, I find that we frequently operate on a different version of Korzybski's statement, one that says, in effect, "The map is not the territory; the map is *better* than the territory." We become attached to our ideas and explanations and prefer to ignore those inconsiderate aspects of reality that do not fit our beautiful maps. Sometimes, reality forces us to redraw our maps; at other times, we neurotically hold onto inaccurate maps all our lives. Science is a good discipline because it reminds us to keep checking back against observation and not to get too attached to the map.

The studies presented in Part II are examples of the kind of observations and experiments that led me to draw the maps presented in Part I. Aside from being interesting in themselves, they give life to the overall schemes and abstractions in Part I. They also remind me that making maps always involves some selection, both conscious and unconscious, of what is important, what I want to emphasize. *All* the observations cannot fit in neatly. I hope that the ones I have chosen are indeed the most important ones. Time will tell.

We shall touch here on telepathic dreams, precognition, remote viewing, and out-of-the-body experiences. There are other studies—on drugs, auras, and many other subjects—that will be the subject of a later work.

Since I want to keep this data accessible to the general reader, I have given just the basic details and findings of the various studies. The reader who wants more information should, of course, go back to the original journal article in which the research was reported (see Bibliography).

6.

A Telepathic Dream

✿✿

My interest in psi increased considerably after I entered the Massachusetts Institute of Technology in the fall of 1955 as a student of electrical engineering. There I met many other students who were interested in psi. Together, we formed a student organization, the MIT Society for Psychical Research, to explore our mutual interests. One of the members, whom I shall call Mr. A, has remained a lifelong friend, and his occasional reports of some of his personal psychic experiences have given me some valuable insights into the nature of psi. This chapter, a study of one of Mr. A's psychic dreams, illustrates some of the complexities of psi that we have discussed in abstract terms in previous chapters. I originally reported on this first case in 1963, in the *Journal of the Society for Psychical Research* [138].

At the time of this dream, Mr. A was working as an electrical engineer in the eastern United States. I have checked his narrative report of the dream against the original tape recording and have interviewed all the persons involved in the case. I am satisfied that their reports are accurate.

Both Mr. A and his wife had been frequent dream recallers since childhood and had been interested in the psychology of dreams for some years. As a result, they had decided to tape-record their dreams when they awoke in the morning for a period of a few months in order to get an overview of their dreamworlds. They had been doing this routinely for several weeks before the events described in this chapter.

On June 24, Mr. A had been planning a trip he was to make the following morning to a city I'll call Metropolis, which was about 113 miles from his home, in order to purchase a new car at a better price than he could get in his hometown. Mr. and Mrs. A had been planning this purchase for several weeks and, because of some rather frustrating mechanical difficulties with their current car, were very involved in their plans. As Mr. A fell asleep on the twenty-fourth at his usual bedtime, he was preoccupied with thoughts of purchasing a car and of seeing his in-laws, the Bs, particularly his sister-in-law, Miss B, who was eighteen and of whom he was quite fond. Because of his preoccupation with these things, he took some time to fall asleep, which was quite unusual for him.

When they awoke in the morning, Mrs. A left their bedroom to prepare the children's breakfast, as usual, while Mr. A taperecorded whatever dreaming he recalled. Considering the distance between the bedroom and the kitchen and the noise made by the children and the preparation of breakfast, Mrs. A could not normally hear what Mr. A was dictating.

Shortly after Mr. A finished recording his dream and left the bedroom, Mrs. A returned and recorded her dreams. Mr. A however, walked past the bedroom door while she was recording and overheard part of her dictation. He was impressed with some apparent parallels to his own dream and so called out that she should record her dreams in detail. He was careful to say nothing else and left the vicinity of the bedroom until Mrs. A had finished her recording.

In the following excerpts from the tape recordings of Mr. and Mrs. A's dreams, the ellipses indicate a little material I have deleted for the sake of brevity because it was not relevant to the question of parallelism. The lines of the narratives have been numbered to facilitate later reference. The names and places have been disguised.

Mr. A's Dream

    Fairly vivid dream. It started out with my being
in my father-in-law's office. . . . He and I then left.
We went down in the elevator, somewhere between eight and
four stories down, and got off and went out of the
5 building. I believe we were going to go back to his
home in Metropolis, but when we got outside the building and
closed the door, for some reason he wanted to go back
into the building again, up to his office. But the door
we [had] just come out of was locked. Se we went around to
10 the rear of the building, and there was a drop of eight or nine
feet onto a lower level where there was some construction
going on, right behind the building. We both jumped over
the fence. He jumped down, and then I jumped down
also by pushing myself over the edge, holding on, and
15 then letting go and dropping down. There was a board
fence, too, right along the edge where we dropped down,
and I followed him over the slightly muddy ground and
went into a back door. Then what happens here is somewhat
confused. But we started up on the elevator, and
20 there were some confusing things, I don't recall exactly,
of getting on and off the elevator several times and the
elevator not exactly lining up with the floor levels
at which it stopped and some things of this nature.*
But then what happened was that I got off the elevator,
25 following my sister-in-law, who is about eighteen. I don't
know what happened to my father-in-law at this point.
My sister-in-law and I were apparently making some kind
of game about going up the stairs the rest of the way.
I was following along a little ways behind her, and she
30 got well ahead of me and a little bit out of sight, and
I became worried over this. I hurried up the stairs after
her because I think at this point I began having
some fear that she [had] committed suicide or something to that
effect. So I ran upstairs, and she and some other girl (and I
35 don't know how this other girl got in the dream except
that she was some friend of my sister-in-law's and

---

  * Although he did not record it immediately, Mr. A is also certain that
the elevator in his dream kept changing its shape and size as he and his
father-in-law were riding on it in the dream.

was about her age) had hung themselves. Some other
people appeared again at this point. I think my father-
in-law was back in here again, and an unknown number of
40 other people, and we got them down and started performing
artificial respiration. . . . She recovered, and her
friend also recovered and didn't seem any the worse
for it. . . . The grief I felt over the potential suicide
was quite intense in the dream. I was quite actively
45 involved in it.

After hearing Mrs. A's dream report, Mr. A immediately
added the following details, which he had not bothered to
mention in his initial report:

When I went into the back entrance of this building,
there was some construction going on around the
building, and it was a relatively new building. The entrance
I went into was something like a service entrance,
50 where there were some pipes overhead on the ceiling, and
it was kind of dirty from a lot of people going in and
out right from this mud. . . .

Mrs. A's Dream

In my first dream, I was in this old office building.
I don't know exactly how high it was, maybe about ninety
55 stories, and I was down in the coffee shop in this building.
I had a job in this building. It was on the eighty-fourth
story. This was pretty important. There was one elevator
in the building and also a flight of stairs, and the
elevator was a very strange elevator because it had
60 buttons in it just for a few of the stories, for the third
and the ninth and the twenty-fifth and a couple of others. But
everything above that was unmarked. There were no buttons
to push, and you had to work this strange contraption
to get to the level that you wanted. I don't remember
65 how I got up to this eighty-fourth story into this new
job that I had, but I got up there somehow. . . . towards
the end of the day, when I wanted to go home, I noticed
that there was nobody in the elevator to work it, and
they said you were supposed to work it yourself. I

70 didn't understand how to work it. I knew I would
   never work it right to get back down to the ground again.
   Also it took a fairly long time for this elevator. It
   was an old, rickety thing to get up all the way to the
   top and back again all the way down and back. So I
75 walked around for a while and found this janitor, and I
   asked him if he could run the elevator for me. We had
   quite a discussion about it, and he told me how to work
   it, and he told me he couldn't work it for me and he
   couldn't take the time unless there were twenty-five people
80 going down. He took me to the elevator and showed me
   how it worked. There was a belt of some sort. If you
   pulled down on it, you would go down. If you pulled up
   on it, you would make the elevator go up. But, of course,
   you had to keep stopping and seeing if you were at
85 the right place because there was no way of telling
   because there was no indicator inside the elevator. As
   the elevator shaft was open, you could see all the way
   down it. The elevator itself was only this wooden platform
   held up by some ropes. When I tried to step on it,
90 it got smaller and smaller, until it was just two or three
   inches across. So I didn't much want to get on the
   thing. I went into the ladies' room and sat down on the
   couch and had a cigarette while I was thinking what to
   do. It was about 4:30. A bunch of people were there
95 waiting for the elevator. I didn't think it was safe to
   go on it, so I decided I would go down the stairs
   even though there were so many flights to go down.
   So I went out to the stairs and started going down,
   and almost before I knew it, I was on the ground. It
100 seemed like I had come down maybe ten flights, and I had
   found it hard to believe that I was on the ground level.
   I went out through some doors in the building. It
   was real new. There was a green one and some parking
   lots. And across the way a little bit another wing of
105 the building where the mechanics and people who worked
   in the building lived. It was strange that on this
   one side of the building it seemed so new because it
   seemed such an ancient building when I first went into
   it. . . . I went inside a big door like a truck entrance.
110 I found myself in this low, steamy tunnel that had pipes

on the ceiling. The floor was damp, and it was very
moist and steamy in there. . . . It gets a little confused
after this, but at some time or other I was back upstairs
again and going up on the eighty-fourth floor. Going down to the
115 ground floor again. And this time a lot of other people
were going down the stairs with me because I persuaded
them it was faster than the elevator. Everybody was
hurrying down just as fast as they could. . . .

Both Mr. and Mrs. A were impressed by the parallelism of a number of elements in their independently recorded dreams, particularly the bizarre elevator. Although they were both fairly sophisticated with respect to the psychology of dreaming and had often traced reasons for their dreams about particular subjects in the past, they had never previously found such striking parallelism, nor could they think of any common experiences in the recent past that could plausibly account for it. Table 6-1 presents a summary of this parallelism, the *A-A′ parallelism*, using line references to the two dream narratives.

Although the A-A′ parallelism is suggestive of psi, there are alternative explanations. For example, despite their inability to discover it, a common life experience may have triggered similar unconscious trains of association in Mr. and Mrs. A, resulting in the A-A′ parallelism. Furthermore, Mr. A has occasionally talked in his sleep, and if he had talked in his sleep about his dream or about the nondreaming sleep thoughts that led up to his dream, he might have strongly influenced the course of Mrs. A's subsequent dream. From a Freudian point of view, both dreams could also be regarded as containing some sexual symbolism, with Mr. A also showing sexual attraction toward his sister-in-law, but this hypothesis does not seem to shed much light on the close parallelism in the manifest (i.e., obvious) content. Another possibility is that Mrs. A unconsciously overheard part(s) of Mr. A's dictation and that this influenced her recollection of her dream. However, this seems rather unlikely, considering the clarity of the recalled dreams.

Mr. and Mrs. A thought of these explanations as they discussed the parallelism on the morning of the twenty-fifth, but they did not feel that they had adequately accounted for it.

Table 6-1

Parallel Dream Elements of A-A′ Parallelism

Element	*Lines in Mr. A's Dream*	*Lines in Mrs. A's Dream*
Action takes place in an office building	1–5	53–4
Mr. A's "8 and 4 stories down," and Mrs. A's "84th story. This was very important."	3–4	56–7
Reenter building by different entrance.	8–12 17–18	102 109
Different entrance is service entrance, has pipes overhead, is unpleasant (dirty and muddy in one case, moist and steamy in other).	17–18 46–52	109–12
Bizarre elevator: changes size and shape; difficult to control, to select level; dreamer gets on and off several times.	19–23[a]	57–64 69–74 81–91
Elevator travels unsatisfactorily, dreamer uses stairs.	24–8	95–8 115–17
Dreamer hurries on stairs in company of at least one other person.	24–33	115–18

Because Miss B played a major part in the second half of Mr. A's dream, he decided to ask her about her dreams and activities on the twenty-fourth as soon as he saw her that afternoon in Metropolis, before telling her anything about his or Mrs. A's dream.

Miss B's Activities

When Mr. A saw Miss B that afternoon, he immediately asked her what she had dreamed about on the previous night, telling her that it was important for her to recollect all that she could about her dreams. Miss B could only vaguely recall a dream that was about either "hanging someone or being hanged." She could recall no other details.

Mr. A then asked her to describe her ,activities on the previous evening. As Mr. A knew, Miss B and her parents had spent the previous evening in their vacation cabin, a place about 88 air miles distant from Metropolis and about 170 air miles distant from the home of Mr. and Mrs. A. Unknown to Mr. or Mrs. A, however, a friend of Miss B's, Miss C, was staying at the cabin with the Bs. Mr. A was not acquainted with Miss C. On the evening of June 24, Miss B had tried an "experiment" that Miss C had suggested to her. It had consisted of lying down and willing herself to die. Miss C had, by her report and by Miss B's, tried this experiment several days before the twenty-fourth. The result was that she had "blacked out" for a few moments, then had gotten bored with the whole thing, and so arose and went about her business. Miss B tried the experiment on the evening of the twenty-fourth, but nothing happened; after a few minutes, she also got bored and gave up.

Mr. A then told Miss B about his and Mrs. A's dreams and asked her to telephone Miss C and, without telling her anything about these events, ask her what she recalled dreaming about on the night of the twenty-fourth while she was staying with Miss B. Miss C could only vaguely recall dreaming about being in a building that was under construction. Although she was subsequently told about the dreams of Mr. A, Mrs. A, and Miss B, this did not stimulate her memory, and she could recall nothing else about her dream.

The similarities between Mr. A's dream and these other events, the A-B and A-C parallelisms, are summarized in Table 6-2; the line references are to Mr. A's dream.

The A-C parallelism is based on too few items to warrant further discussion. The A-B parallelism is a different matter. Miss B is inclined to be rather dramatic about the things she does, as is her friend Miss C. However, she could not be described as depressive or suicidally inclined, and her motivation for trying this unusual experiment seemed to be that it was novel and adventurous. Nevertheless, this particular experiment was quite an unusual thing for *anyone* to do, and the A-B parallelism cannot plausibly be attributed to coincidence.

An interesting feature of this case is that we do not have to

Table 6-2

Parallels Between Mr. A's Dream and Other Events

(A-B and A-C Parallelisms)

Elements in Mr. A's Dream	*Other Events*
Miss B hangs herself. (34–38)	Miss B recalls dreaming about hanging or being hanged.
Miss B hangs herself but does not die and suffers no ill effects. (34–43)	Miss B wills herself to die but does not die and finally stops trying. There are no subsequent ill effects. Dreaming about hanging does not, of course, harm her.
A girl friend of Miss B's appears in the dream quite unexpectedly. She seems about the same age as Miss B, but Mr. A does not know who she is or how she got there. (34–37)	Miss C, a stranger to Mr. A, unknown to Mr. A, was staying with Miss B that night. She is the same age as Miss B.
The girl friend also hangs herself, but like Miss B, she is revived with no ill effects. (34–43)	Miss C had, a few days earlier, tried willing herself to die and had "blacked out" for a few moments but suffered no ill effects. Miss C had suggested this bizarre experiment to Miss B.
The office building is under construction. (46–48)	Miss C dreamed of being in a building that was under construction.

depend exclusively on this commonsense assessment of the improbability of Mr. A's dreaming of Miss B's unusual actions and dream. Mr. and Mrs. A had kept a record of their dreams for some time before the twenty-fourth and continued to do so after that. They allowed me to go through their entire collection of dreams in order to count the frequency with which the various key elements of the June 24 dreams had appeared or recurred. In addition to the dreams described here, there were records of 95 dreams of Mr. A and 165 dreams of Mrs. A. Most of the key dream elements did not appear at all; some appeared in 1 to 2 percent of the other dreams. The probability of their joint occurrence by chance alone would be extremely low, and thus coincidence can almost certainly be rejected as accounting for either the A-A' or the A-B parallelism.

Alternative Explanations

Although some form of psi might be invoked to account for the A-A' parallelism, it need not be (although I suspect it was important). The alternative hypotheses that Mr. A had talked in his sleep and/or that common experiences and trains of association had led to the parallelism could be true.

There are also two alternative theories for explaining the A-B parallelism. One is that some form of psi was operative; the other is that Mr. A's impending visit to Metropolis triggered some intricate series of unconscious associations common to Mr. A and Miss B.

Is there any support for this second theory? In any allegedly parapsychological case, a theory that similar unconscious trains of association account for parallels could best be supported by means of intensive, depth psychological interviews of the participants, utilizing free association and similar techniques. Such a procedure was not feasible in the present case; indeed, it would not be in almost all cases occurring outside of an existing therapeutic setting, where most of the relevant data would already have been collected in the course of therapy. The theory must be judged solely on the basis of internal consistency and plausibility.

The theory of similar unconscious trains of association might suggest that Mr. A and Miss B had an unconscious sexual attraction toward each other and that this attraction was represented in disguised form (playing a game, running up stairs) in Mr. A's dream. This theory would account for Mr. A's dreaming about Miss B on the eve of seeing her. The attraction also produces feelings of guilt in both parties because our culture considers such an attraction illicit. Miss B's guilt feelings are expressed by her action (willing herself to die) and her dream (hanging or being hanged). Mr. A's guilt is transformed into aggression in his dream in which he tries to get rid of Miss B (and thus his attraction and consequent guilt) by having her hang herself.

The unconscious-associations theory makes it very difficult to account for one key fact, and it does not explain the correspondence in the *particular* form of the manifest dream content (hanging). Miss B's behavior was instigated by Miss C, and Miss B's dream also seems to be primarily a function of that behavior. It would indeed be farfetched to stretch the unconscious-association theory to include the possibility that Miss B subtly influenced Miss C to try to will herself to die several days earlier in such a way that Miss C thought it was her own idea and then further influenced Miss C to think she had inspired the idea in Miss B several days later. Furthermore, a young woman who might have been Miss C (Mr. A could not recall his dream imagery well enough to identify Miss C as the girl in the dream when he met her at a later date, although she resembled his imperfect memory image) appears suddenly in Mr. A's dream, much to his surprise (lines 34–37). If this was Miss C, her appearance cannot be explained by an unconscious-association theory.

If coincidence is thus ruled out, the major alternative to a theory involving psi would be that Mr. A and Miss B had similar trains of unconscious associations, probably based on unconscious sexual attraction and guilt, and that these associations were triggered by Mr. A's impending visit to Metropolis. However, such a theory does not explain the close parallelism between the manifest content of Mr. A's dream and Miss B's actions and dreams, which are the *observed* data; and the theory would have to be stretched ridiculously far to account for the fact that Miss C, a complete stranger to Mr. A, was the instigator of Miss B's actions. Thus, although the unconscious-associations theory cannot be absolutely ruled out, and although the history of psychical research is filled with examples of investigators pushing such normal explanations to extreme lengths rather than invoke psi, I feel that in this case some form of psi is a much simpler and more likely explanation.

I have spent considerable time discussing alternative theories in order to illustrate how important it is for the parapsychologist to be certain that he is indeed working with psi. Theories must not be based on data that might not be what they seem. This was a particularly crucial issue in the earlier days of psychical research, when investigators were trying to argue for the *existence* of psi on the basis of spontaneous cases. Now that we have overwhelming laboratory evidence that psi exists, we can be a little more relaxed about studying cases such as this one to see what they show about the mechanisms by which we know psi to work.

Psi Processes in the Dream

I believe that Mr. A's dream involved a genuine manifestation of psi. There are a number of interesting features in the case that aid in understanding psychic dreams in general.

There seems to have been no intentional sender in this case. Miss B might have thought that Mr. A would be interested in her experiment, but she reported that she made no conscious attempt to communicate this to him on the evening of the twenty-fourth. That Miss C was present was, of course, known to Miss B, so there is no need to suspect Miss C of being an active sender for her presence to be known. It also seems unlikely that Mrs. A acted as a sender. This leaves Mr. A, the percipient, as the person who would have used psi to gather information about Miss B's activities and dream.

Two facts support this theory. First, Mr. A was restless and preoccupied with thoughts of Metropolis and Miss B before he fell asleep. Second, Mr. A is interested in psychical phenomena (as many electrical engineers seem to be) and would have been pleased to experience a psychic dream. (He verified this when he became aware of the A-A′ and A-B parallelisms.)

The information that we are assuming was acquired by psi was not, for the most part, presented to Mr. A *directly* in his dream. It was modified and transformed in various ways and accompanied by a considerable amount of irrelevant, nonveridical information. For this reason, Mr. A experienced a reasonably coherent and continuous dream. This can be at least partially explained by what has been learned in recent experiments on dreaming.

What we ordinarily think of as dreaming appears to occur primarily during a particular kind of sleep, named stage 1-REM sleep because of the characteristic electroencephalographic (EEG) pattern that occurs in conjunction with rapid eye movements (REMs). Stage 1-REM dreaming is a d-ASC. It occurs in discrete periods throughout the night. Each period begins approximately ninety minutes after the preceding one, and each period is generally longer than the preceding period. For example, the first period may be about ten minutes long, and the last may be forty or fifty minutes long. The total amount of time spent in stage 1-REM dreaming by most adults (about 20 to 30 percent of total sleep time) is fairly stable from night to night, as is the sequential timing of these dream periods, regardless of normal variations in day-to-day activities. This sleep-dream cycle seems to be quite resistant to experimental modification [151, 160] unless such drastic techniques as sleep deprivation or drugs are used. That is, the control and timing of the physiological state underlying dreaming seems to be controlled primarily by relatively autonomous, internal brain mechanisms.

The effect of sensory stimuli that are not intense enough to wake the dreamer is of particular interest. In general, there seems to be an active inhibition of incoming sensory stimuli, and most such stimuli do not appear in recognizable form in the content of the reported stage 1-REM dreams. William Dement and Edward Wolpert [22] found that only about 25 percent of experimental stimuli were incorporated into stage 1-REM dreams. External stimuli were never the *cause* of dreaming. That is, a stimulus presented to a sleeper who was in EEG stage 2, 3, or 4 and therefore was not dreaming never resulted in the sleeper's beginning to dream.

When external stimuli do appear in a dream, they generally do not control the dream in the sense of strongly determining its content. Rather, they are woven into the fabric of the ongoing dream, they are literally incorporated into the dream action. For example, if a bell were sounded beside a dreamer and he was awakened for a dream report a minute later, the report would rarely be "I dreamed about a bell ringing" (although a report from a sleeper who was not dreaming in stage 1-REM might very well take this form). The dreamer would be more likely to report "I was driving my car down Main Street, talking to my friend John about politics. As we were talking I heard some bells ringing and then a siren, and a moment later, a fire engine raced past us. John and I watched it go around a corner and then continued talking about politics. . . ." The information conveyed by the stimulus is worked into the content of the dream, and this may involve various transformations or modifications (such as representation by a different sensory modality) or perhaps the various types of dream mechanisms postulated by Freud (such as symbolization or condensation). The degree of modification may be related to its degree of congruence or incongruence with the dream content at the time that it occurs.

In some psychic dreams, particularly those dealing with crises, the entire dream seems to be characterized by an exact or symbolic representation of the paranormal information, as if it is a response to whatever psychic stimulus suddenly sprang from a background of mental quiescence. Many of the examples presented in Louisa Rhine's [102] review are of this nature. Other psychic dreams, of which Mr. A's seems to be an excellent example, appear to be instances of psi-acquired information being incorporated into the content of an ongoing dream in very much the same manner that sensory stimuli are incorporated into stage 1-REM dreams. The fact that there seems to be some automatic transformation and modification of incoming stimuli to fit the ongoing dream content would account for some of the distortions and transformations that we find in psychic dreams.

For example, Mr. A's dream presumably combined Miss B's actions (willing herself to die, suffering no ill effects) and dream (hanging) into another form (hanging but recovering because she was cut down). However, the dream was set in Metropolis, not at the vacation cabin where Miss B actually was at the time. Mr. A's preoccupation with his impending trip to

Metropolis seems sufficient to account for his dreaming about Metropolis and the Bs. The information about Miss B's activities and dream acquired by psi was smoothly incorporated into this normal, ongoing dream in the same manner that an external sensory stimulus might have been accommodated.

In some cases, the incorporation of external stimuli into an ongoing dream is not smooth; it contrasts sharply with the ongoing content. In the present case, one item of information, the presence of another woman (possibly Miss C), was not smoothly incorporated. Mr. A seemed surprised at her appearance: "and I don't know how this other girl got into the dream . . ." (34–35). Information about Miss B could apparently be incorporated without much disturbance because Miss B was a highly probable person to appear in a dream about Mr. B and Metropolis, but Miss C, a stranger to Mr. A, was unexpected.

Models of Psychic Dreams

In the first possible model, the percipient is sleeping but not dreaming, a psi message is picked up by the Psi Receptor, a mental process is triggered that immediately creates a stage 1-REM dream (or some d-ASC like dreaming), and the percipient is presented with the content of the psi message expressed as a dream.

In a second model, the percipient is already dreaming when the psi message is received, but the message is so urgent that it is forced into awareness, completely displacing the content of the ongoing dream. This kind of psychic dream seems quite vivid to the dreamer and is totally concerned with the psi message. Rhine's [102] collection gives examples. Like the first model, this is also a variation of the ψ_1 information-flow route we discussed in Chapter 5, from Psi Receptor directly to awareness. Awareness is embedded in the structure of the dream d-ASC, rather than in waking consciousness or in dreamless sleep.

A third possible model is applicable to the present case and also starts with the dreaming percipient. The psi message is received by the Psi Receptor, passed on into parts of the Unconscious mind, and these parts of the Unconscious must then work with whatever other parts of the Unconscious are responsible for producing the dream to modify the dream content in a way that will get at least some of the psi message into the dreamer's awareness. It is what we called the ψ_4 route in Chapter 5. In this complex process, some of the psi information is incorporated, and some is not. Some of the incorporated information appears in the dream in an essentially unchanged form; some is transformed and modified to various degrees. The degree of modification is partly dependent on the nature of the dream content at the time. Some of the transformed information enters smoothly; some may enter in a forced fashion, resulting in a feeling of surprise. Some elements of this information may clash so intensely with the dream content that the dreamer awakens. Transformations also depend upon the personality dynamics of the individual dreamer over and above the general operations involved in incorporating information into ongoing dream content.

Another intriguing aspect of Mr. A's dream is that it seems to be divided into two fairly distinct portions.* In the first portion, the A-A' parallelism occurs; when Mr. A leaves the elevator, the A-B parallelism begins. Why did this shift occur? One possibility is that the events happened in the order presented in the dream. That is, Mr. A acquired information about Mrs. A's dream by psi and/or influenced her dream by talking in his sleep and/or arrived at a similar dream via parallel associative paths; he then acquired the information about Miss B's activities and dream by some form of psi. One could imagine Mr. A "warming up" his psi abilities on his wife and then reaching out all the way to Miss B.

An alternative possibility is that Mr. A acquired the information about Miss B's activities and dream by psi before the first part of his dream began. The A-A' parallelism was then brought about either by sleep talking or by psi, and the information about Miss B was incorporated into it. This possibility provides a function for the A-A' parallelism: calling attention

---

* Actually there are four portions, but the omitted beginning and end of the dream were not relevant to the question of parallelism.

to the part of the dream containing the A-B parallelism. Mr. A told me that he would never have thought to ask Miss B about her activities and dreams had he not been impressed by the A-A′ parallelism. If Mr. A's motivation was to please himself by having a psychic dream, the A-A′ parallelism thus functioned as a marker or attention-getting signal and capitalized on the fact that Mr. and Mrs. A would probably mention their dreams to each other during breakfast.

That possibility is strengthened by the fact that Mr. A had experienced an apparently psychic dream some six months prior to the present events. He had awakened from it with the feeling that there was *something* special about it (as seems to happen in many crisis cases), but he had finally given up trying to make sense out of it and only accidentally discovered later that day that the dream seemed to bear striking resemblances to the actions of friends of his. Thus, a feeling that a dream was special had failed once to alert Mr. A to the need to check the dream; perhaps in the present case, a marker was used as a stronger substitute for a feeling of specialness. A survey of the literature compiled on psychic dreams to determine what caused the dreamers to check their dreams against reality could prove valuable.

7·

Precognition Sneaks
into My Laboratory

✿✿✿

When I wrote the material in Chapters 2 and 3 describing the evidence for the existence of precognition and offering a rough model of how it takes place, I experienced no intellectual difficulties. I have been aware of the evidence for the existence of precognition for many years, and because it is of the highest quality, I had always accepted precognition as a real phenomenon, even though I had never been able to understand quite how it worked. Before I completed the writing of this book, however, some events occurred that made me realize that although I had always accepted precognition *intellectually,* at a deeper level of my being I did not believe in it at all. I was a staunch conservative when it came to time; I believed that the past was dead and gone, that the future did not yet exist, and that only the present was real. Certainly, a nonexistent future could have no influence on the present.

This deep resistance to the idea of precognition had calmly existed side by side with my intellectual acceptance of it, and I had unknowingly arranged my experimental work so that I would never have to deal with it. For example, I had never deliberately done an experiment on precognition, nor had I ever planned to do one. After the events described in this chapter had occurred, a friend whom I had talked to about my resistance to the idea of precognition remarked, "You'll understand it better after you have your first personal precognitive experience." I noticed a remarkable blankness in my mind: the idea that *I* might have a precognitive experience was so inconceivable that I did not even have to defend against it actively. But now, everything has changed.

The chain of events that started this revolution in my thinking began when a colleague at Davis, Dr. Lila Gatlin, of the Genetics Department, walked into my office in the fall of 1975. She is a specialist in information theory, and she had become interested in psi. She asked me for copies of any psi data that might lend itself to analysis through the use of information theory techniques. I had just completed the manuscript of my monograph *The Application of Learning Theory to ESP Performance* [174], so I gave her a deck of IBM cards containing all the target and response data from the first Training Study. I looked forward to a stimulating collaboration that might suggest some interesting new ways of analyzing my data, but I did not realize how stimulating it would be.

Dr. Gatlin showed me several interesting analyses she had made, but the one that has stimulated me the most to date was her finding that there appeared to be significant missing when responses were scored against the next (+1) target, which had not yet been generated, that is an effect I believed showed strong precognitive psi missing. This chapter describes my refinements of those analyses and the theory to which they have led me.

Training ESP Ability

I shall briefly describe the first Training Study in which these precognitive effects occurred. It was intended to test a theory I had put out in the 1960s [142] that said that the reason *declines* (less psi with repeated testing) were so prominent in parapsychological research was that percipients did not get any immediate feedback on the correctness or incorrectness of each of their calls at a target. I understand psi as deliberate "listening to a still, small voice within," trying to pick up an infrequent and subtle quality of your mental processes that conveys psi information. This difficult task must be done against the background of the incessant mental chatter of our ordinary state of consciousness. When you do not get any feedback until results are scored at the end of, say, twenty-five calls, you can't reliably recall whether a certain subtle feeling you had occurred on call eleven, which you *now* know was a hit, or on call twelve, which was a miss, etc. So you gradually get more and more confused, and end up losing your psi ability.

The first Training Study, which has been fully reported on in my *Learning to Use Extrasensory Perception* [178], as well as in the original monograph [174], resulted after putting hundreds of UC Davis college students through preliminary selection procedures to find some with good signs of psi ability. The selected percipients of interest to us in this chapter were ten in number, and they each carried out twenty runs of twenty-five calls each on a special training machine I designed called the Ten Choice Trainer (TCT). This consisted of a console containing ten unlit lamps, arranged on a fifteen-inch circle. When a Ready lamp in the center of the circle came on, this signaled the percipient that his experimenter had, in accordance with instructions from an electronic random number generator, selected one of the ten lamps as the target, and was trying to telepathically send the target identity to him. When the percipient finally decided on what he thought the target was, he would push a button beside that lamp. Immediately the correct target lamp would light up, giving him immediate feedback on whether he was right or wrong.

The experimenters also had a chance to learn to use their sending ability more effectively. A TV camera monitored the percipient's hand movements over the circle of target lamps, so an experimenter could send "hot" and "cold" type messages and visually see if they seemed to have any effect.

The overall psi results of the first Training Study were exceptionally successful. For the total 5,000 trials, we expect 500 hits by chance alone, but the percipients made 722 hits, a result with a probability of 2×10^{-25}, odds of 2 in ten million billion billion! The results were favorable to the learning hypothesis also: no one showed the common decline effect, several showed increases in psi within the runs, where problems of keeping track of internal processes would not be strong, and the degree of learning was proportional to the degree of psi talent each percipient brought to the Training Study.

Although these learning results are very important, space limitations keep me from describing them further here, but the interested reader can refer to [142, 174, 177, 182].

Three years later I, my associates, and students carried out a second Training Study with seven selected students. The results are being prepared for publication [190]. Overall experimental procedure was essentially the same as in the first Training Study.

Scoring Time-Displaced Hits

Figure 7-1 shows the basic procedure for scoring what we shall call *temporal displacements*. The upper third of the figure shows an actual run for the percipient identified as P-5. The twenty-five targets generated by the electronic random number generator are shown in the first row, and P-5's responses to each are shown in the second row. I have circled the hits. This was a highly significant run, with six correct identifications of the GESP stimulus. Six hits would occur by chance about 1 in 100 times.

The middle third of the figure shows the method for measuring the +1 temporal displacement. To do this, the response row is shifted one position to the right. The first response (which was a 4) is scored against the second target (which was a 7), and so on down the line. The twenty-fifth response has no target to be scored against, so one trial is lost to get a run of twenty-four trials. In this particular example, there were no hits on the target in the immediate future, although we would expect two or three (2.4, on the average, to be precise) by chance alone. Note that any significant number of hits here

E1S5, Run #3

Targets   3 7 5 2 7 9 6 0 7 8 3 7 4 8 5 1 4 9 0 7 9 4 3 8 5
Responses   4 8 5 2 4 9 7 5 1 7 2 8 3 9 5 7 4 5 6 7 2 5 0 6 4

REGISTER SHIFT FOR +1 TEMPORAL DISPLACEMENT   #TRIALS = 24

Targets   3 7 5 2 7 9 6 0 7 8 3 7 4 8 5 1 4 9 0 7 9 4 3 8 5
Responses   4 8 5 2 4 9 7 5 1 7 2 8 3 9 5 7 4 5 6 7 2 5 0 6 4

REGISTER SHIFT FOR −1 TEMPORAL DISPLACEMENT   #TRIALS = 24

Targets   3 7 5 2 7 9 6 0 7 8 3 7 4 8 5 1 4 9 0 7 9 4 3 8 5
Responses   4 8 5 2 4 9 7 5 1 7 2 8 3 9 5 7 4 5 6 7 2 5 0 6 4

Figure 7-1. Scoring temporal displacements.

would have to be the result of precognition. While a percipient
was trying to guess any particular target that the experimenter-
sender was trying to send, the next target did not yet exist. The
experimenter did not activate the random number generator
to generate the next target until the percipient had pushed a
button to make his response to the real-time target.

The bottom third of Figure 7-1 shows the method for counting a −1 temporal displacement, that is, scoring each present-
time response against the target of the previous trial. The first
response has no target to be scored against, so again we lose one
trial and end up with a run of twenty-four. One hit occurred in
this particular analysis.

There is an important difference here. Although the +1
future target did not exist at the time the percipient made his
call, the −1 target did exist, not only in the experimental record
but also in the percipient's mind. Because of the feedback, he
knew what the immediately preceding target had been, a point
to which we shall return in the section "Bad Guessing Habits."

Avoiding the Future and the Past

Following Dr. Gatlin's inspiration, I reanalyzed the data from our first Training Study in a way that was more appropriate than her original analysis. We automatically lose 200 of our 5,000 total trials by scoring for +1 hits, and another 10 were lost from experimenter oversight, giving us 4,790 trials where there could have been a +1 hit. But only 318 hits occurred, even though we would have expected 479 by chance. This incredibly significant result would occur by chance only about 8 in 10^{15} times; that is, the odds were over 100 million million to 1. When I later analyzed the results of the second training study, I found a lot of missing on the +1 future hits for some percipients, but it was balanced out by hitting on the +1 increased hits by some other percipients so that the overall group results were not significant.

In spite of great scientific prejudice to the contrary, group results can be only a very general guide to what is going on in reality. What do these findings mean in terms of individuals? Figure 7-2 shows the actual scoring pattern for one of the percipients (P-1) in the first Training Study. The vertical axis represents the Z score of the number of hits or misses, a standard measure of its probability. Z scores greater or less than ±2 are considered statistically significant, and significance rises very rapidly with increasing Z score. P-1's real-time hits were extremely significant; the probability of their occurring by chance was 2 in 100,000. His missing on the immediate future (the +1 time displacement) was also extremely unlikely by chance. With a probability of only 6 in 10,000; he made only twenty-five hits when he should have made about forty-eight. His avoidance of the immediate past (the −1 temporal displacement) was even greater; he made only thirteen hits instead of the forty-eight expected by chance, which has a probability of 1 in 10 million.

I have also shown the −2 and −3 temporal displacements for this percipient. He still significantly avoided the numbers with a −2 temporal displacement from the present-time target, although nowhere near the extent to which he avoided the −1 target; and by the −3 temporal displacement, he had pretty well

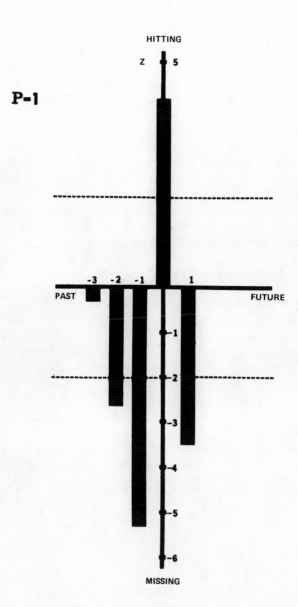

Figure 7-2. Scoring patterns for P-1's real-time and time-displaced hits in the first Training Study.

risen to a scoring level equal to that of chance. P-1's scoring pattern was typical of those of the percipients in both the first and the second Training Studies in terms of avoidance of the past. That pattern was extremely strong avoidance of the immediate (−1) past, fairly strong avoidance of the −2 past, and generally chance scores beginning with the −3 past.

The magnitude with which the percipients avoided the immediate (−1) past did not correlate significantly with the degree with which they hit on the real-time target or the degree with which they avoided the immediate (+1) future. Surprisingly, there was a very strong relationship between real-time hitting and avoidance of the immediate future for the percipients as a group. Figure 7-3 shows this relationship for the percipients in both studies. The solid black bars represent the magnitudes of their real-time hitting (in standard Z scores), and I deliberately lined these up from the most significant hitting at the left-hand side of the graph to zero hitting and on to psi-missing at the right-hand side. The heavy slanted bars represent scoring on the +1 target; most extend below the base line of chance expectation because they represent the magnitude of missing, rather than hitting. The broken lines are statistical regression lines that represent the overall trend of both the real-time hitting and the +1 missing measures. Clearly, the two are strongly related. The correlation coefficient is −0.85 ($P < 0.001$). The more a percipient uses real-time psi, the more he avoids the immediate future. Among those few percipients whose psi seems to have been malfunctioning (they were missing on the real-time psi target they were trying for), there seems to be a tendency for the malfunctioning psi to move over to hitting on the immediate-future target, a sort of poor focusing. (We shall consider the third measure plotted in the figure, strategy-boundness, in the section "Bad Guessing Habits.")

Although the results in Figure 7-3 are for the combined studies, I first found the relationship in the data of the first Training Study. The correlation between real-time hitting and +1 missing was −0.84, a highly significant correlation. When the results of the second Training Study came in, I looked for

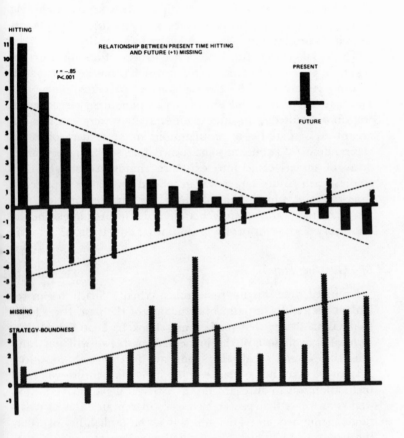

Figure 7-3. Relationship between present-time hitting and future (+1) missing.

the same effect, but I was not sure I would find it because the yield of psi in the second Training Study had been so much lower than in the first, since we started with less talented percipients. Nevertheless, it was there. The relationship between real-time hitting and +1 missing in the second study was strong enough to yield a correlation coefficient of −0.73, which would occur by chance less than 5 in 100 times. The independent occurrence of this relationship in two separate experiments, in spite of the difficulties that traditionally plague second studies, gives me great confidence in its reality.

To my knowledge, this kind of negative relationship between real-time psi and avoidance of the future has not been reported by other researchers. This can probably be accounted for by the fact that the present and future, on an *individual* target level, were not so discrete in other studies as they were in ours. In almost all past studies of precognition, an entire deck of cards was randomized at once at some future time, so that a very large array of targets came into existence simultaneously. In our studies, each future target was generated only after a present-time response, which then called for a future response on the next target and subsequent generation of a future target, and so on—a very discrete series of steps. But what does it mean?

Bad Guessing Habits

I puzzled over this for some time. When I finally began to look at the results in terms of avoidance of the past, I was able to devise a theory that made sense. Look back at Figure 7-2. Typically, avoidance of the immediate past (we will not consider the −2 and −3 displacements any further) was considerably larger than the avoidance of the immediate future. My first inclination was to disregard this as a trivial demonstration of a well-known fact that people have very inaccurate ideas of what random numbers are. They think that the probability of what is called an *XX doublet* (the same number repeating twice in a row) is so very low that they practically never call a target that has just occurred. For example, if the previous target had been a 5, most people would practically never guess a 5 for the next target because they believe that the probability of two 5s in a row is exceptionally low. But in fact, the possibility that a 5 will be immediately repeated is still one-tenth because all targets are generated independently of each other. For this reason, I at first assumed that the −1 avoidance was just a result of this common guessing habit.

Eventually, it occurred to me to try an approach that is not at all common in psychology but that works very well for physicists in their study of the universe. This approach assumes that one of the basic principles of the universe (discussed at more length in *States of Consciousness* [173] Chapter 18) is that all processes are *symmetrical*. For example, if an atomic process creates a positively charged particle, there is probably a negatively charged particle that is in all other respects exactly like it. If the process creates a particle that spins clockwise, physicists look for another particle that spins counterclockwise, and so on. Indeed, some equations in physics that deal with time yield two solutions, one in which time flows forward, in the conventional way, and another in which it flows backward. These backward solutions have been largely ignored because they seem inconceivable, but I suspect that Hal Puthoff and Russell Targ [92] are right in believing that these solutions are a key to some revolutionary advances in physics. At any rate, I decided to assume that if, for each percipient, there was an avoidance of the +1 future of such and such a magnitude because of *pre*cognition (psi operating on the future), then I would assume that the −1 score was made up not only of avoidance of the past target (because memory of it was coupled with maladaptive guessing habits) but also of a *post*cognitive avoidance, again a result of psi, that was equal in magnitude to that percipient's precognitive avoidance. Figure 7-4 illustrates this procedure. The heavy black portion of the −1 score bar has been deliberately drawn to equal the size of the +1 score bar; the remaining portion is assumed to be a result of maladaptive guessing habits based on underestimating the probability of XX doublets. I have called the portion that is left over *strategy-boundness* because it limits, or bounds, a percipient's ability to respond freely to the present situation. The results of making this division are quite profitable, as I shall explain in the section "Trans-temporal Inhibition."

Another Dimension of Time

The theory I have devised to deal with this precognitive avoidance of the future and to distinguish between postcogni-

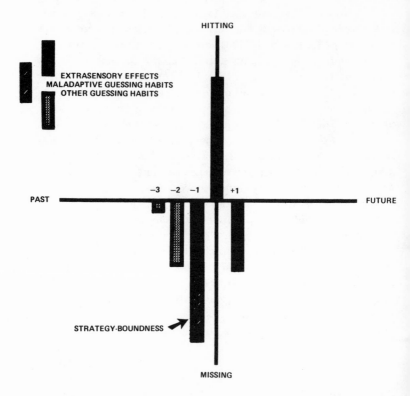

Figure 7-4. Distinguishing strategy-boundness within P-1's total avoidance of the −1 target.

tive avoidance and strategy-boundness is illustrated by the diagram in Figure 7-5. Consider what we call the *now*. Although mathematicians have developed abstractions about time that see the now as an infinitely tiny point of time having no duration at all in itself, a dimensionless point sandwiched between past and future, that particular abstraction does not correspond to my experience or other people's. Our now, my *experienced present,* has a certain duration to it (about several tenths of a second or so). Events in my experience that I call

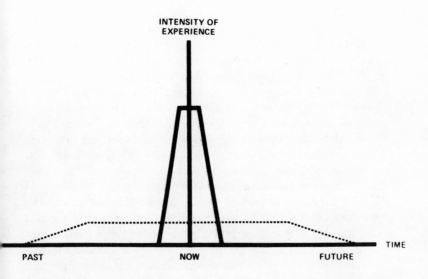

Figure 7-5. Width of the experienced present for ordinary brain and nervous system functioning and for awareness in the postulated second dimension of time.

present are experienced as intense. I have shown this as a tall, narrow band surrounding the present moment (the line at its center) ; this represents the intense experiences of the few tenths of a second duration of our experienced present. The sides of this band slope slightly to indicate that they are not absolutely fixed. That is, by deliberately directing your attention, you can to a small degree widen or narrow your experience of the present. I believe that the width of the experienced present is a function of the physical laws governing ordinary space and time, laws that underlie the operation of our brain structures.

However, my findings and parapsychological findings on precognition in general have forced me to theorize further that there is another dimension of time (and probably of space as well) that some aspect of our awareness can sometimes make contact with. This second dimension acts as the channel for psi information. I theorize that one property of this second dimension of time is that the experienced present of awareness is wider than the experienced present of ordinary consciousness. In my theory of states of consciousness [173], ordinary consciousness is seen as basic awareness modulated by brain mechanisms and thus tied to ordinary time.

The experienced present of the second dimension includes portions of time that from our ordinary point of view are past and future.* I have shown the boundaries of this second experienced present (the dotted line) tapering off toward the past and the future in an indefinite way. I suspect that they can also be moved according to how attention is focused. The overall height of this dimension is shown as quite low to represent the fact that the portions of awareness that are involved in psi phenomena are ordinarily very weak compared with ongoing brain experience in ordinary time. The still, small voice of psi is so quiet that it is generally inaudible; and even when it speaks, we have to listen very carefully.

In electrical engineering terms, we can say that the operation of the brain and nervous system and the ordinary consciousness that results constitutes a high-gain, narrow-band filter dealing with the immediate physical present. This is obviously of high biological significance for our survival. The second dimension of time, which awareness can sometimes work with, is a filter with a much wider band, but its output is ordinarily quite low.

Thus, if a percipient wants to use psi, he must tap into the portion of his awareness that deals with this other dimension of

---

* In response to a preliminary communication about my findings, J. Gaither Pratt wrote that H. F. Saltmarsh had proposed a similar idea of an extended present to account for precognition back in 1934 [110].

time. But there is a problem. If your goal is to achieve information about the *present* via psi, tapping into that other dimension per se is liable to bring you equally strong information
about the immediate past and the immediate future, and that
information is noise. It is not what you want, and its appearance in consciousness is just going to confuse you. It is not
enough, then, just to tap into the other dimension of awareness;
the awareness must also be actively processed to extract the
desired psi information about present-time events and inhibit
the psi information about the immediate past and immediate
future.

Trans-temporal Inhibition

In order to sharpen psi-gathered information about the real-
time target, then, on occasion some form of psi-specific information-processing subsystem had to separate the psi information
into immediate past, present, and immediate future and then in-
troduce a bias into the precipient's mind *against* guessing either
the immediate-past target and/or the immediate-future target, in
addition to producing some information about the present-time
target. Parts of this process might work independently; so on a
given trial, for example, a bias against calling the immediately
forthcoming target might prevail but the information about the
present target might not get through. Ideally the percipient got
information that not only made it much more likely that he
would call the present-time target but also made it unlikely
that he would guess the immediate-past or the immediate-future
target. I have named this process *trans-temporal inhibition*.

Now, consider the process of taking the score for the -1
temporal displacement and dividing it into a portion that I
assume is the result of postcognitive inhibition of the immediate past and a portion that is the result of strategy-boundness.
In the terms of my two experiments, there is no way of proving
that postcognitive inhibition was indeed manifesting (although
that can certainly be done in future experiments that do not
involve immediate feedback about the past target). Nevertheless,
making this assumption leads to very profitable results. I men-

tioned earlier that the magnitude of the −1 avoidance score did not significantly correlate with any other measure. However, the magnitude of the strategy-boundness for each percipient is a very meaningful measure.*

The lower third of Figure 7-3 shows the size of the strategy-boundness factor for each individual percipient, as well as each percipient's real-time hitting and immediate-future missing. The farther the bar representing strategy-boundness extends above the base line, the more the percipient was engaged in a maladaptive strategy (mechanically avoiding repeating whatever the last target had been). For the combined studies, strategy-boundness correlates −0.64 ($P < 0.01$) with real-time hitting and −0.83 ($P < 0.001$) with avoidance of the future. These correlations make perfect sense. The percipient's task on each trial is to be sensitive to whatever is happening in his experiential field *now* that might give him information about the real-time target. Because the electronic random number generator generates each target completely independently of the previous one, any strategy for coming up with a response that is based on remembering what the previous target was is a waste of time. In fact, it is positively detrimental. We have only so much awareness available, and if some of it is bound up in the past, trying to outguess the random number generator, then less awareness is left for paying attention to the current experiential field. The highest-scoring percipients had very little strategy-boundness. For percipients who had few real-time hits or who tended toward psi-missing, strategy-boundness generally went up. Of course, the relationship is not perfect; the measures have a certain amount of chance variability superimposed on them. Furthermore, according to the theory of trans-temporal inhibition, successful psi discrimination of the real-time targets involves the inhibition of the immediate past and the immediate

---

* There are a lot of positive and negative scores here, representing hitting and missing. Measured in this way, strategy-boundness is greater as it goes more negative because we are dealing with a negative deviation in the first place. However, I find that this gets confusing, so in the text, I will speak of strategy-boundness in a positive way; that is, the bigger it gets, the more a percipient is bound in his strategy by mechanical avoidance of the target he knows was immediately past.

future. Therefore, low levels of strategy-boundness (more now-ness, more focus on the psi task) were associated with strong inhibition of the immediate future (and, by assumption, of the immediate past), and high levels of strategy-boundness were associated with less inhibition of the immediate future and, in some cases, a tendency to call the immediate-future target correctly.

A Universal Information-Sharpening Technique

A conversation about these data with Enoch Callaway of the Langley-Porter Neuropsychiatric Institute, provided me with the final link in understanding the significance of this avoidance of the immediate past and the immediate future. Callaway suggested that the effect was analogous to *lateral inhibition,* an information-processing strategy used in all ordinary sensory systems [198]. This can be illustrated by an example of the sense of touch. Figure 7-6 is a schematic representation of the pressure receptors in the skin. These receptors are arranged in a lateral network; that is, they run side by side all through the skin. If you press down on the skin with a pointed object, such as a pencil point, you obviously stimulate the receptors immediately below the point, but because the skin surrounding the point of pressure is being stretched, touch receptors immediately lateral to the stimulated point are also stimulated. It's as if you were being touched by a wider, blunted object. The little spike trains, shown just above the receptor ends in the skin, represent what happens neurophysiologically. The receptors that are most distant from the point of stimulation occasionally fire spontaneously at fairly long intervals; the closer the receptors are to the stimulation point, the more rapidly they fire. Thus, at this first stage, the output signals from the touch receptors are going to give you a pattern of a wide, blunt stimulating object.

However, because of lateral inhibition, you will recover the sensation of being stimulated by a sharp point. The various levels in Figure 7-6 show lateral connections between the neurons from the touch receptors. These connections have the property of inhibiting one another's activities. The firing of the

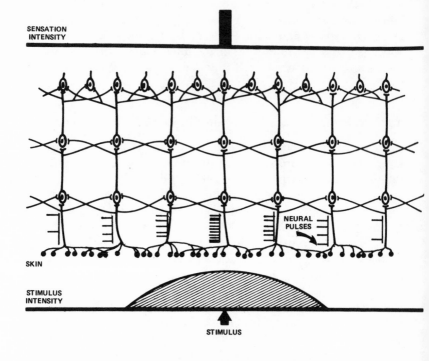

Figure 7-6. Lateral inhibition in touch receptors.

receptor that receives the most stimulation produces the most
active inhibition signals, so it tends to inhibit the firing of the
lateral receptors. This occurs in several stages, until, by the
highest level, there is strong firing only from the directly stimulated neuron, and the perceived sensation is of a sharp point,
rather than of a wide, blunt object.

Lateral inhibition, then, is a sharpening, or contrast-en-
hancement process that makes the relevant stimulus much
sharper by suppressing activity in adjacent neurons. This kind
of lateral inhibition is an example of a universally useful information-processing mechanism. Under another name, *edge de-
tection,* it is used in computer processing of pictures such as

those sent back by the Viking Mars probe, producing an incredibly detailed picture from a noisy, blurry signal.

I believe that I have discovered a temporal analogue of lateral inhibition. Because psi involves using a dimension of the mind that extends over a much wider segment of time than our ordinary consciousness, some part of the mind must identify and actively inhibit the immediate past and the immediate future in order to increase the detectability of a particular segment of that extended present (in the case of our two Training Studies, the real-time target) by sharpening its contrast. It is very exciting to discover that a universally useful information-processing technique, which I call trans-temporal inhibition because it extends across ordinary time (rather than across ordinary space), should appear to function for psi.

Broadening the Focus

There are many implications of this new theory to be worked out yet, and I shall discuss only one of them here. The psychological situation in both Training Studies, required that the percipients focus directly on the immediate present. That situation implicitly defined the boundaries of the present as the immediate-past (-1) target and the immediate-future $(+1)$ target. As I noted in the preceding section, the width of the ordinary experienced present can be varied somewhat simply by changing the focus of attention, and this is probably true for the experienced present of the second dimension of time. What would happen if we changed the psychological definition of the desired present target and its boundaries? In the analogous terms of electrical engineering, I would expect that we could deliberately shift the center frequency of the filter and/or shift its bandwidth by controlling attention. That is, we could shift what target(s) a percipient was trying to get; this should shift the place where the inhibition occurs.

A first confirmation of this has occurred recently. Ingo Swann had heard me talk about the phenomenon of trans-temporal inhibition at a meeting of parapsychological researchers, and he became intensely interested in both that and the learning possibilities on ADEPT (Advanced Design Extrasensory Perception Trainer, an improved version of the ten-choice feedback trainer). A few days later, he briefly visited my laboratory and had time to do five runs. Because he had heard me talk about the effects that occurred on the +1 target, and because of his own interest in precognition, I suspected that the present to which his interest extended clearly included the +1 target as well as the real-time target. Although I did not say anything to him, I predicted that this would shift the inhibitory points in his scoring. It did.

Figure 7-7 shows Swann's scoring pattern. He gave a very impressive performance, coming into a new working situation and, in only five runs,* significantly demonstrating psi. He made 21 real-time hits in his five runs, when only 12.9 would have been expected by chance; this has a probability of 9 in 1,000. However, he did almost as well on the +1 scoring. Rather than avoiding the +1 target, he made 19 hits, when only 12.4 would have been expected by chance; this has a probability of only 3 in 100. Indeed, his precognition score was even more significant than that because he tended to have bursts of hitting twice in a row; the probability of such results occurring by chance alone are 1 in 1 million.

His score on avoidance of the immediate past (the −1 hits) was only 7 hits, when 12.4 were expected; this would occur 5 in 100 times by chance. On the +2 targets, he only scored 7 hits, when 11.9 would have been expected by chance; and although this does not reach the usual level $(P \leq 0.05)$ for statistical significance, it is quite low $(P = 0.07)$. It is significantly less than the +1 scoring. Indeed, 4 of these hits occurred because of a rather unusual conjunction of target repeats; thus, these particular hits may have resulted artificially from using psi successfully to identify real-time and +1 targets. Consequently, I suspect that his +2 score should be much lower. We can see a widening of the bandwidth of his transtemporal inhibition filter to include both the +1 future and the real time with an inhibition surrounding this.

---

* In one run, he did 29 trials, instead of the usual 25, because of experimenter oversight. Thus, his five runs contained a total of 129 trials.

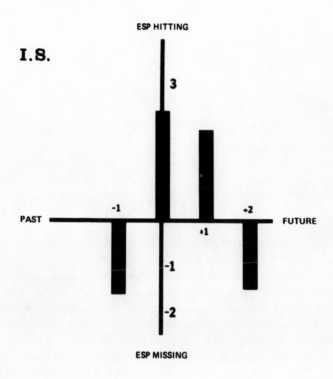

Figure 7-7. Ingo Swann's scoring pattern.

It is also noteworthy that Swann's avoidance of the −1 past is only slightly greater than his avoidance of the +2 future, which gives an extremely low strategy-boundness score, indicating that he was not restricted by maladaptive guessing habits.

Other experiments suggest themselves. For example, if we could get a talented percipient to focus on trying to guess the +5 target, would we see missing on the +4 and +6 targets? This is the kind of result that would further support the concept of trans-temporal inhibition. I shall touch upon some of the other implications of trans-temporal inhibition in Chapter 10. Further technical details of this study can be found in [189].

8.

Remote Viewing

❍❍

In 1964 and 1965, I had many stimulating conversations with Russell Targ about parapsychology, particularly about two of our most prominent mutual interests: teaching people more reliable psi ability and out-of-the-body experiences (OOBEs). My primary interest was in the dramatic kind of OOBEs that seemed to imply a drastic dissociation of consciousness and bodily functioning (the subject of Chapter 9), whereas Targ was interested in a wider view. He and his Stanford Research Institúte colleague Harold Puthoff went on to develop an extremely successful technique for eliciting psi that they termed *remote viewing*. Their studies of remote viewing are described in their recent book *Mind-Reach* [136] and in technical publications [92, 135].

The term *remote viewing* was deliberately chosen because it is a naturalistic description of what percipients are asked to do: namely, view something that is at a location remote to them. It is usually a GESP procedure, in which a percipient tries to describe a remote location that is being viewed by an agent, or *traveler,* at the remote site. Targ and Puthoff have been extremely successful with this technique in work with individual percipients, and it is one of the most exciting developments in parapsychology today. I shall briefly describe two illustrative remote-viewing studies carried out at the University of California (Davis) by my colleague John Palmer, my students Thomas Whitson and David Bogart, and myself and one carried out by Arthur Hastings and myself. The technical report on the first study has appeared in the *Proceedings of the Institute of Electrical and Electronic Engineers* [205].

The First Davis Study

We had been excited by Puthoff and Targ's highly successful remote-viewing studies, especially by their claim that they had found at least some remote-viewing ability in almost every percipient they had worked with. If the ability was indeed so widely distributed, their technique ought to be successful when used by other researchers. Our percipients were students in a Davis art class. They were selected, not because they had any reputed psi abilities, but because they were quite good at drawing and describing their visual images. Unlike the Puthoff and Targ experiments, this was a group experiment, with all percipients working simultaneously, although they made their drawings and written descriptions individually, without discussing them with one another.

Whitson and Bogart made color slides of some thirty sites that were within ten minutes' driving time from the campus and then narrowed these down to a target pool of ten slides of sites that visually were clearly distinct from each other. The target pool included such things as a palm tree, a Hammond organ, a bike tunnel in an underpass, and a gravestone statue of an angel. Each slide was sealed in an envelope, along with travel instructions. Before meeting with the class, Whitson thoroughly randomized the envelopes while Bogart, who was to be the agent and traveler to the remote site, was absent.

Whitson and Bogart first went to the class together, introduced themselves, and described the successful remote-viewing experiments at Stanford Research Institute, emphasizing the fact that remote viewing might be a widely distributed ability. They described the procedure that would be followed and then left and allowed the class to go on as usual. Thus, the percipients were left to draw for a couple of hours, warming up, as it were, before actually attempting the remote-viewing task.

Bogart randomly selected one of the envelopes from the target pool without Whitson (who was to remain with the percipients during the experiment) knowing what the choice was. He traveled to the target site and arrived there at the designated time of the experiment. He remained there for fifteen minutes, looking at the prominent features of the target site.

Meanwhile, Whitson had returned to the art class at the designated time. He asked the percipients to try to visualize the remote location that Bogart was viewing. After the percipients had attempted remote viewing for fifteen minutes, Whitson asked them to try to produce a drawing of their images of the remote site. He then collected the drawings and promised the percipients feedback on their work at the next class meeting.

After he had viewed the remote site for fifteen minutes, Bogart returned to a designated room, removed the slides from their envelopes, added the slide of the correct target site to them, and randomized them a second time. Whitson, who had no idea what the correct site had been, then returned to the room to get the stack of randomized slides and took them to an outside judge, an employee of the UC Davis art department. This judge, who was not informed that this was a psi experiment, was asked to examine each drawing and then to pick the slides that were the closest and second-closest matches. Table 8-1 gives the results of the judging.

As the table indicates, the correct target site, the bike tunnel, received eleven of the judge's first and second choices, which was not only the highest number of first and second choices but also far ahead of the next highest, which received only six choices. That seems quite significant statistically. I say "seems" because there are some technical problems involved in exactly what assumptions are valid for making a statistical test; for that reason, we did not make a formal evaluation, although it would have been extremely significant. The main problem is: what if tunnellike images corresponding to the bike tunnel site hap-

Table 8-1
Judging Results of the First
Davis Remote-Viewing Study

Target Site	First Choice	Second Choice	Combined First and Second Choices
Angel	1	3	4
Banjo	1	4	5
Bean pole	3	2	5
Bikes	3	3	6
Bike tunnel[a]	**5**	**6**	**11**
Dirt mounds	3	2	5
Logs	4	0	4
Organ	3	2	5
Palm tree	1	3	4
Tractor	3	1	4

[a] Actual target site.
[b] The judge gave no one second choice for logs.

pened, by coincidence, to be something that Davis art students drew frequently? We would need some way to assess this factor before we concluded that we had indeed demonstrated remote viewing.

The Second Davis Study: A Mixed-Motivation Experiment

Our second experiment was done with mixed motivation, and in retrospect, I do not recommend the procedure. We wanted to do a second group remote-viewing study in which the bike tunnel was again a *possible* target, although it would not actually be chosen, in order to get a control check on how often tunnellike images appeared. We also wanted to get successful remote-viewing results again. We did not clearly realize this at the time of the experiment, but it was a mixed set of motives to want simultaneously to fail and to succeed.

The second experiment followed essentially the same procedures as the first, except that we used a new group of art students and a new judge, a graduate student in the art department. Whitson again conducted the procedure in the class, and Bogart again acted as the traveler. Whitson noted (before the results were in) that this class seemed less interested and involved in the experiment than the first class had been.

The results of this experiment are presented in Table 8-2. Tunnellike images that were matched with the slide of the bike tunnel were quite rare, so we had our control to demonstrate that the possibility of an artificial inflation of the significance of the first experiment was very unlikely. The target this time was some bicycles in a bicycle rack. Although the target slide received the third-highest number of matches, that is not an impressive result, and we concluded that we did not have remote viewing operating in the experiment.

It is statistically legitimate to combine the results of the two experiments for an overall evaluation, and we did so. Of the ninety possible pairs, the actual target pairs received the third-highest possible number of matches. Because this result is associated with a probability of 3 in 100, our results support Puthoff and Targ's work.

Table 8-2
Judging Results of the Second
Davis Remote-Viewing Study

Target Site	First Choice	Second Choice	Combined First and Second Choices
Angel	0	0	0
Banjo	3	3	6
Bean pole	1	2	3
Bikes[a]	**3**	1	4
Bike tunnel	1	0	1
Dirt mounds	0	2	2
Logs	2	1	3
Organ	4	4	8
Palm tree	0	0	0
Tractor	0	1	1

[a] Actual target site.

Why were our results less successful than the striking results Puthoff and Targ routinely got? One reason may be that we used a group procedure and thus did not give a lot of attention to individual percipients, which we suspect is an important factor in Puthoff and Targ's research. Another reason may be the fact that we used university art students, whereas Puthoff and Targ regularly used visitors to their laboratory who are usually scientists, managers, contract monitors, and other highly successful, educated, middle-class people who have been more selectively screened for accomplishment than have college students. We suspect that the use of this kind of percipient holds great promise for psi research.

The Nebraska Experiment

In May 1976, I was asked to teach a two-day workshop on consciousness and extrasensory perception for the professional staff of the Nebraska Psychiatric Institute. By that time, I was quite excited about the possibilities of adapting the remote-viewing paradigm to group settings, both because of our own initial results and because of a study that Arthur Hastings and David Hurt [33] had done.

During a meeting of the Parapsychology Research Group in Palo Alto, Hastings went through a sophisticated psychological procedure (to be described at length in a future publication) to get the percipients to allow themselves to use psi. David Hurt and a companion then randomly selected a sealed envelope, and after opening the envelope in their car, drove to the selected target site (which was one of six possible targets). They observed and interacted with the remote site for ten minutes and, after a planned delay, returned to the meeting place.

While the agent team was gone, the percipients worked and sketched their impressions of the site. Then, before the agents returned, Hastings named and briefly described the six locations in the target pool. He was, of course, ignorant of which one had actually been chosen. The percipients voted on which possible site their individual impressions most closely matched.

Amazingly, twenty of the thirty-six participants voted for the correct site, a playground area with a log structure in a nearby park. Hastings and Hurt report that obtaining such a result by chance alone would happen less than 1 in 1 million times.

The playground had a circular play area full of sand. There was a log-platform structure, with chains hanging from it, in the circular area and a slide on one side. The agent team climbed on the structure, stood on the platform, slid down the slide, and took off their shoes in the sand. There were also swings next to the play area and a jungle gym next to the sidewalk.

The percipients' perceptions included mental pictures of swings, trees, sand, and things that could be interpreted as a log structure. Two percipients reported images of the agent team taking off their shoes, and one drew a circle and wrote *playground* in it. One of the remote agents later reported that he had indeed drawn a circle in the sand and written *playground* in it.

I was particularly impressed by the sophisticated psychological procedures that Hastings had used to put percipients in a group at ease and bring out their psi abilities, so he and I discussed them at length, and I worked out a protocol for incorporating them into my workshop. I wrote ahead to the workshop organizer, Dr. Marjorie Hook-Gegoud, indicating that I was going to conduct a remote-viewing experiment and asking her to get me large numbers of slides of relatively distinct locations that were within a twenty-minute drive of the Nebraska Psychiatric Institute.

By the time I arrived in Omaha, she had collected about sixty slides of possible target sites. When I was alone in my room that night, I went through them and chose six slides that I felt were visually quite distinct. I then sealed each slide, along with a set of instructions that I made up then and there on appropriate things that could be done to interact with the site, in an opaque envelope.

I spent the first morning of the workshop on a general discussion of psi phenomena. This gave us all a chance to get to know each other. The remote-viewing experiment began in the afternoon. I began with a lecture on some of the results of the Stanford Research Institute remote-viewing studies, stressing how widespread success had been. Then I gave instructions on psychological procedures for eliciting psi for remote viewing. These procedures included dividing the participants into teams of two people each. One member of the team would be the viewer; the other would be the coach. The coach's main functions were to take notes of the viewer's imagery, ask questions to help elaborate imagery, and so on.

A Successful GESP Test

To give the teams a chance to practice relaxing, visualizing, and trying to get their psi talents to operate, I then conducted a GESP test in which the task was to try to get impressions of a color slide that was sealed in a double, opaque envelope in my pocket. I had picked this slide from a set of four slides of artworks (Chagall's *The Yellow Rabbi,* Dali's *The Sacrament of the Last Supper,* Tamayo's *Animals,* and Dali's *Persistence of Memory*) before leaving for Nebraska. These works had all been used as successful targets in the Maimonides studies of dream telepathy [193, 194, 195]. The particular slide that I had selected was Dali's *The Sacrament of the Last Supper,* a beautiful and unearthly painting showing Christ and his twelve disciples seated at a long, low table, celebrating the Last Supper. (The painting and responses from the Maimonides study are described in Chapter 3.)

Because I knew what the slide in the envelope was, even though I did not open it during the test procedure, this was a GESP test. That is, the percipients could get information about it directly by telepathy or by clairvoyance. In order to avoid saying anything that could give cues to the slide content, I stuck to a detailed, formal protocol about what I was to say and do during the test.

One reason for presenting this part of the experiment here is concretely to illustrate the human dimension in science. The fact that I knew what the target slide was, and that I was in the physical presence of the percipients, allows any results obtained to be interpreted by an alternative theory of some sort of un-conscious, sensory cueing from me to the percipients, even though I stuck to a protocol that apparently allowed no possibility of this. By contemporary parapsychological standards, this part of the experiment cannot conclusively demonstrate psi. That's the logic, but I was there, and I am personally convinced that I did not give any cues about the target slide, so I present this part of the experiment here, both for its inherent interest and to demonstrate some of the humanness that goes into science.

Immediately after the percipients had turned in their response sheets, I unsealed the envelope and projected the target slide. Many percipients commented that they believed their imagery had corresponded quite well to various aspects of the painting. After I returned to California, I tested this objectively by giving the set of four slides to Arthur Hastings, who had no idea what the correct target was, and asking him to match each team's responses (both written notes on mental impressions and drawings) to the slide it most closely resembled.

I had responses from twenty-eight teams. Hastings correctly matched *The Sacrament of the Last Supper* to twenty-four of these, an event that would happen by chance less than 1 in 10 million million times. On the whole, then, the workshop participants had shown an extremely high level of psi.

Hastings was familiar with the Maimonides dream telepathy work, and he thought the kinds of responses to *The Sacrament of the Last Supper* in this remote-viewing study were quite different from those obtained at Maimonides. There, the percipients frequently had *associations* to the target (such as dreaming about a Christmas catalog rather than perceiving Christ directly in the painting). However, with the Nebraska group, which was working in a psychological atmosphere that encouraged remote viewing, the indicators that went into successful judging dealt primarily with the *form* of the target (such as the geometric structure surrounding the painting, its windowlike quality, and the ocean and mountains in the background).

Trying for the Remote Site

After a brief break, we began the actual remote-viewing experiment. Marjorie Hook-Gegoud and her husband had agreed to be the agents who would travel to the remote site, and they were introduced to the workshop participants. Most of them already knew Dr. Hook-Gegoud. I had brought along my HP-25 scientific calculator with a random number–generating program in it, and I instructed our travelers to push the Generate button until the last digit of the random number generated contained a number between 1 and 6. That number instructed them how far down in the stack of shuffled envelopes to go to pick the target. Strangely, they had to push the button many times before they got a number between 1 and 6. At the time, I thought it was just coincidence, but in retrospect, they found it meaningful.

They got a number, which they did not reveal to us, took the stack of six envelopes, and left. They got into their car and started to drive away. At that point, they were to open the target envelope, drive to the target site, timing their driving (by circling the area if necessary) to arrive there in twenty minutes, at which time the workshop participants would try to remote view.

We went through our remote-viewing procedure, and I collected all the notes and drawings that the teams had made of their impressions. Once all the drawings were collected, I unsealed an envelope containing slides of the six possible target sites and copies of the instructions to the agents on what to do there. These were projected so that everyone could see them clearly. Each team then ranked how strongly their impressions matched each of the six possible sites. There was a team vote for each team and separate votes for the viewer and the coach. This was to allow for the fact that the coach might either have had psi impressions himself or have come to a different conclusion about the viewer's comments than the viewer himself had come to. The results of these ratings for the combined first and second choice responses for each site are shown in table 8-3.

The six sites were a mortuary, a room with a fountain in an art museum, a church with rather striking architecture, a Wool-

Table 8-3

Judging Results for the Nebraska
Remote-Viewing Study

| Target Site | *First and Second Choices* | | |
	Viewers	Coaches	Teams
Mortuary	17	12	13
Museum	11	11	9
Church[a]	**10**	7	**7**
Woolworth's	8	9	10
Bookstore	4	2	1
Printshop	0	1	0

Note: Because some participants had to leave early, results are for 25 viewers, 21 coaches, and 20 teams.

[a] Actual target site.

worth's store at a shopping center, a bookstore, and a printshop. We did a quick blackboard tally of these results immediately after I collected all the rating sheets, and there was a clear preponderance of first and second choices for the mortuary as the target site; the second-place vote went to the room in the art museum; the third choice was for the church. By that time, I knew the traveling agents should have returned to another office at the institute, so we turned the blackboard over to hide our votes and sent a messenger to invite the agents to return and tell us about where they had gone.

Dr. Hook-Gegoud, whom I had regarded as the principal agent because she was known to the percipients, immediately apologized for "messing up the experiment." She explained that as they were driving away, they had picked the fifth envelope (chosen by the calculator) in the stack and found that the designated target site was the room in the art museum. Her husband immediately commented that the museum was closed on Mondays and so they could not go to the target. A quick check of the telephone book they happened to have in the car revealed that the museum was indeed closed on Mondays. Dr. Hook-Gegoud was very upset by this, but her husband suggested that if the fifth target envelope was impossible, then it did not count and that counting down five envelopes from the top meant that they would have to open the next envelope down. They opened it and found that the target site was the church, which they got to on time.

The principal agent also told us that throughout the experiment, she had been hoping that the mortuary would be picked as the target site. (Remember that the agents did know that the mortuary was one of the sixty possible target sites, although they did not know that it was one of the six I had chosen.) She had wanted to go to the mortuary for two reasons. First, an old friend of hers had died a few days before, and his funeral had taken place (at a different mortuary) earlier that afternoon. She had wanted to attend the funeral but felt that she could not because of her obligation to act as the agent for the experiment. Second, the agents did not start out until late in the afternoon, and Dr. Hook-Gegoud was worried that they might not be able to get a parking place at many of the possible target sites; she was sure, though, that they would be able to get a parking place at the mortuary.

In terms of the percipients' votes for the target actually traveled to, the experiment was a failure. Yet, the viewers' choices showed a clear preponderance of first and second choices for the mortuary (the target site that the principal agent had strongly *wanted* to go to), a second-place vote for the room in the art museum (where the agents had been *supposed* to go), and a third-place vote for the church (the site they had *actually* visited). The coaches' separate votes and the team votes also showed a preference for the mortuary, with the room in the art museum and the church also getting a very high number of votes.

Because the slide-viewing experiment had shown that this group had a high level of psi, I am strongly tempted to interpret these results retrospectively, not as a failure of psi to manifest at all, but as a displacement of psi from the target site per se to the psychological processes of the principal agent. Indeed, one percipient insisted (before we knew the results) that the agents had not been able to get to the target site they were supposed to go to. Russell Targ has told me that they have often seen displacement to the agent's psychological processes in the Stanford Research Institute experiments, although their percipients still generally identify the target sites correctly.

I believe that the Nebraska experiment is an excellent illustration of one of the main problems in doing psi experiments. We can instruct the percipients to try to use their psi to focus on designated targets, and although I think such instructions are fairly effective, they are not totally so. But because we do not know what the *limits* of psi are, we cannot assume that the experimenter is independent of the experiment.

9.

Out-of-the-Body Experiences

✿✿✿

One of the central claims of practically all religions is that we each have some kind of soul, a nonphysical center of being and consciousness that may or does survive physical death. Although the majority of people in America and in the world today believe they have a soul, the idea has been totally dismissed by science as something certainly not fit for scientific inquiry.

As soon as I became interested in parapsychology, I started coming across accounts of *out-of-the-body experiences (OOBEs)*. The people who have had OOBEs describe them as a feeling that their consciousness has temporarily left the physical body and has journeyed to some other location. They also report their firm conviction that this was *not* some kind of dream or hallucination, that it was *real,* as real as ordinary experience. They generally felt their state of consciousness during the OOBE was basically their ordinary state and therefore rational. Furthermore, the usual result of having an OOBE is to convince the experiencer that he does indeed have some kind of soul or nonphysical self that will survive death. This reaction is sometimes summed up in a statement such as this: "I no longer *believe* I have a soul that will survive death. I *know* I do because I have experienced being conscious without my physical body."

It struck me that the OOBE was obviously the basis for the religious idea of a soul. Throughout history, people have had OOBEs and have communicated to others their experiences and the conviction that they have souls. This experiential, psychological basis for the soul idea deserves serious investigation in the study of the psychology of religion. I regret to say that this key experience has not received much investigation at all.

If OOBEs were nothing more than psychologically powerful experiences that strongly affected belief systems about survival after death, they would demand scientific study. This would be the case even if you thought that the experience was an illusion (i.e., that there was no something or soul that actually left the body) that it was just some sort of altered state in which the OOBE was vividly hallucinated.

However, people who have OOBEs sometimes give accurate accounts of events at the distant place to which they believe their consciousness was projected, events that they could not have known anything about through normal information channels. Thus, some OOBEs have a psi component that makes them especially interesting because they give support to the theory that perhaps there is a something that can temporarily leave the physical body. The slightest possibility that we can scientifically show that OOBEs are what they seem to be makes them a fit subject for an immense amount of scientific investigation. After all, good answers to questions of whether this life is all there is or whether we go on to something else, whether religions are just arbitrary belief systems that are useful for promoting social order or whether they are dealing with a vitally important reality, are very important to each one of us.

The government is not, of course, providing funds for a National Institute of Soul Research. The question of the nature of the OOBE is not even asked in orthodox scientific circles, the whole area of psi having been thrown out a long time ago; not because the evidence was scientifically examined and found to be nonsensical, but because of various social factors connected with the struggle between science and religion, as science became a force in society. So we have practically no scientific information on the nature of the OOBEs and their implications for the idea of a soul that might survive death.

The Landau Case

Let me illustrate an OOBE with a report from England originally published in the *Journal of the Society for Psychical Research* [48]. Figure 9-1 shows the physical locale of the incident, which is known as the *Landau case*.

I knew my wife, Eileen, for quite a number of years before we were married and she frequently used to talk to me about her out-of-the-body experiences. These were of the usual kind and on some occasions, I was able to verify that something paranormal had in fact occurred. For example, she went to bed one afternoon, saying she would try to see what our friend, who was on holiday in Cornwall, was doing. When she woke up, she was able to give an accurate description of a rock plant, which our friend was photographing, the details of the surroundings, and also of a gentleman who was with him. All this was subsequently confirmed, and, what was interesting, our

Figure 9–1. The Landau case.

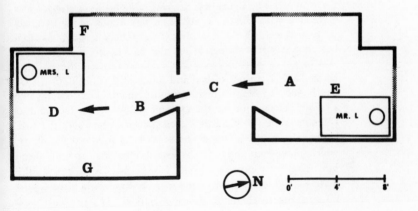

friend was under the impression that a shadowy figure passed near him at the time.

At the beginning of September 1955, I was not very well. Much fuss was made about it, but a thorough medical examination failed to show any real trouble. Eileen, who was then living with her mother in Kent, spent several nights in my house, occupying the spare bedroom which was opposite mine, across the landing, on the south-western corner of the house. [Figure 9-1 shows her sleeping position; it's marked "Mrs. L."] One morning she told me that she came into my bedroom during the night, minus her physical body, to check on my pulse and respiration. I asked her to do this again the following night, this time trying to bring some object with her; I gave her my small diary, weighing 38 grammes.

That night we left the doors of both bedrooms open, as I could hardly expect a physical object to pass through solid wood. [That really gets to me. He obviously expects Eileen to leave her physical body and float across the hallway carrying his diary, but he is not going to entertain any odd ideas such as a physical object passing through the door! We learn a lot about our assumptions when we study psi material.] Before falling asleep I asked myself to awake, should anything unusual occur in my room.

I woke up suddenly: it was dawn and there was just about enough light coming through the partly drawn curtains to enable one to read. At the point marked "A" stood the figure of Eileen, facing north-west and looking straight ahead towards the window. The figure was wearing a night dress, its face was extremely pale, almost white. The figure was moving slowly backwards towards the door, but it was otherwise quite motionless; it was not walking. When the figure, progressing at the rate of about one foot per five seconds, reached the position marked "C" I got out of bed and followed. I could then clearly see the moving figure which was quite opaque and looking like a living person, but for the extreme pallor of the face and at the same time the head of Eileen, asleep in her bed, the bedclothes rising and falling as she breathed. I followed the figure, which moved all the time backwards, looking straight ahead but apparently not seeing me. I kept my distance and ultimately stood at the door of the spare bedroom when the figure, now having reached the position marked "D", suddenly vanished. There was no visible effect on Eileen, who did not stir and whose rhythm of breathing remained quite unchanged.

I moved quietly back to my room, and at point "E", on the floor, found a rubber toy dog, which belonged to Eileen, and which stood on a small chest of drawers in position marked "F" when I last saw it. The dog weighed 107.5 grammes.

In the morning after breakfast, I questioned Eileen about the diary. She said that she first went to the desk on which it was, and somehow could not pick it up. She then thought it would be easier to carry something that belonged to her, and she decided on the rubber toy, which she managed to take with her to my room. It was a pity that I woke up some thirty seconds too late. [48, pp. 126–127].

Mrs. Landau added the following note to her husband's report:

I remember getting out of bed (but do not recall exactly how), going over to the desk and seeing the diary. As a child, I had been told never to handle other people's letters or diaries, so probably for this reason I did not want to touch this one. Instead I lifted my rubber toy dog, and I remember taking it through the door, across the landing, to the other room, but do not remember actually *walking*. I did not find the dog heavy or difficult to hold. I have no recollection of what I finally did with it. I felt very tired and wanted to go back to bed. Up to this moment my consciousness appeared to me normal, and so did my ability to see my surroundings, which also appeared normal to me. I do not remember anything about going backwards to my room, or entering my body. [48, pp. 127–128]

In some ways, this is an atypical case. In almost all OOBE cases, the person having the experience is not perceived by other people as an apparition or as any kind of figure, and it is almost unheard of for a person having this kind of experience to be able to affect the environment physically, to carry something or otherwise cause some kind of physical effect. People often try to have some kind of physical effect but find that they cannot.

But in other ways, this case is typical. Eileen was a person predisposed to having this kind of experience, so she was able to exercise some control in the sense of wanting to have the experience, thus having it happen. She had strong motivation to do this. Her fiancé was sick, and she was concerned about his condition. They both had a mutual interest in, and acceptance of, this kind of thing, which helped provide a certain amount of emotional impetus to make the OOBE happen and to make it acceptable. Eileen glided rather than walked. Apparitions often seem to do this. She was sure that she experienced normal consciousness almost all the way through, and then she apparently fell asleep while still having the OOBE.

An Archetypal Delusion?

In terms of ordinary physical science, the event described in this report is impossible. Either Mrs. Landau was having some kind of hallucination or delusion (good words that explain it away), or perhaps the writer is lying, or both. The trouble is that if this is a delusion or a lie, then it is what we would call an *archetypal* delusion or lie. It is clearly something very basic to human beings because OOBEs have been recorded for thousands of years. There are examples of OOBEs in many cultures. Obviously, people in all these cultures, separated by thousands of years and miles, have not read each other's books. Nevertheless, these descriptions show a great deal of agreement about the main characteristics of the experience. And almost everyone who has this experience says something to the effect that they no longer simply *believe* that they will survive death, they *know* it to be true because they have had the experience of consciousness existing outside of their physical bodies.

Of course, this conclusion is not entirely logical. It could be argued that the physical body was still functioning at the time, so it may be necessary for consciousness. But regardless of logic, OOBEs do produce an almost unshakable conviction in almost everyone who has them that they will survive death.

We do not know how many people have OOBEs. It might be 1 person in 100 or 1 in 1,000 or 1 in 10. Most people in our culture are too "smart" to say anything.

Most parapsychologists have ignored OOBEs, simply because they have not known how to work with such an elusive thing. The most they could do was collect post hoc reports from people who had had the experience and examine them for any general patterns that would tell something about it (see, e.g., [16, 17, 18, 29, 60]). I have been collecting detailed accounts of people's OOBEs for some years, and my colleague John Palmer and I hope to complete a thorough psychological analysis of these cases and publish the results within a couple of years in a book to be titled *The Flight of the Soul: Psychological Studies of an Archetypal Experience.*

I would like to do even more extensive psychological studies of OOBEs in the future. If you had had one or more OOBEs and are willing to fill out a very detailed questionnaire about them, please write to me (Department of Psychology, University of California, Davis, Calif. 95616) and ask for the OOBE questionnaire, indicating in your letter how many OOBEs you have had so that we will know which questionnaire to send. I cannot promise any immediate feedback about your experience because I'm still behind on analyzing the cases I already have information about, but you will be contributing something toward our future understanding of OOBEs.

In spite of the elusiveness of OOBEs, though, a few other investigators and I have always been interested in finding more active ways to supplement the case study approach. I have been able to carry out two laboratory studies of OOBEs, which I shall describe briefly: The full technical reports can be found in the *Journal of the American Society for Psychical Research* [148] and in the *International Journal of Parapsychology* [145]. My colleague John Palmer has begun working on ways of experimentally inducing OOBEs [72, 73, 75].

Miss Z

Miss Z, as I shall call her to protect her privacy, is a young woman whom I knew socially. As my wife and I became well acquainted with her and she learned of our interest in unusual experiences, she told us that ever since her childhood it had been a routine experience for her to awaken in the middle of the night, often several nights a week, and find herself floating near the ceiling of her bedroom, looking down at her sleeping physical body lying in her bed. The experiences generally lasted less than a minute, then she would fall asleep again. After the surprise of the first few experiences, Miss Z became rather bored with them: After all, it's not very exciting to watch yourself sleeping over and over again for years!

At my suggestion she carried out an experiment to determine for herself whether there was a psi component to her OOBEs. After lying down in bed she would blindly reach into a box containing randomized pieces of paper with the numbers one through ten on them and, without looking, lay one on her bedside table. She could not see it from the bed. If she had an OOBE, she was to memorize the number and check for accuracy in the morning.

When she told me, several weeks later, that she had tried this home experiment seven times and had always been correct, I was naturally excited! The experimental standards of parapsychology wouldn't allow me to accept self-reports like this as really evidential, but they certainly made me want to try the experiment under controlled laboratory conditions.

Before she had to move to another part of the state, Miss Z spent four nights sleeping in a psychophysiological laboratory I was able to use, wired up for brain wave (EEG), eye movement, and autonomic nervous system measures (skin resistance, blood pressure, and pulse rate). Since OOBEs were often reported by people who had almost died, or even been declared clinically dead and then revived, I thought there might be profound physiological changes when Miss Z experienced being out of her body. I also placed a five-digit random number on the shelf near the ceiling after she was wired up and ready to go to sleep. She was to try to float high enough to read the number and then wake up and report it to me. This would test for a psi component to her OOBEs.

Miss Z awoke a number of times and reported OOBEs, although she usually reported she had not floated high enough to see the number, so she had no idea what it was. Her OOBEs were generally associated with a unique brain wave pattern of a type I had never seen before. It seemed a mixture of the stage 1 pattern ordinarily associated with nocturnal dreaming, plus a lot of slowed down alpha activity (technically termed alphoid activity). Alpha activity is normally associated with relaxed wakefulness. The other measures were solidly within the ranges expected for normal sleep, so while Miss Z was in a novel physiological state, it certainly was not a "near death" state.

On the one occasion when Miss Z reported that she had floated high enough to see the target number, she correctly reported that it was 25132. The odds against correctly guessing a five-digit random number, making only one guess at it, are 100,000 to 1, so this argued strongly for a psi component to Miss Z's OOBEs.

It was very disappointing when she moved to a distant city, and we could not continue the laboratory research.

Robert Monroe

Robert Monroe is a Virginia businessman whom I met in 1965. He had been having OOBEs for some years by then, and although he knew nothing about OOBEs when they started and had been frightened by them, he had since explored them thoroughly and had worked on developing techniques to try to induce them at will. He felt he had been somewhat successful in bringing them under control; he couldn't guarantee an OOBE on demand, but there was a fair chance of one if he tried.

Our laboratory procedure was similar to that for Miss Z, although a technician generally monitored the equipment rather than I, and the borrowed laboratory was rather uncomfortable compared to the one I had been able to use for the work with Miss Z. Mr. Monroe had two brief OOBEs in the time available for research (this time I had to move across the country and so terminate the research). He reported not being able to control OOBE movements well enough in either one to get a look at the target number, but in one he did report a description of the technician's activities that was suggestive, although not conclusive evidence, of a psi component.

Unlike Miss Z, Mr. Monroe's OOBEs occurred in conjunction

with a brain wave pattern usually associated with ordinary dreaming, a stage 1 EEG, although there were not as many rapid eye movements, as there usually are in ordinary dreaming. Since the reported qualities of his consciousness during OOBEs are quite different from what he experiences as nocturnal dreaming, it seemed that OOBE activity had supplanted the mental activity ordinarily resulting in dreaming in stage 1.

These two case studies mainly illustrate the possibility of studying an exotic phenomenon like OOBEs in the laboratory, rather than giving the final word on the nature of OOBEs. They had the desired effect of stimulating some other investigators to study talented OOBE people in laboratory conditions, and we shall briefly look at the results of this work later. First let us begin to look at how we can understand what an OOBE is, what kinds of theories seem to explain them.

Theories about OOBEs

Theories about OOBEs have run along two general lines. One of these takes the experience pretty much as given: namely, that the person experiences himself at a location distant from his physical body. The theoretical explanation of this is that consciousness is indeed associated with some nonphysical (in terms of currently known physics) vehicle or second body (often called the "astral body" in older metaphysical literature), and that this second body is capable of temporarily leaving the physical body. The other theoretical line considers the idea of a second body or a soul to be far too extreme, and explains the OOBE as a purely subjective experience. According to this point of view, the experience of traveling to and/or being in a distant location is considered hallucinatory, in the same way that our experience of being somewhere else and having a second body in a dream (but without the clear consciousness characteristic of OOBEs) is hallucinatory.

When an OOBE has psi components (bringing back information about the distant location), the first theoretical line sees it as a straightforward consequence of literally being at the distant location. Because perception is a function of consciousness and consciousness is there, it sees things at the distant location. The second line of explanation sees psi operating by the ψ_4 route from the Psi Receptor to the unconscious. Here the unconscious mind, responsible for the production of the hallucinatory experience that consciousness is involved in, simply uses the psi-obtained knowledge to make sure that the hallucinations actually convey information about the distant event.

Which theory is true—that is, which best accounts for our observations? We cannot say at present, and we may never be able to decide between the two. The theory of an independently traveling consciousness certainly stays close to the experiential data and is strongly supported by those rather rare OOBE cases in which the OOBE traveler is perceived by witnesses at the distant scene as some sort of apparition. Obviously, if there is something there, there is something for witnesses to see, although seeing it must involve some sort of psi perception. A major difficulty with this first theoretical line, however, is that people who experience OOBEs often find themselves not only possessed of a second body, but the body is *clothed*. Although many people are willing to concede that *you* have a soul, they are not willing to attribute a soul to your pajamas.

The second theoretical line (hallucination plus psi) has no difficulty in dealing with the OOBE traveler's pajamas or with other things that are experienced during the OOBE but that have no corresponding physical reality. The OOBE body itself is considered a hallucination, and a normal one at that, because we ordinarily hallucinate a second body of sorts for ourselves every night during stage 1-REM dreaming. The problem with this second line, however, is that it is *too* general. You could equally well argue from it that your experience of being located here in your present physical body is a purely subjective hallucination; it only happens to be consistent with the rest of your knowledge because this hallucination is constantly tuned up with unconscious psi. We do not know what limits (if any) exist for psi functioning. Thus, it is difficult to make the hallucination plus psi theory specific enough to identify instances to which it would not apply. For any theory to be scientific, it has to be capable of being disproved.

Varieties of OOBEs

To complicate the matter further, I am convinced that we use the term OOBE too widely, that it actually covers at least two and perhaps more quite different types of experiences with different characteristics. Lumping them together indiscriminately in this way is bound to produce a certain amount of confusion.

Consider, for example, the kind of OOBEs that Miss Z and Robert Monroe have had. These are what I call full-scale or classical or *discrete* OOBEs (d-OOBEs). During the OOBEs, neither Miss Z nor Mr. Monroe felt any contact with the physical body. In terms of conscious experience, there is what I call a *full-scale disconnect*. During the OOBE, all perceptions and actions performed are relevant to the OOBE location. In order to reexperience sensations from the physical body or to control it, both Miss Z and Mr. Monroe must terminate the OOBE and go through a transition back to ordinary being. Because this is an all-or-none transition between two quite different patterns of experience, I call it a d-OOBE [169] just as I distinguish discrete states of consciousness [173].

Another kind of experience that unfortunately has been labeled OOBE is one that focuses on internal imagery about distant scenes. This is the remote-viewing experience discussed in Chapter 8. I believe it is comparable to being absorbed in anything. For example, if you are watching a movie in a theater and are very involved in a scene taking place in medieval Europe, in an experiential sense you *are* in medieval Europe at that time. You will usually have little or no awareness of bodily sensations. But if someone asks you, or if you ask yourself, where you really are, your answer will be: "I am sitting here in a movie theater but thinking about medieval Europe." If Miss Z or Mr. Monroe were to ask that question during an OOBE, the answer would be that they are at the distant location, not in their physical bodies.

Which of the two types of theorizing best fits Miss Z's and Mr. Monroe's experiences? We can make them fit the hallucination plus psi theory, but this involves disregarding the primary quality of their experiences: the immediate experience of being located elsewhere than the physical body and knowing *at the time* that they are so located and that their state of consciousness is clear and reasonably ordinary.

If we retain this primary bit of data, how well do their experiences fit the theory that something does indeed leave the body?

Some of Miss Z's experiences certainly fit this theory well. Her only guess at the target number, for example, was given on the one occasion when she experienced herself as being located in the right position to see it clearly. Robert Monroe frequently experienced clear communication with someone at an OOBE location, without that person later recalling anything about it. He found this extremely frustrating, particulary when these experiences first began to occur, because some kind of objective verification of his OOBEs was tremendously important to him. Occasionally, he did get reports from acquaintances that they had had an unusual experience while he was there that partly corresponded to his OOBE; but most of the time, these people remembered nothing about it. Sometimes this meant that part of his description of the OOB location was correct, implying that psi was operating, but that other parts of it were plainly incorrect. Let me give an example.

Flying to California

Shortly after finishing the first series of laboratory experiments with Monroe, described in my introduction to *Journeys Out of the Body* [56], I moved to California. Several months later, I decided to try an experiment in which my wife and I would concentrate intensely for about half an hour to create a sort of "psychic beacon" to try to help Monroe have an OOBE and travel to our home. If he could accurately describe our home, this would be good evidence for a psi component in his OOBE because he had no idea what our new home was like.

I telephoned Monroe and told him that we would try to guide him across the country to our home at some unspecified time during the night of the experiment. That was all I told him. That evening I randomly selected a time to begin concentrating; the only restriction I put on my choice was that it would be sometime after I thought Monroe had been asleep for a while. The time turned out to be 11:00 P.M. California time (2:00 A.M. eastern standard time). At 11:00, my wife and I began our concentration; but at 11:05, the telephone rang. We never get calls late at night, so this was rather surprising and disturbing, but we did not answer the phone. We tried to continue concentrating and did so until 11:30 but the interruption had seriously disrupted our effort.

The following day, I telephoned Monroe and noncommittally told him that the results had been encouraging but that I was not going to say anything more about it until he had mailed me his written account of what he had experienced.

His account was as follows:

> The evening passed uneventfully, and I finally got into bed about 1:40 am, still very much wide awake. The cat was lying in bed with me. After a long period of calming mind, a sense of warmth swept over body, no break in consciousness, no pre-sleep. Almost immediately felt something (or someone) rocking my body from side to side, then tugging at my feet! (Heard cat let out complaining yowl.) I recognized immediately that this had something to do with Charley's experiment, and with full trust, did not feel my usual caution (about strangers!). The tugging at my legs continued, and I finally managed to separate one second body arm and hold it up, feeling around in the dark. After a moment, the tugging stopped and a hand took my wrist, first gently, then very, very firmly and pulled me out of the physical (body) easily. Still trusting, and a little excited, I expressed feeling to go to Charley, if that was where he (it) wanted to lead me. The answer came back affirmatively (although there was no sense of personality, very businesslike). With the hand around my wrist very firmly, I could feel a part of the arm belonging to the hand (slightly hairy, muscular male). But could not "see" who belonged to the arm. Also heard my name called once.

Then we started to move, with the familiar feeling of something like air rushing around my body. After a short trip
(seemed around 5 seconds in duration), we stopped, and the
hand released my wrist. There was complete silence and dark-
ness. When I drifted down into what seemed to be a room. . . .
[56, p. 13]

I will add that when Monroe finished this brief OOBE and got
out of bed to telephone me, it was 2:05 A.M. his time, 11:05 P.M.
our time. Thus, the time match with the start of our concentration was extremely good; he experienced a tug pulling him
from his body within one or two minutes of the time we started.
On the other hand, the portion of his account that I have
omitted, his description of our home and what my wife and I
were doing, was quite inaccurate. He perceived too many
people in the room, perceived my wife and me performing actions that we did not do, and gave a rather vague description of
the physical arrangement of the room.

Was he actually there? His experience of being located there
and the synchrony of timing would seem to suggest that he was,
but his description of events would not suggest any psi.

If there is one certain fact with respect to OOBEs, it is that
the direct experience of being at a particular physical location
while out of the body does not guarantee that the perception of
that location will in any way match its physical reality. Although both Miss Z and Monroe seemed to experience
d-OOBEs, we should also note that these probably did not
occur in the same physiological state. Miss Z's seem to occur in a
unique psychophysiological state, a mixture of stage 1-drowsy
pattern with prominent alpha wave activity, whereas Monroe's
seemed to occur from stage 1 EEG activity. Neither one of them
show pronounced heart rate or other autonomic nervous system
changes. So they are similar in that respect. But the records
from my laboratory of two people who have had d-OOBEs of
two apparently different physiological states do not suggest that
there is a simple, unitary phenomenon involved.

The publication of my research on Miss Z and Robert
Monroe had a major effect in reminding other parapsychol-

ogists about OOBEs and in demonstrating that this rather exotic phenomenon could be brought into the laboratory for more precise study. Have the three research studies reported since my studies clarified any of the issues raised above? Let us briefly look at them.

Ingo Swann's Remote Viewing

Apparent OOBEs were one among many apparently psychic experiences that Ingo Swann experienced as a child. They are described in his fascinating book, *To Kiss Earth Goodbye* [132]. Like many children who had unusual experiences, he was made painfully aware by the taunts and jeers of adults and other children that he did not fit in, and he suppressed most of these phenomena. Later in his adult life, he redeveloped some of them.

An initial study of his ability to focus his consciousness outside his body and perceive from that location was carried out by Karlis Osis and Janet Lee Mitchell at the American Society for Psychical Research in New York City [55]. Although Mitchell describes this as a study of OOBEs, I would classify it as a study of remote viewing. Swann describes his perception of a remote location while it happens, so he can hardly be said to be fully disconnected from his body. Other remote-viewing experiments with Swann have been described by Russell Targ and Hal Puthoff [92, 135, 136] in terms of psi content, but we will focus on the Osis and Mitchell study here because it included physiological measurements.

The experiments were similar to those that I carried out with Miss Z and Monroe in that Swann sat in a comfortable chair with electrodes attached for measuring brain waves and various autonomic functions. He attempted to focus his consciousness outside his body and see target material, which was located in an open-top box hung from the ceiling. The material would be readily visible from a position above the box but invisible to anyone in the room. Initially, a five-digit random number was used as a target, as in my study of Miss Z, but Swann did not feel he was able to see clearly enough to make this rather fine distinction; he was only able to get a less focused impression of the target material.

In the experimental procedure that evolved, the target would be a randomly selected object or objects. Swann described his impressions of the objects verbally and made drawings of them. Eight sessions were carried out; then Swann's drawings and descriptions were given to an outside judge, who attempted to match them with the stimulus objects. Naturally, the judge did not know which drawings were supposed to go with which objects. Nevertheless, he correctly matched all eight drawings with the correct targets, a result that would occur by chance less than 1 in 40,000 times. There is no doubt that Swann's remote-viewing impressions involved a great deal of psi. Swann did not show any obvious changes in autonomic functioning, a similar finding to that from Miss Z, and for some of Monroe's OOBEs. But he did show some decrease in the abundance and amplitude of EEG alpha rhythms during his remote viewing. It was not the quality of pattern shift toward alphoid activity that Miss Z showed, but more the sort of decrease that we would expect from any task that involved concentration, so I do not believe there are any unique EEG correlates of Swann's remote viewing.

Sharpening the Methodology

Osis and his associates were very aware that although correctly identifying a target near the ceiling can be evidence for psi, it does not really discriminate between the theory that something leaves the body and the theory of hallucination plus psi. Therefore, they designed a more ingenious type of experiment that could yield data favoring one theory or the other, even though it would not prove either. They constructed some targets consisting of a box with a viewing window on one end. The person trying to have an OOBE is instructed that if he succeeds in having one, he should position himself in front of that viewing window, look into it, and note what he sees.

Although the person trying to have the OOBE is not given any details, the window does not provide an accurate view of the contents of the box; instead, it consists of various mechanical and optical systems that deliberately distort the image of the target material. If the OOBE percipient is indeed viewing the target from a position in front of the viewing window, as if he had some sort of "eye" there, his description of the target would reflect this distortion. But if he is just hallucinating being at that location and unconsciously using psi clairvoyantly to make his hallucination correspond to what the target object is, he would see it without the distortions. Clear-cut results one way or the other should thus favor one of the theories, although you could always argue for a far more complicated case where the results would seem to favor the consciousness-in-front-of-the-viewing-window-theory, while actually results were achieved by hallucination plus psi. Here we have a sort of superpsi, plus supercomputing on an unconscious level, in which psi must be used to determine how the distorting system performs and also what the target object is and then make appropriate transformations in the hallucinated imagery. This is obviously a rather cumbersome hypothesis. We shall see the first results of this sophisticated test below.

The Flyby Experiment

An important practical issue in OOBE research is that you need talented percipients who can have OOBEs almost at will. How do you get them? I had great luck in finding Miss Z and Robert Monroe, and Osis was lucky in finding Ingo Swann for his initial experiments. But how do you go on beyond that?

Osis spread the word that he was looking for people who could have OOBEs at will. For those who contacted him, he arranged for a *flyby experiment* at a designated time. The self-professed OOBE traveler was to try to have an OOBE and travel to a laboratory room at the American Society for Psychical Research. He or she was to mail a description of that room to Osis. About 100 persons have been tested this way, but Osis reports that, unfortunately, about 85 percent of them showed no awareness of the stimulus objects or persons in the target area, even though they believed that they had had an OOBE and had seen what was in the room [66].

Work has gone on with a few OOBE people who showed some promise. Some of the most interesting work has been done with Alex Tanous, another person who, like Swann, had had many apparently psychic experiences as a child but had had to suppress them in order to get along. He describes his childhood in his book *Beyond Coincidence: One Man's Experience with Psychic Phenomena* [133]. He was selected from the flyby experiment.

In the account he first sent in, he mentioned that when he found himself in the target room, he was bent over and floating over the display with his arms and legs dangling and that he could not get out of this rather absurd position. Osis had a psychic observing the area during that particular flyby experiment, and she reported that she saw someone hovering over the target display who was bent over like a jackknife.

Osis has told me that a number of experiments have been carried out with Tanous and the sophisticated target displays described in the preceding section. Some of the results have been statistically significant and have favored the theory that Tanous's consciousness was indeed in front of the viewing window. Unfortunately, these significant analyses involve partially correct identifications of various complex target characteristics and in general represent a statistically significant but rather weak level of psi. Clearly, there is a tremendous amount of noise in these results, and they do not help much in choosing between the two theories. Although there seems to be a psi component to Tanous's experiences, it is certainly not what you would expect if in some sense he had some equivalent of an eye located right in front of the viewing window and capable of giving full, accurate descriptions of what was seen. Furthermore, because Tanous, like Swann, describes his experience as it is happening, I again think this is probably an example of remote viewing occurring in a d-ASC, rather than a d-OOBE.

Work with Blue Harary

To the outside observer, remote viewing can sometimes seem to be a rather casual affair. A person sits down, relaxes, closes his or her eyes, and simply begins describing impressions of the remote target. At other times, as with Alex Tanous, considerable mental preparation is required; and even though there is obviously considerable contact with the physical body, because the person is still talking, a profound d-ASC apparently occurs.

Such a d-ASC seems to be involved with another talented percipient, Blue Harary, who is both a scientific investigator and an experiencer of OOBEs, probably of the discrete kind. He has worked with William Roll, Robert Morris, John Hartwell, Joseph Janis, and D. Scott Rogo at the Psychical Research Foundation in Durham.

The basic experimental procedure with Harary is for him to spend an entire day before an evening's experiment preparing himself to have an OOBE. For the experiment itself, he is wired for measuring brain waves and autonomic functions, and he reclines on a cot in a soundproof room in a psychophysiology laboratory at Duke University. He goes through a deliberate mental procedure for relaxing and preparing himself, called a *cool-down stage,* and then attempts to leave his body and travel to a target room in the Psychical Research Foundation, which is about half a mile away. In various experiments, he may attempt to identify target objects in the target room and/or to influence various physical, human, or animal detectors there. Usually, he has two OOBEs in a single experimental session, and two control periods are also interspersed. The observers at the target location are not informed of the times when Harary is attempting to travel to the room. These OOBEs are demanding on Harary, and he is often disoriented after a session. For a few minutes, he sometimes walks unevenly, his vision is distorted, and he sometimes feels pains in his chest [103]. He does not describe anything about his experiences until they are over because he feels totally "out" during them. For this reason, I think he is having d-OOBEs.

The cool-down stage is characterized by large and consistent physiological changes. Harary usually takes several big, slow breaths at the start of the cool-down stage, but his breathing becomes shallow and extremely regular by its end. Changes in the electrical voltage of his skin indicate relaxation, and his blood vessels enlarge for a relaxed flow of blood, necessitating a slightly increased heart rate to compensate for the decreased blood pressure. During the OOBE, however, physiological recordings indicate only a relaxed, normal waking state. There are occasional REMs and lots of alpha waves but no signs of sleep or any abnormalities [32].

In terms of identifying a psi component to his OOBEs, much of the work with Harary has been frustrating. The results have not been clear-cut enough to say there was definitely a psi component. However, there have been enough occasional flashes and near hits to suggest that some kind of psi is manifesting. The one highly successful experiment involved using an animal detector to determine when Harary was experiencing himself in the target room, a procedure that I proposed in 1965 [140] and that I am glad is starting to be used.

Harary had a couple of pet kittens, named Spirit and Soul [103]. Because Spirit showed exceptionally strong affection for Harary, he was used in the formal experiment, which was devised by Robert Morris. An activity-measurement board was used. It was a shuffleboardlike apparatus, thirty by eighty inches, marked off into twenty-four numbered squares. An observer could measure Spirit's activity by noticing how many squares he walked into during a given period of time and by counting his meows. Spirit was a very active kitten, and under base-line conditions would wander all over the board and meow frequently. For the experiment itself, Harary would try to have an OOBE and keep Spirit company; during control periods, he did not.

The results were striking. Spirit was quite active during control periods, but when visited by Harary during OOBEs, he rarely moved about. The difference was significant at the 0.01 level. The difference in number of meows is also striking. Spirit meowed thirty-seven times during control periods but not at all during OOBE periods [57].

Harary's OOBEs are quite profound, but like the others discussed in this chapter, they do not lend themselves to simple understanding. If he were in the target room in a simpleminded way, he ought to be able to describe everything about it accurately, but he seemed to get only fragments of it.

Part III: Speculation

Introduction

I find that the last chapter ends unsatisfactorily, without really explaining what OOBEs are or their full significance. This is a function of scientific honesty: We simply know so little about OOBEs, or about psi in general, that many times in this book I have had to say that we just don't know. In this book, I have theorized or tried to explain various things, but I have followed the rule of staying fairly close to my scientific data base and limiting myself to ideas that can be checked against that base within the near future. I have larger views about the nature of psi and consciousness, of course. As a human being, I do not like to feel that I do not understand things, and so I think about them. Chapter 10 sketches some of these ideas, but by and large, it is a prescientific chapter, and the ideas are much more tentative than those in the rest of the book. The concepts are too big for present-day science to work with in the immediate future, but I believe them all capable of investigation by a more mature science.

Chapter 10 will leave more questions asked than answered, and that is probably a good state of affairs for curious beings. My research on psi and on consciousness will continue.

IO.

What and Where Are Consciousness and Awareness?

✿✿✿

What do we mean when we say, "I know something," or "I understand such and such"? The exact meaning will vary with the circumstances, but, as we discussed in Chapter 1, we generally mean that an experience is happening to us, that someone is telling us about something, or that we are looking at a situation. Rather than feeling puzzled or confused by the experienced situation, it is familiar to us; we comprehend it and know how to act in accordance with our understanding and values. More specifically, knowing something means that when a certain experience happens to us, we already have an appropriate mental map or set of concepts that usefully places the ongoing experience in a context of past experiences and learnings.

I glance around me as I write this and ask myself, Where am I? I answer, "I am in my study." I can expand that to street address, city, state, to where it is with respect to certain hills or rivers, and so forth. I map my physical location and say, "I know where I am." Similarly, if I look into a physics textbook and see the equation $F = MA$, I know the meaning of this equation. I immediately remember that F stands for force; M, for mass; A, for acceleration; and the equals sign, for numerical equivalence. But if I read further in the physics book and come across the equation

$$\tan \phi = \frac{4\pi^2 n^2 LC - 1}{2\pi n RC}$$

I do not know what it means. That is, it does not fit in with any of the maps of my experience. I have not been trained in the maps of the area of knowledge we call physics.

This understanding of knowledge assumes that there is an observer or experiencer to whom experiences happen and that this experiencer judges the degree of matching between ongoing experience and another special subset of experience, maps, or concepts: knowledge stored in memory. When I did not recognize or understand the second equation, the observing part of me immediately knew there was no match between any available maps and ongoing experience.

In thinking about knowledge this way, I am implicitly dividing the totality of experience into certain useful subcategories. I have clusters of experience relating to physics, clusters of experience related to eating, and so on. A more basic distinction that we have implicitly been making is that of a subset of experiences about what we call the *external world* and another subset of internal experiences called *knowledge,* the remembered experiences that we draw upon to make sense out of ongoing experience. I want to emphasize that this is a useful division of experience per se, without involving such complexities as the ultimate reality of a division between inside and outside or whether the external world is more or less real than our internal world.

Consistency and Reality

For most of us, the subset of experiences we call our perception of the external world shows an extremely high degree of consistency and lawfulness. There is change, but in ways we can fit on our maps. Every time I jump off something, for example, I land on the ground with a certain intensity of experienced shock, and that intensity is generally in direct proportion to the height from which I have jumped. However, most, though not all, of the experiences that we consider internal show far less consistency and predictability. For example, I perceive that my study has the same shape and size every time I walk into it; but an internal visualization of my study or a dream about it is liable to show considerable variations in shape, size, furniture, and so on.

The difference in consistency and lawfulness between experiences belonging to the external world and those belonging to the internal or subjective world is the basic difference between them as far as any *direct* knowledge goes. That is our experience. We usually go a step farther, though, and say that because external experiences are so consistent, they are independently *real*. We may do this because we like the idea of a solid, lawful, ultimate reality that we are not responsible for, or for other reasons. As a result, we take an experiential quality of consistency and come to believe automatically that this consistency is inherent in the nature of these experiences, that there really is an external, lawful world. Thus, it becomes all too easy to mistake our maps, our concepts about this subset of experiences, for real knowledge about what we think is the real world. The map becomes the territory. In our discussion of the nature of scientific inquiry, we saw the blindnesses that can result from mistaking the map for the territory. *It is an excellent working hypothesis in most instances to believe in the independent reality of the external world, but it is a mistake to believe it totally.*

I must admit that this is easier to state than it is to live by. I, too, believe totally in the reality of the external world most of the time, forgetting that I am probably experiencing my internal maps about it rather than paying attention to the totality of my ongoing experience, but I cannot emphasize the above points too strongly.

Psi phenomena are considered paradoxes or apparent violations of physical laws. Actually, psi phenomena are a part of reality, a part of our experiential potentials, but they just do not fit onto some of our cherished maps. At times, I think it might be useful to rename them *paraconceptual* (rather than paranormal) phenomena. If a majority of Americans believe that they have had such experiences [28], they are certainly normal.

Location

Because the subset of our experiences we call the external world shows such high consistency and lawfulness, the concept of *location* in three spatial dimensions and one temporal dimension has proved to be extremely useful. "My study is in a room under my garage" and "I will be meeting a colleague in my study at 3:15 P.M. on January 24, 1978" are highly useful statements. The next time I want to go from my house to my study, it will be far more useful to go to the back of the garage than to go down the street or up on the roof. If I actually want to meet that colleague, it will best be in my study at the designated time, rather than some other time. I am not so sure that space and time actually really exist out there, but as abstractions that are part of my mapping system, three dimensions of space and one dimension of time work exceptionally well in my everyday life. Sometimes, however, these abstractions of three spatial dimensions and one temporal dimension do not work well for making sense of experience. And that is what happens when we deal with psi. Furthermore, the concept of spatial and temporal location does not always work very well when we deal with our internal experiences.

The concept does work fairly well for one part of that subset: bodily experience. We have an exquisitely detailed spatial map of some parts of our body. For example, if you want to touch a particular tooth with the tip of your tongue, your tongue can touch it directly, without error. Somewhere in your mind, the space inside your mouth is represented in great detail. This is biologically very adaptive because it keeps you from biting your own tongue when you chew food. Some other bodily experiences are not so well localized. Think of all the vague and shifting aches and pains you have had in the past or of sensations that you may be having now. For example, your back is crudely mapped compared with the inside of your mouth. Have a friend touch you lightly on your back, sometimes with one finger, sometimes simultaneously with two fingers spread an inch or two apart; you will find that many times you cannot reliably distinguish between the two touches.

Where do you spatially locate an intuitive insight into something? Or love? Or hope? Or the answer to the question, "What is the sum of two plus seven?" Where is the observer who is observing particular experiences or sensations that he attributes to the outside world or to his body? If you have a dream about being in a castle on the Rhine, is the observer (your consciousness) in a castle on the Rhine or at home in bed? Because we have been taught that dreams are not real, we tell ourselves, *after* the dream, that we were really at home in bed the whole time; we deny our immediate experience in favor of faith in a map about where consciousness is really located. But suppose that dream was really an OOBE, that you not only experienced yourself in that castle on the Rhine but also felt that your consciousness was just as clear, rational, and lucid as it is right now? Or suppose you remember an actual visit to a distant place and spend a few minutes completely absorbed in the memory? Where are you then? Where is the mind during trans-temporal inhibition, and in what time? Answers to these questions are not at all straightforward.

Talking Ourselves Out of Direct Experience

In the development of our consciousness from infancy, as I understand it [77, 173], I find that we have performed an amazing trick. Although we do not know for sure what an infant's consciousness is like, the data we do have suggest that there is nothing but experience and that the infant does not have very clear distinctions (if any) between himself or herself and the external world. In the course of being educated through interaction with the external world, the infant gradually builds up a series of internal maps about outside and inside and about the nature of that external world (particularly the *consensus reality* of its culture) that allow the infant to survive and operate effectively in it.

A lot of infants over the past few hundred years have grown up to be scientists who have gone on to investigate our sense organs and the brain and nervous system. Using the scientific techniques developed for dealing with the external world, we have begun to understand how the brain and nervous system work and have found that, to some extent, variations in the functioning of the brain can be related to how we behave and what we experience. For example, a severe head injury with corresponding brain damage or surgical removal of a part of the brain can lead to changes in an individual's external behavior and changes in his or her report of what is experienced. If the brain is electrically stimulated during surgery, as in the well-known work of the surgeon Wilder Penfield [78], specific memories of the past may flash back to the patient. There seems little doubt that the brain and nervous system play a major role in what we experience as our consciousness.

Now here is where the neat trick comes in. Whenever we have mental maps that work well, we tend to forget that they are abstractions we use to make sense of our experience and begin to think that they are truth. We become emotionally attached to these useful maps and regard questions about their adequacy as personal attacks. This is what has happened with our maps, our scientific theories about the external world and the brain. In innumerable ways, they are exceptionally good maps. But we have come to believe in them so much that if something that happens cannot be adequately located on the map, we can readily talk ourselves into believing that it did not happen in the way in which we experienced it, that it was a mistake. We have faith that it really does fit on one of our maps, that we just missed something that would help us fit it in.

By using maps prepared by physical science methods, we have achieved some useful understanding of how the brain and nervous system work, and we know that they are related to conscious experience. Consciousness or awareness per se, on the other hand, is not something external to yourself that you can

conveniently look at with the techniques developed for studying the external world. For this reason, some scientists and
philosophers of science explicitly (and most, implicitly) have rejected consciousness or awareness per se as objects of scientific
study. Yet, even these people can hardly deny that they themselves have conscious experiences, even if those experiences are
not fit for scientific study.

What do we do with consciousness? By a simple extension of
the tremendous attachment to and faith in the maps of external
reality we already have, we equate consciousness with the operations of the brain. In formal terms, we accept the reality of
the *psychoneural identity hypothesis,* which says that every
little nuance of experience is identical to, is caused by, and can
be reduced to specific neural processes within the brain and
nervous system. What is real is what is physical, and consciousness is just an interesting manifestation of basic physical laws
within the physical structure of the brain.

This is a neat trick, indeed. We start as creatures with nothing but experience; we separate some of that experience into
the category of the external world; we elaborate our maps of
that part of our experience; and then we come to believe that
those maps totally explain the very act of experiencing itself.
Instead of experience being the primary data from which to
develop a world view, it now becomes a rather minor side effect
of basic physical processes that we believe are totally independent of us.

Orthodox Scientific View of Consciousness

On purely psychological grounds, it is useful to distinguish
between consciousness and basic awareness. *Consciousness* is a
complex, content-filled thing that fills the great bulk of our experience; whereas *basic awareness* is that something behind consciousness, that pure kind of knowing that simply knows that
something is happening, rather than knowing that at this very
moment I am sitting in my study looking out a glass window at
rain falling after a long dry season.

Awareness per se cannot be defined in any satisfactory manner

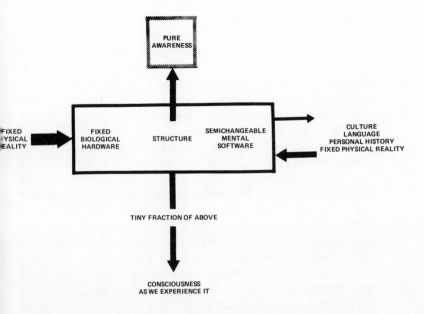

Figure 10-1. Orthodox scientific view of consciousness.

because definition is a function of verbal knowledge and verbal knowledge and its complex grammar is a matter of consciousness, of very complex, interconnected content. I am aware at this very moment, just as I am conscious. You can have the same experience. At various moments in life, especially those connected with meditative practices, people often experience their mental state moving toward simpler basic awareness and away from the highly complex and articulated consciousness that is our normal state.

Although it is useful to distinguish consciousness and awareness in a psychological way, the orthodox scientific view of consciousness (what I call the *conservative* or *physicalistic* view of the mind in *States of Consciousness* [173]) is that basic awareness is only a discriminable subfunction of the brain and nervous system. Figure 10-1 illustrates this view.

The brain and nervous system are seen to consist of an

extremely large number of structures, the neurons that make them up, and their even more numerous interconnections. Some of these structures can be seen as fixed in their function, as biological hardware with which the brain comes prewired. The instructions on how your kidneys should work, for example, are already wired into your body. There is a great deal of semi-changeable software: the specific physical changes that will occur in your brain as a result of our culture, the language you learn, your particular personal history within the culture, and your interactions with a fixed, lawful physical reality. This will enable you to speak, to think, to act, to fantasize, and so forth. All these physical processes in the brain and nervous system, both hardware and software, constitute the mind, according to the orthodox view.

A small subset of structures, which would probably be considered partially isolated from many other structures, give rise to the experience of pure awareness. Figure 10-1 shows pure awareness as something arising from the operation of the brain structure. In this view, it arises from, and is identical to, the operation of these particular parts of the structure of the brain. The operation of the brain itself is controlled by the laws of fixed physical reality; hence, the heavy arrow to the left of the structure of the brain shows the ultimate determinants of mental processes. This is a one-way arrow. Although we may to some extent alter our own culture rather than be totally controlled by it, there is no way of getting around the fixed laws of physical reality that ultimately determine all brain processes.

Consciousness as we experience it is a tiny fraction of the activity of all the structures of the brain and nervous system, primarily those subsystems having to do with the software.

Some Implications of the Orthodox View

Many implications follow readily from this orthodox view of consciousness. In terms of scientific emphasis, it becomes obvious that the ultimate key to understanding the mind is an understanding of the brain. We know that the brain is incredibly complicated. Therefore, any real understanding of the mind (i.e., a reduction of mental experience to specific brain processes) depends on technological progress: bigger and better computers, more highly refined brain surgery, and so on. Spiritual traditions, which arose in pretechnological cultures, obviously deal with inherently soft, psychological data and so have little to contribute. It also defines the possibility of consciousness surviving death as inherently absurd. If consciousness is nothing but brain functioning and the brain obviously stops functioning and disintegrates with death, there is nothing to survive, so research on survival is a waste of time.

I find a number of other implications flowing from this view, although not everyone would agree with these reactions. For example, this view means that ultimately each of us is completely alone. My sense of I is nothing but an electrical pattern in my brain; I am totally locked within my skull, receiving only indirect electrical messages about what I presume to be out there and sending out electrical messages that seem to affect what is out there through my muscles. But there is no direct contact. I am a prisoner in a permanently sealed room, even though I have a TV set and some other senses in there and have some buttons I can push that change the images on the TV set.

If chemical and electrical patterns in my brain are my only reality, then these are my only real concern. What happens to others, from whom I am ultimately isolated, is really a very secondary concern. I may treat them decently so that they will treat me decently because it maximizes my pleasure and minimizes my pain, but this is a strategy of convenience and adaptation. If I can get away with things that give me more pleasure, even if they cause pain to others, it is all right as long as I am not caught. After all, their pain has no direct reality for me; only *my* pleasure and pain are direct, are *real*.

I can maximize my pleasure and minimize my pain through the usual routes of the senses; as science progresses, I will be able to do it more effectively. Already, science has provided me with analgesic and tranquilizing drugs that can make it difficult for me to feel physical or emotional pain and some that can provide me with pleasure. These are certainly more direct ways to happiness than living in a world with unreliable others. Yet, even drugs are technologically crude compared with the promise that science seems to hold out: as brain research advances, I should be able to have electrodes implanted in pleasure centers of my brain so that I can feel good any time I want to just by pushing the right button.

If we look at the mystical experiences (or some psi experiences) that have changed people's lives from this point of view, they are clearly nothing but hallucinations. For example, if you believe that you have talked to God, your belief demonstrates what odd and interesting patterns of electrical and chemical activity can be stimulated in your brain. That is what is real. Many scientists would be personally upset by your talking to God or being at one with all life, but the more sophisticated among them would realize that as long as it stayed within socially acceptable bounds, enjoying your hallucinations might be good for your mental health. Some day, some clever scientists will try to see where electrodes can be located in your brain to give you the experience of talking to God just by pushing the appropriate button, and there will be another button to push to control the intensity of the experience so that you will not get more excited by it than you want to be.

I have painted a deliberately stark picture of some of the implications that readily flow from the orthodox model of consciousness. The maps we make and believe about the ultimate nature of reality have important effects on us, and I wanted to illustrate some of the effects that flow from that approach. Many other effects can already be observed in the world around us and perhaps in ourselves.

Can Psi Fit into the Orthodox View of Consciousness?

The orthodox view of the nature of consciousness stems from a philosophical approach that gives ultimate reality to physical things; this approach is incorrectly equated with scientific method [164]. But one of the things that makes psi phenomena so interesting is that they do not fit into the current physical view of the universe. Of course, our idea of what is physical depends upon our current conceptions; perhaps expanded conceptions in physics could handle psi phenomena and still retain the conventional view of consciousness. But if you take expansion to mean rather straightforward extensions of current physical concepts, I do not think this will happen.

For example, consider telepathy between two people. Might we be able to fit this psi phenomenon into a straightforwardly expanded physics? We know that the isolated consciousness inside a single skull can control muscles, which, in turn, control external physical energies such as sound; these physical energies then transmit information to another person's receptors, which, in turn, convert physical energies into neural impulses that reach the percipient's otherwise isolated consciousness. Could it be that we have some kind of physical organ modulating an undiscovered physical energy that conveys the psi information and affects an appropriate receptor organ in the percipient?

If telepathy were the only psi phenomenon we had to deal with, research along these lines might be very profitable. For instance, Persinger's theory [79] that extremely low frequency radio waves might convey telepathic impressions would be one possibility for study. But the total variety of psi phenomena seem to defy a possible explanation in terms of a straightforward expansion of physics.

Consider clairvoyance experiments, in which percipients successfully guess the order of a deck of cards that is stacked in a sealed box. What kind of physical energy could convey this information? Consider the problem of selectivity (e.g., not knowing where the target deck of cards is). What about precognition? Some equations in physics do have mathematical solutions that suggest information or energy traveling backward in time, but I do not know whether that will lead us to an explanation of precognition. Even if it does, that is not exactly a straightforward expansion of physics; it is an extremely radical change in concepts. Consider OOBEs. When Miss Z experienced herself floating near the ceiling and correctly reported a five-digit target number, where was she, really?

Overall, the few psi phenomena for which we have some fairly good scientific data fit very poorly into a theory of consciousness as being nothing but electrical and chemical reactions confined inside a skull. And this theory does not deal with the problem of understanding the more exotic psi phenomena.

Radical View of Consciousness

Figure 10-2 is what I consider a more adequate model of consciousness, which I call the *radical view of consciousness* [173]. The term *radical* is, of course, relative. This view is radical compared with today's scientific orthodoxy, but it is quite conventional in terms of the beliefs of most people throughout history and of most Americans today.

The radical view of consciousness has much in common with the orthodox view. The complex structures of the brain and nervous system obviously continue to occupy a central place. The software of the mind—the particular bits of consciousness programmed by our culture, language, history, and interaction with external reality—are still very prominent, and consciousness as we experience it is still only a tiny fraction of the total amount of activity going on. But there are two major differences. First, basic awareness is something that is added to the structure of the brain from outside, rather than something that arises from it. That is, the nature of basic awareness is qualitatively different from that of brain functioning. Second, whereas the orthodox view holds that brain structure is absolutely determined by completely fixed physical laws, the radical view recognizes an interaction with a semichangeable physical reality, an external reality that can sometimes be partially shaped by our mental processes, using some kind of PK. The laws of physical reality are still quite important in setting many basic constraints, but they are no longer all-embracing.

In postulating this radical theory of consciousness, I have drawn primarily on two sources; my investigations of altered states of consciousness, in which I have explored some of the very radical alterations in the ways in which people perceive themselves and the world, and psi phenomena.

In this theory, awareness is distinguished from consciousness not only as a convenience in working with certain kinds of

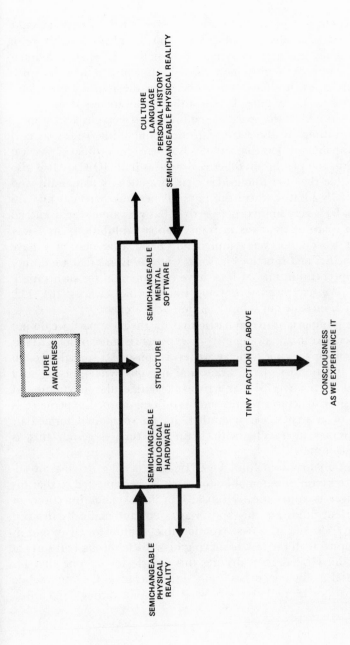

Figure 10-2. Radical view of consciousness.

psychological phenomena but also because the nature of basic awareness is inherently different from the physical structure of the brain and nervous system. I do not know what that different nature is; I only have some hints about it from people's experiences in altered states and from the implications of psi phenomena. My guess is that although awareness is ordinarily located within the space of the brain and nervous system or at least intimately associated with the brain and nervous system, it is capable of locating itself elsewhere in ordinary physical reality and perhaps in other realities (as in d-OOBEs). It is also possible that the whole idea that awareness is temporally and spatially located where the physical nervous system is may, in fact, be a very limited perspective. Basic awareness may extend over space or time (as in trans-temporal inhibition) in a way that we do not yet comprehend. Basic awareness may have capacities and functions in some wider universe that we do not comprehend or may at least have the potential for such capacities. We may need to develop state-specific sciences [164, 172, 173] to increase our comprehension of awareness.

It is important to emphasize that for the most part, we do not experience basic awareness; we experience consciousness. That is, our capacity for basic awareness is constantly spread through the functioning of the brain and nervous system, acting as a kind of energy [173] that activates or guides the functioning of physical structures within the brain. Our normal experience is not of awareness per se; rather, it is a compound formed by awareness interacting with brain structure, a gestalt that is consciousness.

An analogy is helpful here. Imagine a man driving an advanced form of automobile to which he is connected so that his hunger is automatically satisfied by intravenous injections of nutrient fluids and his body wastes are automatically drained away. He sits in a very comfortable contoured chair and is occupied with the task of driving his vehicle through all sorts of terrain. He has been driving this vehicle for so long that his mental body image has long since included the automobile as part of himself. He sees what is visible through the windshield. If he wants to go forward, he presses down on the accelerator; if he wants to stop, he pushes down on the brake pedal; if he wants to turn, he turns the steering wheel. He has been so continuously absorbed in the driving of the car in appropriate ways that his understanding of his self (i.e., his feelings and his maps) , has become a system, a gestalt of vehicle-plus-driver.

What happens if he has to cross very rocky ground? He does the obvious thing and drives around it because he knows that he cannot drive over rocky ground. That is, he automatically conceptualizes himself as having all the advantages of a driven automobile, but he also takes on the limits of the automobile. He forgets that it is possible to stop, climb out of the automobile, and walk over rocky ground. In other words, from the perspective of his ordinary consciousness, he forgets that he can use a "paranormal" power to shift the locus of his awareness.

If an accident suddenly throws our driver from the automobile, he may be confused and frightened by his experience. He finds himself lying on the ground and wants to get back into his automobile. He presses down with his right foot, but he does not move forward. He wants to change direction, so he moves his arms in the motion of turning the steering wheel, but this does not turn him. He is a different being outside the automobile. His capacities and qualities are different because the gestalt has been broken, although at first he may carry the habits that work in the automobile-plus-driver gestalt with him.

If he remains out of the car for a while, he may learn to walk and use his body in other ways, to expand his capacities and horizons; or he may find the experience terribly traumatic and quickly repress it. He may be so distressed while he is out that his unconscious defense mechanisms come to his aid, so that he hallucinates that he is still safely in his car. As a psychologist, I know that such a hallucination would not be at all improbable.

The analogy to d-OOBEs is deliberate here. Awareness per se suddenly finds itself outside the body that it has been "driving" and that has provided for it all its life. Confusion and fear sometimes occur, although great joy is far more typical. I be-

lieve that the person who has OOBEs usually takes his condi-
tioning and habits with him. That is, he hallucinates a second
body that is like his ordinary one and constructs what he
perceives in the same way he has been sensorily constructing his
ordinary world. In this way, his habits construct his ordinary
state of consciousness, and he does not experience a d-ASC, although the physical structures of his brain and body are not
there to pattern his awareness. Perhaps this body is real in some
way. Some theorists have postulated a *psychic ether,* a kind of
stuff that is flimsy by ordinary physical standards but fairly
solid to the naked mind, from which the second body and other
things are molded by the thoughts (mainly unconscious and
habitual) of the experiencer. But when long-standing habits
(car-plus-driver habits) break down, the nature of the d-OOBE
can change considerably, becoming a d-ASC as well as a d-OOBE.

I do not want the reader to take the car-plus-driver analogy
too literally. I am not saying that we definitely have some fully
developed soul inside us that just happens to be temporarily
driving the physical body and can do all sorts of wonderful
things the instant it is released. Certainly, some people have
claimed that this is the case, and it might be possible, but I do
not know. With our current level of scientific knowledge, this
elaborate theoretical concept is too complex to support or re-
fute; it is too big a jump from what we know to what might or
might not be. Nevertheless, the analogy illustrates a concept
that is congruent with altered-states phenomena and psi phenomena: in terms of current physical knowledge, basic awareness is something that seems to be of a quite different nature
than the phsyical brain and it is not always bound by the temporal and spatial constraints that limit the physical body.

Insofar as we conceptualize awareness as an entity or thing,
its interaction with the physical brain must take place through
the psi processes of clairvoyance and PK. Basic awareness clairvoyantly perceives the state of the brain and nervous system in
order to know what is going on in the body and uses PK to
influence the firing of the motor neurons that control the
body. That is, consciousness as we normally experience our

minds is our basic awareness, absorbed in reading and controlling brain processes. Thus meditative techniques that quiet the normally frenzied three-ring circus of consciousness and lead to an experience of more basic awareness should be conducive to psi. Because basic awareness is the instrument of psi, more of it should be available to direct elsewhere if we can free it from being totally absorbed in reading and controlling brain processes.

This view offers interesting possibilities for understanding brain functioning. Until recently telephone-switchboard theories of brain functioning have been dominant. Such theories see the brain as lots of specific connections between neurons that are wired in relatively fixed ways. However, modern research suggests that a lot of brain areas seem to function almost at random, with many interacting neurons poised to fire. The problem is, how do you get controlled, lawful functioning out of such seemingly diffuse, random activity? Perhaps the brain is organized by slight amounts of PK being focused on critically poised firing patterns.

There are some interesting suggestions that although the physical body functions relatively normally during short d-OOBEs, pathological changes increase during prolonged d-OOBEs; it is as if the brain can function for a while on its own but then starts to make slight errors in the absence of the patterning influence of basic awareness.

In this view, clairvoyance and PK are with us all the time; they are the normal mode of awareness-brain interaction. The kinds of clairvoyance and PK that happen at a distance, in life or in the laboratory, are infrequent extensions of a process that ordinarily is almost totally confined to a single brain. Why is it ordinarily so confined? Perhaps the requirements of biological survival make it imperative to keep close track of what is happening to our bodies physically and take appropriate actions. Perhaps—? If this is the normal mode of operation of clairvoyance and PK, it suggests that PK experiments should generally be more successful with extremely complex, semi-random, critically poised physical systems, such as brains (or

perhaps huge computers), rather than simple, highly determined objects such as dice.

Some Consequences of the Radical View

The scientific consequences of the radical view of consciousness are quite different from those of the orthodox view. For
example, brain research remains very important. After all, basic
awareness operates through, is influenced by, and forms a
gestalt with, brain functioning; therefore, a sophisticated understanding of brain functioning must be part of our ultimate
understanding of consciousness. But psychology and parapsychology become sciences that are just as fundamental to an
ultimate understanding of consciousness as brain research is
because we have to begin to understand not only the brain per
se but also awareness per se and its interactions with the brain.
The brain becomes an important transmitter and modifier of
awareness, with subsequent creation of consciousness, rather
than the generator of consciousness.

The question of personal survival of death is no longer
automatically nonsensical. It could be that basic awareness,
even though different from brain functioning, could exist only
in conjunction with a living brain. But it is also possible that
basic awareness could exist on its own. Because the question of
whether individuals will survive bodily death and go on to
some other sort of existence makes a tremendous difference in
what people do with their lives, intensive research on the possibility of survival of death becomes one of our highest priorities.

The orthodox view sees each of us totally isolated in the
prison of our skulls; the radical view holds that although we
may ordinarily live there, the constraint is no longer absolute.
This can have important personal and ethical implications. For
instance, if you are suffering, and if there is a very real sense in
which we are connected (or even potentially connected) on
some level, then your suffering becomes my suffering. (This
connection is even more important if you are suffering because
of the way I am treating you.) As we develop effective psi, this
could become a direct experiential reality for some of us, not

just a deduction based on scientific knowledge. The kind of ethics and values that would evolve from such shared experience would be very different from those developed by isolated egos that are concerned only with maximizing their own pleasures and minimizing their own pains.

The radical view of consciousness would also imply that we ought to take spiritual experiences more seriously. I feel hesitant to say this because I fear some will misinterpret it as meaning that parapsychology says religion is true. That is not at all what I mean. Religions are complex, historically evolved social and intellectual systems, mixtures of wisdom, superstition, and nonsense. They include practices and ideas about and based on altered-states experiences and psi experiences. But if we accept the fact that we have good evidence for the radical view, then if someone reports a mystical experience in which he directly experienced that we are all one, we might be more inclined to give him a telepathy or clairvoyance test next time he has such an experience, rather than automatically consigning him to psychiatric care. To some extent, we might be able to develop an experimental science of the spiritual.

Spirituality and Paranormality

I hesitate to discuss the concept of spirituality, both because we have so many irrational and neurotic biases about it and because as a scientist I have no real qualifications to speak with authority about spirituality. But as a person who has tried to learn some things about both the paranormal and the spiritual, there is one point I must discuss: the naïve equation of the two.

Many people believe that psi abilities per se are a manifestation of some sort of higher force or spirituality. Thus, if a person does something apparently psychic, he is given great authority and power. Others believe that psi manifestations are a manifestation of primitive or evil forces and so people associated with them are automatically thought to be primitive or insane or wicked. I would prefer the metaphysical theories that see psi as a manifestation of higher forces and claim that they can only be used for good. But because everything in life seems to be capable of being used for good or for evil, depending on the user and the purpose, I do not see why psi should be an exception.

I have known many people who have claimed to be psychics. Some of them have demonstrated psi abilities under laboratory conditions; others are self-professed psychics. Some of them struck me as highly mature, loving, and aware, as having the kind of qualities that I hope are associated with being spiritual. Some exuded sentimental spirituality all over the place and believed it themselves, but they struck me as being as neurotic as the rest of us (or more so). Many were quite unremarkable. The limited laboratory studies that have looked for personality correlates of psi ability have not had any particular success [96], and my own impressions of psychcis have not suggested any connection between personality and psychic ability.

You and I can do something that, by the standards that have governed all human life until quite recently, is magic and paranormal. We can talk to each other over a distance of thousands of miles. We call it talking on the telephone. But it is important to remember that the fact that we can do it over a great distance does not guarantee that the conversation will be uplifting or useful.

We shall probably see a development of practical applications of psi in the next few decades, as well as increased theoretical understanding of it. Such practical applications will be at least as revolutionary as the development of nuclear energy was. I doubt that there is anything inherent in the nature of psi that will keep us from using it for evil ends as well as desirable ones, so while we need to continue researching psi and its possible implications (it's too late to turn back), we have an even greater need to develop a more comprehensive psychology that can lead us to develop maturity and wisdom, as well as technical skill, to maximize our positive use and minimize our abuse of psi.

Bibliography

1. Allison, P. Social aspects of scientific innovation: The Case of Parapsychology. Unpublished M.A. thesis, University of Wisconsin, 1973.
2. Alton, K., and Braud, W. Clairvoyant and Telepathic Impressions of Musical Targets. In J. Morris, W. Roll, and R. Morris (eds.). *Research in Parapsychology, 1975.* Metuchen, N.J.: Scarecrow Press, 1976, pp. 171–174.
3. André, E. Confirmation of PK action on electronic equipment. *J. Parapsychol.,* 1972, *36,* 283–293.
4. Barry, J. General and comparative study of the psychokinetic effect on a fungus culture. *J. Parapsychol.,* 1968, *32,* 237–243.
5. Beloff, J. ESP: the search for a physiological index. *J. Soc. Psych. Res.,* 1974, *47,* 403–420.
6. ———, and Evans, L. A radioactivity test of psychokinesis. *J. Soc. Psych. Res.,* 1961, *41,* 41–54.
7. ———, and Mandleberg, I. An attempted validation of the "Rýzl technique" for training ESP subjects. *J. Soc. Psych. Res.,* 1966, *43,* 229–249.
8. ———. An attempted validation of the "waiting technique." *J. Soc. Psych. Res.,* 1967, *44,* 82–87.
9. Braud, W., Smith, G., Andrew, K., and Willis, S. Psychokinetic Influences on Random Number Generators during Evocation of "Analytic" vs. "Nonanalytic" Modes of Information Processing. In J. Morris, W. Roll, and R. Morris (eds.). *Research in Parapsychology, 1975.* Metuchen, N.J.: Scarecrow Press, 1976, pp. 85–88.
10. Brier, R. PK on a bio-electrical system. *J. Parapsychol.,* 1969, *33,* 187–205.

Note: The following abbreviations are used: *Amer.,* American. *Assn.,* Association. *Clin.,* Clinical. *Exp.,* Experimental. *IEEE,* Institute of Electrical and Electronic Engineers. *Int.,* International. *J.,* Journal. *Neuropsychiat.,* Neuropsychiatric. *Parapsychol.,* Parapsychological. *Proc.,* Proceedings. *Psych.,* Psychical. *Psychoanal.,* Psychoanalytic. *Psychol.,* Psychological. *Psychophysiol.,* Psychophysiology. *Res.,* Research. *Rev.,* Review. *Soc.,* Society.

11. Cadoret, R. Some applications of information theory to card-calling performance in ESP. *J. General Psychol.,* 1961, *65,* 89–107.

12. Carpenter, J. The differential effect and hidden target differences consisting of erotic and neutral stimuli. *J. Amer. Soc. Psych. Res.,* 1971, *65,* 204–214.

13. Cox, W. The PK placement of falling water. *J. Parapsychol.,* 1962, *26,* 266.

14. ———. PK tests with a thirty-two channel balls machine. *J. Parapsychol.,* 1974, *38,* 56–68.

15. ———. Note on some experiments with Uri Geller. *J. Parapsychol.,* 1974, *38,* 408–411.

16. Crookall, R. *The Study and Practice of Astral Projection.* London: Aquarian, 1961.

17. ———. *More Astral Projections: Analyses of Case Histories.* London: Aquarian, 1964.

18. ———. *The Techniques of Astral Projection.* London: Aquarian, 1964.

19. Dean, E. Long Distance Plethysmograph Telepathy with Agent under Water. In W. Roll, R. Morris, and J. Morris (eds.). *Proc. Parapsychol. Assn.,* 1969 (6), 41–42.

20. ———. Precognition and Retrocognition. In J. White and E. Mitchell (eds.). *Psychic Exploration: A Challenge for Science.* New York: Putnam's, 1974, pp. 153–178.

21. ———, and Mihalasky, J. *Executive ESP.* Englewood Cliffs, N.J.: Prentice-Hall, 1974

22. Dement, W., and Wolpert, E. The relation of eye movements, body motility, and external stimuli to dream content. *J. Exp. Psychol.,* 1958, *55,* 543–553.

23. Eisenbud, J. *The World of Ted Serios.* New York: Morrow, 1967.

24. ———. *Psi and Psychoanalysis.* New York: Grune & Stratton, 1970.

25. ———. Psychic Photography and Thoughtography. In J. White and E. Mitchell (eds.). *Psychic Exploration: A Challenge for Science.* New York: Putnam's, 1974, pp. 314–332.

26. Grad, B. Some biological effects of the "laying on of hands": A review of experiments with animals and plants. *J. Amer. Soc. Psych. Res.,* 1965, *59,* 95–129.

27. ———. "The laying on of hands": Implications for psychotherapy, gentling, and the placebo effect. *J. Amer. Soc. Psych. Res.,* 1967, *61,* 286–305.

28. Greeley, A. *The Sociology of the Paranormal.* Beverly Hills, Calif.: Sage Publications, 1975.

29. Green, C. *Out-of-the-Body Experiences.* Oxford: Institute of Psychophysical Research, 1968.

30. Haddox, V. A pilot study of a hypnotic method for training subjects in ESP. *J. Parapsychol.*, 1966, *30*, 277–278.

31. Hansel, C. *ESP: A Scientific Evaluation*. New York: Scribner's, 1966.

32. Hartwell, J., Janis, J., and Harary, B. A Study of Physiological Variables Associated with Out-of-Body Experiences. In J. Morris, W. Roll, and R. Morris (eds.). *Research in Parapsychology, 1974*. Metuchen, N.J.: Scarecrow Press, 1975, pp. 127–129.

33. Hastings, A., and Hurt, D. A confirmatory remote viewing experiment in a group setting. *Proc. IEEE*, 1976, *64*, 1544–1545.

34. Honorton, C. Review of Hansel's, "ESP: A Scientific Evaluation." *J. Parapsychol.*, 1967, *31*, 76–82.

35. ———, and Barksdale, W. PK performance with waking suggestions for muscle tension versus relaxation. *J. Amer. Soc. Psych. Res.*, 1972, *66*, 208–214.

36. ———, Davidson, R., and Bindler, P. Feedback-augmented EEG alpha, shifts in subjective state, and ESP card-guessing performance. *J. Amer. Soc. Psych. Res.*, 1971, *65*, 308–323.

37. ———, and Krippner, S. Hypnosis and ESP performance: A review of the literature. *J. Amer. Soc. Psych. Res.*, 1969, *63*, 214–252.

38. Jacobson, E. *Progressive Relaxation*. Chicago: University of Chicago Press, 1938.

39. Johnson, M., and Nordbeck, B. Variation in the scoring behavior of a "psychic." *J. Parapsychol.*, 1972, *36*, 122–132.

40. Kanthamani, H., and Kelly, E. Awareness of success in an exceptional subject. *J. Parapsychol.*, 1974, *38*, 355–382.

41. ———. Card experiments with a special subject. II. The shuffle method. *J. Parapsychol.*, 1975, *39*, 206–221.

42. Kanthamani, H., and Rao, H. A Study of the ESP-Memory Relationship Using Linguistic Forms. In J. Morris, W. Roll, and R. Morris (eds.). *Research in Parapsychology, 1974*. Metuchen, N.J.: Scarecrow Press, 1975, pp. 150–154.

43. Keil, H. A wider conceptual framework for the Stepanek focusing effect. *J. Amer. Soc. Psych. Res.* 1971, *65*, 75–82.

44. ———, and Pratt, J. G. Further ESP tests with Pavel Stepanek in Charlottesvil.e dealing with the focusing effect. *J. Amer. Soc. Psych. Res.*, 1969, *63*, 253–272.

45. Kennedy, J., and Taddonio, J. Experimenter effects in parapsychological research. *J. Parapsychol.*, 1976, *40*, 1–33.

46. Krippner, S. *Song of the Siren: A Parapsychological Odyssey*. New York: Harper & Row, 1975.

47. Kuhn, T. *The Structure of Scientific Revolutions*. Chicago: University of Chicago Press, 1962.

48. Landau, L. An unusual out-of-the-body experience. *J. Soc. Psych. Res.*, 1963, *42*, 126–128.

49. LeShan, L. *Toward a General Theory of the Paranormal: A Report of Work in Progress.* New York: Parapsychology Foundation Monograph no. 9, 1969.

50. Maslow, A. *The Psychology of Science: A Reconnaissance.* New York: Harper & Row, 1966.

51. Matas, F., and Pantas, L. A PK Experiment Comparing Meditating versus Nonmeditating Subjects. In W. Roll, R. Morris, and J. Morris (eds.), *Proc. Parapsychol. Assn.,* 1971, No. *8,* 12–13.

52. McMahan, E. An experiment in pure telepathy. *J. Parapsychol.,* 1946, *10,* 224–242.

53. Millar, B., and Broughton, R. A Preliminary PK Experiment with a Novel Computer-Linked High-Speed Random Number Generator. In J. Morris, W. Roll, and R. Morris (eds.). *Research in Parapsychology, 1975.* Metuchen, N.J.: Scarecrow Press, 1976, pp. 83–84.

54. Mitchell, E. An ESP test from Apollo 14. *J. Parapsychol.,* 1971, *35,* 89–107.

55. Mitchell, J. Out-of-the-body vision. *Psychic,* 1973, *4,* 44–47.

56. Monroe, R. *Journeys Out of the Body.* New York: Doubleday, 1971.

57. Morris, R. The Use of Detectors for Out-of-Body Experiences. In W. Roll, R. Morris, and J. Morris (eds.). *Research in Parapsychology, 1973.* Metuchen, N.J.: Scarecrow Press, 1974, pp. 114–116.

58. ———. The Psychobiology of Psi. In J. White and E. Mitchell (eds.). *Psychic Exploration: A Challenge for Science.* New York: Putnam's, 1974, pp. 225–246.

59. ———. Biology and Psychical Research. In G. Schmeidler (ed.). *Parapsychology: Its Relation to Physics, Biology, Psychology, and Psychiatry.* Metuchen, N.J.: Scarecrow Press, 1976, pp. 48–75.

60. Muldoon, S., and Carrington, H. *The Phenomena of Astral Projection.* London: Rider, 1951.

61. Nicoll, M. *Psychological Commentaries on the Teachings of Gurdjieff and Ouspensky.* London: Stuart & Watkins, 1970.

62. Onetto, B. PK with a Radioactive Compound: Cesium 137. In W. Roll, R. Morris, and J. Morris (eds.). *Proc. Parapsychol. Assn.,* 1968, No. *5,* 18–19.

63. Orme, J. Precognition and time. *J. Soc. Psych. Res.,* 1974, *47,* 351–365.

64. Orne, M. On the social psychology of the psychological experiment, with particular reference to demand characteristics and their implications. *Amer. Psychologist,* 1962, *17,* 776–783.

65. Osis, K. ESP over distance: A survey of experiments. *J. Amer. Soc. Psych. Res.,* 1965, *59,* 22–46.

66. ————. Perspective for Out-of-Body Research. In W. Roll, R. Morris, and J. Morris (eds.). *Research in Parapsychology, 1973.* Metuchen, N.J.: Scarecrow Press, 1974, pp. 110–113.

67. ————, and Bokert, E. ESP and changed states of consciousness induced by meditation. *J. Amer. Soc. Psych. Res.,* 1971, *65,* 17–65.

68. ————, and Turner, M. Distance and ESP: a transcontinental experiment. *Proc. Amer. Soc. Psych. Res.* 1968, *27.*

69. ————, Turner, M., and Carlson, M. ESP over distance: Research on the ESP channel. *J. Amer. Soc. Psych. Res.,* 1971, *65,* 245–288.

70. Palmer, J. Scoring in ESP tests as a function of belief in ESP. Part I. The sheep-goat effect. *J. Amer. Soc. Psych. Res.,* 1971, *65,* 373–408.

71. ————. Scoring in ESP tests as a function of belief in ESP. Part II. Beyond the sheep-goat effect. *J. Amer. Soc. Psych. Res.,* 1972, *66,* 1–26.

72. ————, and Lieberman, R. The influence of psychological set on ESP and out-of-the-body experiences. *J. Amer. Soc. Psych. Res.,* 1975, *69,* 193–214.

73. ————. ESP and Out-of-Body Experiences: A Further Study. In J. Morris, W. Roll, and R. Morris (eds.). *Research in Parapsychology, 1975.* Metuchen, N.J.: Scarecrow Press, 1976, pp. 102–106.

74. Palmer, J., Tart, C., and Redington. D. A Large-sample classroom ESP card-guessing experiment. *European J. Parapsychol.,* 1976, *1,* No. 3, 40–56.

75. Palmer, J., and Vassar, C. ESP and out-of-the-body experiences: An exploratory study. *J. Amer. Soc. Psych. Res.,* 1974, *68,* 257–280.

76. Panati, C. (ed.). *The Geller Papers: Scientific Observations of the Paranormal Powers of Uri Geller.* New York: Houghton Mifflin Co., 1976.

77. Pearce, J. *Exploring the Crack in the Cosmic Egg: Split Minds and Meta-Realities.* New York: Julian, 1974.

78. Penfield, W., and Roberts, L. *Speech and Brain Mechanisms.* Princeton, N.J.: Princeton University Press, 1959.

79. Persinger, M. *The Paranormal: Part II, Mechanisms and Models.* New York: MSS Information Corp., 1974.

80. Pratt, J. The meaning of performance curves in ESP and PK test data. *J. Parapsychol.,* 1949, *13,* 9–22.

81. ————. Further significant ESP results from Pavel Stepanek and findings bearing upon the focusing effect. *J. Amer. Soc. Psych. Res.,* 1967, *61,* 95–119.

82. ————, and Jacobson, N. Prediction of ESP performance on selected focusing effect targets. *J. Amer. Soc. Psych. Res.,* 1969, *63,* 38–56.

83. Pratt, J., et al. A transitional period of research on the focusing effect: From confirmation toward explanation. *J. Amer. Soc. Psych. Res.*, 1969, *63*, 21–37.

84. Pratt, J., and Keil, H. The focusing effect as patterned behavior based upon habitual object-word associations: A working hypothesis with supporting evidence. *J. Amer. Soc. Psych. Res.*, 1969, *63*, 315–337.

85. ————. Firsthand observations on Nina S. Kulagina suggestive of PK upon static objects. *J. Amer. Soc. Psych. Res.*, 1973, *67*, 381–390.

86. ————, and Stevenson, I. Three-experimenter ESP tests of Pavel Stepanek during his 1968 visit to Charlottesville. *J. Amer. Soc. Psych. Res.*, 1970, *64*, 18–39.

87. Pratt, J. and Ro l, W. Confirmation of the focusing effect in further ESP research with Pavel Stepanek in Charlottesville. *J. Amer. Soc. Psych. Res.*, 1968, *62*, 226–245.

88. Price, G. Science and the supernatural. *Science*, 1955, *122*, 359–367.

89. ————. Apology to Rhine and Soal. *Science*, 1972, *175*, 359.

90. Puharich, A. *Beyond telepathy.* New York: Doubleday, 1962.

91. Puthoff, H., and Targ, R. PK Experiments with Uri Geller and Ingo Swann. In W. Roll, R. Morris, and J. Morris (eds.). *Research in Parapsychology, 1973.* Metuchen, N.J.: Scarecrow Press, 1974, pp. 125–128.

92. ————. A perceptual channel for information transfer over kilometer distances: Historical perspective and recent research. *Proc. IEEE*, 1974, *64*, 329–354.

93. ————. Physics, Entropy, and Psychokinesis. In L. Oteri (ed.). *Quantam Physics and Parapsychology.* New York: Parapsychology Foundation, 1975, pp. 129–150.

94. Randall, J. An áttempt to detect psi effects with protozoa. *J. Soc. Psych. Res.*, 1970, *45*, 294–296.

95. ————. Biological Aspects of Psi. In J. Beloff (ed.). *New Directions in Parapsychology.* Metuchen, N.J.: Scarecrow Press, 1975, pp. 77–94.

96. Rao, K. R. *Experimental Parapsychology.* Springfield, Ill.: Charles C. Thomas, 1966.

97. Rhine, J. B. *Extrasensory Perception.* Boston: Bruce Humphries, 1934 (reprinted 1964).

98. ————. A review of the Pearce-Pratt distance series of ESP tests. *J. Parapsychol.*, 1954, *18*, 165–177.

99. ————. Comments: Security versus deception in parapsychology. *J. Parapsychol.*, 1974, *38*, 99–121.

100. ————. Comments: A new case of experimenter unreliability. *J. Parapsychol.*, 1974, *38*, 215–225.

101. ————, Smith, B., and Woodruff, J. Experiments bearing on the

precognition hypothesis: II. The role of ESP in the shuffling of cards. *J. Parapsychol.*, 1938, 2, 119–131.

102. Rhine, L. Psychological processes in ESP experiences, part II, Dreams. *J. Parapsychol.*, 1962, 26, 172–199.

103. Rogo, D. *Exploring Psychic Phenomena: Beyond Mind and Matter.* Wheaton, Ill.: Quest Books, 1976.

104. Roll, W. The psi field. *Proc. Parapsychol. Assn.*, 1957, 64 (1), 32–65.

105. ―――. ESP and memory. *Int. J. Neuropsychiat.*, 1966, 2, 505–521.

106. ―――, and Tart, C. Exploratory ESP matching tests with a "sensitive." *J. Amer. Soc. Psych. Res.*, 1965, 59, 226–236.

107. Rosenthal, R. *Experimenter Effects in Behavioral Research.* New York: Appleton-Century-Crofts, 1966.

108. Rýzl, M. Training the psi faculty by hypnosis. *J. Soc. Psych. Res.*, 1962, 41, 234–252.

109. ―――, and Pratt, J. G. The focusing of ESP upon particular targets. *J. Parapsychol.*, 1963, 27, 227–241.

110. Saltmarsh, H. Report on cases of apparent precognition. *Proc. Soc. Psych. Res.*, 1934, 42, 49–103.

111. Schmeidler, G. PK effects upon continuously recorded temperature. *J. Amer. Soc. Psych. Res.*, 1973, 67, 325–340.

112. ―――, and McConnell, R. *ESP and Personality Patterns.* New Haven, Conn.: Yale Univ. Press, 1958.

113. Schmidt, H. Clairvoyance tests with a machine. *J. Parapsychol.*, 1969, 33, 300–306.

114. ―――. A PK test with electronic equipment. *J. Parapsychol.*, 1970, 34. 175–181.

115. ―――. PK tests with a high-speed random number generator. *J. Parapsychol.*, 1973, 37, 105–118.

116. ―――. Observation of Subconscious PK Effects with and without Time Displacement. In J. Morris, W. Roll, and R. Morris (eds.). *Research in Parapsychology, 1974.* Metuchen, N.J.: Scarecrow Press, 1975, pp. 116–121.

117. ―――. PK Experiment with Repeated, Time Displaced Feedback. In J. Morris, W. Roll, and R. Morris (eds.). *Research in Parapsychology, 1975.* Metuchen, N.J.: Scarecrow Press, 1976, pp. 107–109.

118. ―――, and Pantas, L. Psi tests with internally different machines. *J. Parapsychol.*, 1972, 36, 222–232.

119. Schultz, J., and Luthe, W. *Autogenic Training: A Psychophysiologic Approach in Psychotherapy.* New York: Grune & Stratton, 1959.

120. Scott, C. Models for psi. *Proc. Soc. Psych. Res.*, 1961, 53, 195–225.

121. Shapin, B., and Coly, L. (eds.). *Education in Parapsychology: Proceedings of an International Conference Held in San Fran-

cisco, California, August 14–16, 1975. New York: Parapsychology Foundation, 1976.

122. Smith, J. Paranormal effects on enzyme activity. Proc. Parapsychol. Assn., 1968, No. 5, 15–16.

123. Soal, S., and Bateman, F. Modern Experiments in Telepathy. London: Faber & Faber, 1954.

124. St. James-Roberts, I. Cheating in science. New Scientist, 1976, 72 (1028), 466–469.

125. Stanford, R. An experimentally testable model for spontaneous psi events. I. Extrasensory events. J. Amer. Soc. Psych. Res., 1974, 68, 34–57.

126. ———. An experimentally testable model for spontaneous psi events. II. Psychokinetic events. J. Amer. Soc. Psych. Res., 1974, 68, 321–356.

127. Stanford, R., and Fox, C. An Effect of Release of Effort in a Psychokinetic Task. In J. Morris, W. Roll, and R. Morris (eds.). Research in Parapsychology, 1974. Metuchen, N.J.: Scarecrow Press, 1975, pp. 61–63.

128. ———, and Stio, A. Associative Mediation in Psi-Mediated Instrumental Response (PMIR). In J. Morris, W. Roll, and R. Morris (eds.). Research in Parapsychology, 1975. Metuchen, N.J.: Scarecrow Press, 1976, pp. 49–53.

129. Stanford, R., et al. Motivational Arousal and Self-concept in Psi-Mediated Instrumental Response. In J. Morris, W. Roll, and R. Morris (eds.). Research in Parapsychology, 1975. Metuchen, N.J.: Scarecrow Press, 1976, pp. 54–58.

130. Stanford, R., et al. Psychokinesis as psi-mediated instrumental response. J. Amer. Soc. Psych. Res., 1975, 69, 127–134.

131. Stephenson, C. Cambridge ESP-hypnosis experiments (1958–64). J. Soc. Psych. Res., 1965, 43, 77–91.

132. Swann, I. To Kiss Earth Goodbye. New York: Hawthorne, 1975.

133. Tanous, A., and Ardman, H. Beyond Coincidence: One Man's Experience with Psychic Phenomena. New York: Doubleday, 1976.

134. Targ, R. Precognition and Everyday Life: A Physical Model. In W. Roll, R. Morris, and J. Morris (eds.). Research in Parapsychology, 1972. Metuchen, N.J.: Scarecrow Press, 1973, pp. 49–51.

135. ———, and Puthoff, H. Information transmission under conditions of sensory shielding. Nature, 1974, 251, 602–607.

136. ———. Mind-Reach: Scientists Look at Psychic Ability. New York: Delacorte, 1977.

137. Tart, C. Physio ogical correlates of psi cognition. Int. J. Parapsychol., 1963, 5, 375–386.

138. ———. A possible "psychic" dream, with some speculations on the nature of such dreams. J. Soc. Psych. Res., 1963, 42, 283–298.

139. ———. The influence of the experimental situation in hypnosis

and dream research: A case report. *Amer. J. Clin. Hypnosis,* 1964, 7, 163–170.

140. ———. Application of instrumentation to the investigation of "haunting" and "Poltergeist" cases. *J. Amer. Soc. Psych. Res.,* 1965, 59, 190–201.

141. ———. Models for explanation of extrasensory perception. *Int. J. Neuropsychiat.,* 1966, 2, 488–504.

142. ———. Card guessing tests: Learning paradigm or extinction paradigm? *J. Amer. Soc. Psych. Res.,* 1966, 60, 46–55.

143. ———. ESPATESTER: An automatic testing device for parapsychological research. *J. Amer. Soc. Psych. Res.,* 1966, 60, 256–269.

144. ———, and Hilgard, E. Responsiveness to suggestions under "hypnosis" and "waking-imagination" conditions: A methodological observation. *Int. J. Clin. Exp. Hypnosis,* 1966, 14, 247–256

145. ———. A second psychophysiological study of out-of-the-body experiences in a gifted subject. *Int. J. Parapsychol.,* 1967, 9, 251–258.

146. ———. Psychedelic experiences associated with a novel hypnotic procedure, mutual hypnosis. *Amer. J. Clin. Hypnosis,* 1967, 10, 65–78.

147. ———. Random output selector for the laboratory. *Psychophysiol.* 1967, 3, 430–434.

148. ———. A psychophysiological study of out-of-the-body experiences in a selected subject. *J. Amer. Soc. Psych. Res.,* 1968, 62, 3–27.

149. ———. Hypnosis, Psychedelics, and Psi: Conceptual Models. In R. Cavanna and M. Ullman (eds.). *Psi and Altered States of Consciousness.* New York: Garrett Press, 1968, pp. 24–41.

150. ———, and Smith, J. Two token object studies with the "psychic," Peter Hurkos. *J. Amer. Soc. Psych. Res.,* 1968, 62, 143–157.

151. ——— (ed.). *Altered States of Consciousness: A Book of Readings.* New York: Wiley, 1969.

152. ———. A further psychophysiological study of out-of-the-body experiences in a gifted subject. *Proc. Parapsychological Assn.,* 1969, 6, 43–44.

153. ———. Did I Really Fly? Some Methodological Notes on the Investigation of Altered States of Consciousness and Psi Phenomena. In R. Cavanna (ed.). *Psi Favorable States of Consciousness: Proceedings of an International Conference on Methodology in Psi Research.* New York: Parapsychology Foundation, 1970, pp. 3–10.

154. ———. Marijuana intoxication: Common experiences. *Nature,* 1970, 226, 701–704.

155. ———. *On Being Stoned: A Psychological Study of Marijuana Intoxication.* Pa o Alto, Calif.: Science & Behavior Books, 1971.

156. ———. Introduction. In R. Monroe, *Journeys Out of the Body.* New York: Doubleday, 1971, pp. 1–17.

157. ———. Work with marijuana: II. Sensations. *Psychology Today,* 1970, *4* (12) , 41–45, 66–68.

158. ———. ESP and pot. *Psychic,* 1971, *3* (2), 26–30.

159. ———. Scientific foundations for the study of altered states of consciousness. *J. Transpersonal Psychol.,* 1972, *3,* 93–124.

160. ——— (ed.) . *Altered States of Consciousness.* 2d ed., revised. New York: Doubleday, 1972.

161. ———. Sleep EEG study of out-of-the-body experiences. *Psychophysiol.* 1972, *9,* 140.

162. ———. Concerning the scientific study of the human aura. *J. Soc. Psych. Res.,* 1972, *46,* 1–21.

163. ———. La ciena y el alma humana. (Science and the human soul.) *Tribuna Medica,* 1972, *9* (425) , 12.

164. ———. States of consciousness and state-specific sciences. *Science,* 1972, *176,* 1203–1210.

165. ———, et al. Some studies of psychokinesis with a spinning silver coin. *J. Soc. Psych. Res.,* 1972, *46,* 143–153.

166. ———. Parapsychology. *Science,* 1973, *182,* 222.

167. ———. Preliminary Notes on the Nature of Psi Processes. In R. Ornstein (ed.) . *The Psycho ogy of Consciousness: A Book of Readings.* San Francisco: W. H. Freeman, 1973, pp. 468–492.

168. ———. On the Nature of Altered States of Consciousness, with Special Reference to Parapsychological Phenomena. In W. Roll, R. Morris, and J. Morris (eds.) . *Research in Parapsychology, 1973.* Metuchen, N.J.: Scarecrow Press, 1974, pp. 163–218.

169. ———. Some Methodological Problems in Out-of-the-Body Experiences Research. In W. Roll, R. Morris, and J. Morris (eds.) . *Research in Parapsychology, 1973.* Metuchen, N.J.: Scarecrow Press. 1974, pp. 116–120.

170. ———. Out-of-the-Body Experiences. In E. Mitchell and J. White (eds.) . *Psychic Exploration.* New York: Putnam's, 1974, pp. 349–374.

171. ———, and Fadiman, J. The case of the yellow wheat field: a dream-state explanation of a broadcast telepathic dream. *Psychoanal. Rev.,* 1974–75, *61,* 607–618.

172. ——— (ed.) . *Transpersonal Psychologies,* New York: Harper & Row, 1975.

173. ———. *States of Consciousness.* New York: Dutton, 1975.

174. ———. *The Application of Learning Theory to ESP Performance.* New York: Parapsychology Foundation, 1975.

175. ———. Discrete States of Consciousness. In P. Lee, R. Ornstein,

D. Galin, A. Deikman, and C. Tart, *Symposium on Consciousness.* New York: Viking, 1976, pp. 89–175.

176. ———. Samsara: A Psychological View. In T. Tulku (ed.). *Reflections of Mind.* Emeryville, Calif. Dharma Press, 1975, pp. 53–68.

177. ———. Studies of learning theory application, 1964–1974. *Parapsychol. Rev.*, 1975, *6*, 21–28.

178. ———. *Learning to Use Extrasensory Perception.* Chicago: University of Chicago Press, 1976.

179. ———. Causality and synchronicity. *Forum for Correspondence and Contact*, 1976, *8* (1), 9–20.

180. ———. Drug-Induced States of Consciousness. In B. Wolman, et al. (eds.). *Handbook of Parapsychology.* New York: Van Nostrand/Rheinhold, in press.

181. ———. The basic nature of altered states of consciousness: A systems approach. *J. Transpersonal Psychol.*, 1976, *8* (1), 45–64.

182. ———, and Neubert, R. ESP training. *Psychic*, 1976, *7*, April, 12–15.

183. ———. Sex and Drugs as Altered States of Consciousness. In K. Blum (ed.). *Social Meaning of Drugs (Principles of Social Pharmacology).* New York: Harper & Row, in press.

184. ———. A Systems Approach to Altered States of Consciousness. In J. Davidson, R. Davidson, and G. Schwartz (eds.). *Human Consciousness and Its Transformations: A Psychobiological Perspective.* New York: Plenum. in press.

185. ———. Studying Out-of-the-Body Experiences. In T. X. Barber et al. (eds.). *Advances in Altered States of Consciousness Potentialities.* New York: Psychological Dimensions Press, 1976, pp. 579–586.

186. ———. Review of The Amazing Randi. *The Magic of Uri Geller*, C. Panati (ed.). *The Geller Papers: Scientific Observations on the Paranormal Powers of Uri Geller;* and U. Geller. *Uri Geller: My Story. Psychology Today*, 1976, *10* (2), 93–94.

187. ———. Reply to O'Brien. *J. Parapsychol.*, 1976, *40*, 240–246.

188. ———. Toward humanistic experimentation in parapsychology: a reply to Stanford. *J. Amer. Soc. Psych. Res.*, 1977, *71*, 81–102.

189. ———. Improving real time ESP by suppressing the future: trans-temporal inhibition. Paper, Electro 77 meeting of the IEEE, New York City, April 1977.

190. ———, Palmer, J., and Redington, D. Effects of immediate feedback on ESP performance: a second study. Submitted for publication.

191. Terry, J., and Honorton, C. Psi information retrieval in the ganzfeld: Two confirmatory studies. *J. Amer. Soc. Psych. Res.*, 1976, *70*, 207–218.

192. Troffer, S., and Tart, C. Experimenter bias in hypnotist performance. *Science,* 1964, *145,* 1330–1331.
193. Ullman, M., and Krippner, S. *Dream Studies and Telepathy.* New York: Parapsychology Foundation Monograph no. 12, 1970.
194. ———, and Feldstein, S. Experimentally induced telepathic dreams: Two studies using the EEG-REM monitoring technique. *Inter. J. Neuropsychiat.,* 1966, *2,* 420–438.
195. Ullman, M., Krippner, S., and Vaughan, A. *Dream Telepathy.* New York: Macmillan, 1973.
196. Van de Castle, R. The facilitation of ESP through hypnosis. *Amer. J. Clin. Hypnosis,* 1969, *12,* 37–56.
197. Vasiliev, L. *Experiments in Distant Influence.* New York: Dutton, 1976.
198. von Békésy, G. *Sensory Inhibition.* Princeton: Princeton University Press, 1967.
199. Wadhams, P., and Farrelley, B. The investigation of psychokinesis using beta particles. *J. Soc. Psych. Res.,* 1968, *44,* 736.
200. Watkins, G., and Watkins, A. Possible PK influence on the resuscitation of anesthetized mice. *J. Parapsychol.,* 1971, *35,* 257–272.
201. Wells, R., and Klein, J. A replication of the "psychic healing" paradigm. *J. Parapsychol.,* 1972, *36,* 144–149.
202. White, R. A comparison of old and new methods of response to targets in ESP experiments. *J. Amer. Soc. Psych. Res.,* 1964, *58,* 21–56.
203. ———. The influence of persons other than the experimenter on the subject's scores in psi experiments. *J. Amer. Soc. Psych. Res.,* 1976, *70,* 133–166.
204. ———. The limits of experimenter influence on psi test results: Can any be set? *J. Amer. Soc. Psych. Res.,* 1976, *70,* 333–370.
205. Whitson, T., et al. Preliminary experiments in group "remote viewing." *Proc. IEEE,* 1976, *64,* 1550–1551.

Index